Academic Distinctions

Academic Distinctions

Theory and Methodology
in the Sociology of School Knowledge

by James G. Ladwig

ROUTLEDGE
New York and London

Published in 1996 by

Routledge
29 West 35TH Street
New York, NY 10001

Published in Great Britain in 1996 by

Routledge
11 New Fetter Lane
London EC4P 4EE

Copyright © 1996 by Routledge

Printed in the United States of America
Design: Jack Donner

Library of Congress Cataloging-in-Publication Data

Ladwig, James G.
    Academic distinctions: theory and methodology in the sociology of
        school knowledge / James G. Ladwig
            p.   cm.
    Includes bibliographical references.
    ISBN 0-415-91187-7. — ISBN 0-415-91188-5 (pbk.)
    1. Educational sociology—Research—Methodology. 2. Critical theory. 3. Critical
        pedagogy—Research. 4. Education—Curricula. I. Title.
    LC191.L26   1995
    370.19'072—dc20   95–540
                                                                              CIP

for my parents
Velma R. and Harman A. Ladwig

contents

#32665788 CIP

c1996
x, 194 p.; 24 cm.
bibl. p. [179]-194, no index

acknowledgments

O VER THE COURSE OF WORKING on this project I have continually re-learned that academic work is best lived collectively, thus my thanks:

To my friends, colleagues and families who sustained me while this work began in the United States: M. Bruce King, Karen Fennema, David Chawszczewski, Leslie McCall, James Beane, Barbara Brodhagen, Ross Davies, Mark and Ann Berends, Didacus Jules, Graham Walter Fennema King, Peter Berends, Rudy Careaga, Michael Apple, Thomas Popkewitz, Michael Olneck, Adam Gamoran, Martyn Nystrand, and Fred Newmann;

To my newer colleaugues and friends in Australia who encouraged me to complete this project: Allan Luke, Carmen Luke, Bill Green, Marie Brennan, Fazal Rizvi, and Lawrie Angus;

To my fellow nomads, whose friendship and intellect continue to help me make sense of this world: Cameron McCarthy, Hannu Simola, and Tomaz Tadeu da Silva;

To the Australian Association for Research in Education, who sponsored a series of seminars which allowed me to rehearse this work; and to those colleagues who joined in those discussions;

To the Faculty of Education at the University of Newcastle for providing much needed research support just when it appeared little would be found;

To the Department of Education at The University of Newcastle, for giving me a job;

To Terry Lovat, Jennifer Doyle, Pam Nilan, Melissa Monfries, and Eileen Sedunary for making our Department enjoyable and professionally interesting;

To Thomas Griffiths and Gavin Hazel for all their help and interest;

To Jayne Fargnoli at Routledge for all her encouragement and patience;

And especially to Jennifer Gore: my intellect, my global companion, my love.

one

Introduction

IN THE MIST OF A VERY ACADEMIC LECTURE AND DEBATE which took place in the Social Science Building on the campus of the University of Wisconsin, Madison on 4 April 1989, Pierre Bourdieu was questioned about the degree to which his sociology provides a fuzzy picture of the social world. The questioner clearly did not see this fuzziness as a virtue. But in response, Bourdieu explained that while he generally declines from making universal proclamations about how sociology ought to be conducted (forevermore), there was one tenet he himself tried to follow. In Bourdieu's words, when constructing his sociological accounts, the one rule he has tried to follow has been, "Do not be more clear than reality."

Some of the audience chortled in turn, some did not (there were more than a few analytical Marxists in the audience). Turning to the side of the audience from which a significant portion of the snickers had come, Bourdieu said, "You laugh, because you are on the same side as me."

Taking sides seems to me to be more than a pasttime among the academics with whom I work. If fact, with an analytical heritage built on making "significant" or "illustrative" distinctions, taking sides seems more the rule than the exception in my part of the world. It is from within that world that I have attempted to construct the descriptive analysis of the academic field presented in this book. The field to which I am referring I have named in this analysis the "Radical Sociology of School Knowledge" (RSSK). I would like to make explicit very early on that, in a sense, I really don't take this to be a field at all. There are no academic departments (that I know of) with such a title.

There are no academic journals exclusively devoted to such a discipline. And, in fact, I know of very few other people on this planet who would call themselves sociologists of school knowledge.

Nevertheless, there is a body of literature with bridges across multiple disciplinary lines that questions the relationship between societal relations of power and school knowledge. Only some of this literature refers to itself as a sociology of school knowledge; though most of it that I would see as "radical" I think does. Hence, I place this work within the intellectual context of contemporary radical sociological accounts of school knowledge.

Here I am referring to both more and less than the theoretical arguments put forth by those who claim similar areas of academic interest. As Mannheim (1936) reminds me, one ought not separate intellectual assertions from their socio-historical context. In this regard, when I speak of "contemporary radical sociological accounts of school knowledge," I minimally shall be referring to three things: the social field of schooling, the social field of intellectuals who study schooling, and the linguistic/ theoretical assertions made by these intellectuals about the role of knowledge in both aforementioned social contexts. In that I shall be examining both intellectual arguments and the social contexts about which and in which these arguments are made, I take the object of my analysis to be "more" than most sociologies of school knowledge.

I am also referring to "less" than many sociologies of school knowledge in that I seek to limit my analysis to works done in the U.S. whose central interests are claims about the social practices related to knowledge within schools. To be sure, following the lead of Mannheim, as a sociological analysis of knowledge, much of this work is concerned with how knowledge about schools is produced and consumed. This concern is evident in the ubiquitous critiques of (ostensibly) positivistic educational research found within radical curricular work. In delimiting the area of my study, I seek to concentrate on those works which have directly addressed a study of the social practices of knowledge within schools. I shall say more later about how I selected the literature I analyze below. But with at least this sense of the field of study into which this study enters, I would like to outline below some of the arguments I attempt to build.

OUTLINING THE ARGUMENT

Early in the 1970s, educational researchers in England argued that a central task of the sociology of education ought to be the systematic investigation of the relationship between societal structures of power and curriculum. Broadly speaking, this agenda was identified as the central problematic of the so-called New Sociology of Education. Brought into the U.S. educational literature by such prolific writers as Michael Apple and Henry Giroux, *inter alios*, the agenda of the New Sociology of Education has become intellectually linked to

< 2 >

a larger array of research which more generally can be named radical sociologies of school knowledge. Given the proliferation of "critical" analyses of curriculum, particularly within the U.S. curriculum field, it is interesting to note that few educational scholars would suggest that the original task of the New Sociology has been met (Sadovnick, 1991). With more than two decades of research on which to rest, it is important to note that even Basil Bernstein, one of the central figures in the formulation of the New Sociology, holds a somber view of what the sociology of school knowledge has accomplished. Writing in 1990, Bernstein said, "this programme, whatever else it produced, did not produce what it called for" (1990, p. 166).

This book seeks to respond to the current demise of the sociology of curriculum in two ways. First, the book will provide an analysis and overview of extant literature which can be known as U.S. radical sociologies of school knowledge. In brief, the book begins by constructing an answer to the grounding question, "What happened to the sociology of curriculum?" Second, the book begins the analytical groundwork needed to construct a research agenda not yet taken up by radical sociologists of education in the English-speaking world. I have named his alternative research agenda, "constructing a science with an attitude." Since the analysis of the field and the alternative research agenda have been constructed to complement each other, this volume presents both.

In sum, I shall argue that the theory and methodology of RSSK have developed specifically in relation to struggles within academic fields, and that for radical educational scholars in the United States, these struggles have constructed a particular identity with a specific associated stance toward research methodology. As a consequence, I further argue, current radical educational research limits its own potential in such ways that it cannot meet the basic tenets of conventional science, and it will not be persuasive to anyone not already in agreement with the basic tenets of radical theories of education.[1] In this light, the stances of radical educational research have been very effective for opening and defending nonconventional positions in academic space. However, if the initial agenda of the New Sociology is to be met, and if a wider audience of educational scholars is to be persuaded by radical educational insights, an alternative research agenda clearly is needed. My own "science with an attitude" is one such agenda.

AN OUTLINE OF THE CHAPTERS

The following chapter begins the study of RSSK with a specific focus on the original U.S. reformulation of the English New Sociology of Education. Using the "Parallelist Position" of Michael Apple and the early analyses of Henry Giroux and Jean Anyon as prime heuristic points of reference, this chapter demonstrates how it is that U.S. sociologies of school knowledge have become

< 3 >

entwined in analytical cul-de-sacs, stuck in perpetual debates that show little or no sign of resolution. This chapter demonstrates that the Structural Neo-Marxist framework initially adopted by RSSK is self-contradictory. While the Structural Neo-Marxist agenda is clearly responsive to a political logic of oppositional appeal (much like the more popular "politically-correct" logic), it remains incoherent in conventional empirical terms.

The third chapter expands the boundaries of what is known as the sociology of school knowledge by outlining four analytical positions within the U.S. literature which address the relationship between power and curriculum. These four positions (a continuing structural neo-marxist position, a post-structural position, a structural feminist position, and a post-structural feminist position) are evident in recent educational literature, particularly since the advent of post-structural analysis in U.S. educational research. The primary aim of this chapter is to present each position as unique, responding to separate concerns and particular political agendas. Research analyzed in this chapter includes work by Mark Ginsburg, Carnoy and Levin, Madeleine Grumet, Nilen and Kelly, Wexler, Patty Lather, and Elizabeth Ellsworth, among many others.

The fourth chapter carries a central analytical task and provides the pivotal "framing" of the research previously analyzed. That is, where Chapters Two and Three attempt to present each analytical position in the field as a unique contribution to the field, Chapter Four takes up the task of finding common theoretical stances among the various positions. Here, each position will be recast through the analytical lens of a sociology of science, each argument understood in terms of Bourdieu's logic of distinctions (following Bourdieu, 1981). This chapter presents the argument that these "partially equivalent" dispositions can be seen as elements of a radical educational research social identity. In this view, the theoretical debates in the field can be seen as strategies of social differentiation within one very small academic field that is reflective of debates rehearsed in many academic subfields throughout the 1980s (particularly in the social sciences and humanities).

The fifth chapter begins the task of excavating the implications of viewing the sociology of school knowledge as a social field. In direct terms, since all the research analyzed earlier shares, in part, the identity of "radical" educational research, the question now becomes "'radical' compared to whom?" To answer this question, Chapter Five turns back to some of the initial arguments on which the radical sociologies of school knowledge were based, identifies the "critique of positivism" as a central point of strategic distinction, and reassesses those initial formulations by asking the question, "Was the critique of Positivism a mistake?" Here the main question is not one of assessing some sort of inherent validity in the original criticism voiced by radical educational researchers. The point of this chapter is to assess the relationship established

< 4 >

between radical educational theory and "mainstream" educational research on three levels—the philosophical, the political, and the social.

The sixth chapter specifically focuses on identifying weaknesses in the relationship which radical sociologies of school knowledge have established between themselves and mainstream educational research. To make this issue plausible, however, it is necessary to begin viewing educational science in a radically different light. That is, one way to question how social relationships are established through scientific practices is to view science as a form of rhetoric, an art of persuasion. Thus, Chapter Six explicitly sets out this image of science as rhetoric and demonstrates how a radical sociology of school knowledge fails to meet conventional canons of science in such a way that its basic persuasiveness can be seen as problematized. Where conventional criticisms of radical educational research pose similar charges by employing criteria rejected in radical theory, this argument poses the problem in terms radical sociologists could ill-afford to ignore. Some basic philosophical and political defenses of this image of science are also presented in Chapter Six.

The seventh chapter of this work offers an outline of the alternative research agenda which I have (in the spirit of Feyerabend and Public Enemy) named "constructing science with an attitude". That is, in addition to providing some specific points of departure for the theoretical and methodological positions taken up in constructing a science with an attitude, Chapter Seven outlines briefly an assessment of current theories available to sociologies of school knowledge and proposes a working theoretical framework for a research agenda that would respond to the initial call set out in the establishment of a sociology of school knowledge.

This framework, perhaps not surprisingly, builds on a growing acknowledgment of the merit of theories of "cultural difference" (such as Bourdieu's) for explaining the relationship between power and curriculum. In all, combined with the rationale which follows in this Introduction, I hope to demonstrate that radical sociologies of school knowledge can potentially connect with a very wide range of current research interests. Potentially connecting with mainstream sociological analyses of educational inequity, social-psychological explanations of social identity formation, institutional analyses of schooling as a global world culture, and post-colonial theories of racism, the socio-theoretical agenda opened by accepting the scientific heterodoxy I propose for the sociology of school knowledge provides an agenda that is at once reflexive and, I believe, profoundly expansive.

ON USING MULTIPLE "FRAMES"

Throughout this project I have attempted to employ a multitude of analytical frameworks or conceptual lenses. By and large I also have attempted to explicitly name the frameworks from within which I construct various claims, but

< 5 >

not always within the main text itself. Employing this textual tactic, I must admit, was a rather difficult task. There were times when I found myself constructing some claims I would immediately want to wipe off my computer screen, but left them in with heavy (and almost immediate) qualifications, for illustrative purposes. Temporally adopting various conceptual lenses, however, involved something of a forced Gestalt shift; and having made that shift while writing (and in reading over drafts) I cannot claim to have become consciously aware of all the subtexts this text has generated. But the main purpose in constructing my text in this manner, forcibly shifting my analytical frameworks, was to make explicit some of the conceptual consequences of each framework.

This procedure may at first sound similar to those employed in recent postmodern educational discourses. And in many ways it is. But my "privileged" frame is one that is usually not taken to be in alliance with postmodernism at all. In fact, as I hope will be apparent, many of the metaphors and methodological procedures I employ and thereby contribute to RSSK are precisely those that postmodern critics have attacked. Let me explain.

I have intentionally made use of visual metaphors. For readers of recent feminist theories, social theory, and literary criticism, this may seem a dangerous choice. Mine is an intellectual context where I am keenly aware of critiques that point out the devastating historical associations between visualist sciences and, to name only a few, "the male gaze," "colonizing voyeurism," and a utopian "enlightenment." I also embrace science (as a historically grounded phenomenon). For readers of twentieth century social thought, feminist critiques of science, and Critical Theory, this choice too will appear risky. Since I have just raised the issue, it is perhaps predictable that the connections between science and light metaphors, and my highlighted use of both, is no accident. My acceptance of both, and the overall project I have attempted to practice in this book, I take as an exercise in the attempt to find a way to make social science work for radical sociologies of school knowledge without carrying with it the Grand Theory, marginalization, domination, and utopian vanguardism that have been associated with its past.

Speaking of theory: while this is undoubtedly a theoretical monograph, as might be fashionable to say, *Ceci n'est pas une theorie*. No, this is not a theory. And it certainly is not a new theory. The theoretical framework I have attempted to deploy here is built largely from my reading of the sociological and anthropological analyses of Pierre Bourdieu—which have been available in English for nearly thirty years.

And the methodological tenets I have adopted were first sketched out in a text that was originally written more than twenty years ago in Bourdieu, Chamboredon, and Passeron's *Le Métier de Sociologue*, which was originally published in 1968. Luckily, since I can't read much French, with the

< 6 >

translation of this text into English as *The Craft of Sociology*, I have been able to check what I thought I saw happening methodologically and epistemologically in Bourdieu's other texts against the explicit statements of methodology he and his colleagues laid out very soon after I was born. More specific explication of the ways in which I used Bourdieu's concepts (particularly in relation to 'capital', 'habitus', and 'fields') can be found in Ladwig (1994a).

Built within the very French, Durkheimian sociological tradition, Bourdieu's methodological stance begins from the epistemological presumption that (in Poincare's words) "facts do not speak." Yet, at the same time, in the endeavor to construct a sociology of my ostensibly sociological field, I am more than willing to speak about the facts I have constructed.

With that statement of authority made, I must make clear that even as I have attempted to use Bourdieu's sociological insights, I have attempted to do so neither with utmost loyalty nor with reverence. All of my appropriations of social theory, philosophy, educational theory and sociology have been guided by my singular (empirical) task of trying to describe what I see happening in RSSK.

ON SELECTING LITERATURE

In this ostensibly postmodern academy, valid generalizations seem quite rare. One generalization I have come to accept, however, is that there are a number of problems faced when delimiting the literature to be included in any study. This study is no exception.

Overall, it should be noted that my "survey" of the literature is not exhaustive. I make no claim to have analyzed, much less summarized, all of the literature that may fit into the categories I have created. Whether or not such a study is at all possible in these times is open to debate. But such a debate I take to be beside the point. Completeness is neither necessary, nor valued, in this study. The research I have chosen to consider or "study" is meant to be illustrative of the kinds of research relevant to the main arguments of this book. However, I have attempted to find theoretical and methodological arguments relevant to my concerns and, in that sense, have sought to "cover" the relevant literature for my study.

This general concern is most problematic, I think, in considering feminist and non-feminist works on gender and curriculum. There are (at least) two problems I faced in making my selection of feminist works. First, it is sometimes difficult to differentiate between radical feminist and mainstream feminist work. After all, in some sense, to name one's work feminist in the United States is to be considered at least mildly "radical." And there are a great number of studies about gender and the curriculum which distinguish themselves from the "mainstream" in that they do in fact address gender. In educational literature, one could probably find examples of such studies in every

< 7 >

subarea of curriculum, such as mathematics education, science education, or health education. Many of these studies are considered "feminist," and some are self-proclaimed feminisms. But most of this work, to my knowledge, is not intended to be nor functions as transformative, and therefore because of my focus on "radical" sociologies of school knowledge, I have ignored a great deal of important work done within what I call the "mainstream."

Put another way, finding studies of gender differentiation in schooling and curriculum is rather straightforward; but much of this work is rarely cited by, and almost never refers to, non-feminist, self-identified "radical" sociologies of education. In this construction, some feminist studies of schooling seem more an internally subordinate fragment of the "mainstream" than part of the radical field I seek to understand. It is very important to recognize that this selection criteria potentially centers the male-dominated "radical" works of the New Sociology by virtue of its conception of what "radical" work is.

A second problem lies in considering all the feminist studies done of gender differentiation and the curriculum and then "selecting out," as not radical, some prime examples of simplistic structural understandings of gender. In the familiar feminist divisions of "liberal," "radical," and "socialist" feminisms, what I take to be mainstream is most closely identified with liberal feminisms. Because I have not surveyed the curricular work on gender which is not radical, however, I cannot make this claim strongly. I simply do not know if most of the literature I have termed "mainstream" feminist curricular work is actually "structural." I do know of some works, however, that clearly are structural. To me, for example, Rapheala Best's (1983) work would be an example of "mainstream" structural feminism since her work universally applies very simplistic gender differences to all members of both sexes *and* declares no intent for advancing radical social transformation. Where authors such as Best clearly argue for the need to alter social formations, their studies are not presented as transformative in themselves. And where Best does consider the construction of gender (as opposed to "sex differentiation"), she also tends to conflate sex and gender, making broad proclamations about all girls and boys.

The turn toward post-structural feminist arguments initiated in my second chapter responds to both of the problems faced in selecting from among the feminist works. On the one hand, the threefold typology of feminisms employed above has recently been expanded to include a fourth category known as either "deconstructive" or "post-structural" feminisms (de Lauretis, 1990; Lather, 1991). In this view, taking the post-structural feminists' word for it, an example of any one of the liberal, radical or socialist feminisms available in educational literature would suffice as a structural argument. On the other hand, decentering male-dominated research is one of the intentions and benefits (I think) of the post-structural turn in feminisms.

< 8 >

I would also like to discuss one final problem in selecting the relevant literature for this study: namely, my U.S.-centric view. My choice of focusing on the sociology of school knowledge in the United States is directly related to both my questions and responses about how one understands power relations between social groups. Because my questions emanated from a concern about how RSSK relates to "mainstream" educational research communities, it was necessary to focus on specific social fields and contexts. Given that I was located in the United States when this work began, my chosen focus was also made relative to the social world I then knew best. This I take to be consistent with my analysis.

While I suspect partially equivalent claims may be "transported" to other contexts, the specific legitimating principles and social distinctions would probably vary greatly from "society" to "society." To give an example, it may be true that educational research in Europe faces the same privileging and mimicking of the natural sciences as can be found within the U.S. educational sciences, and perhaps even the same dominance of psychologically based research, but I do not think the notion of an academic pursuing openly political research would be as "radical" to most European academics as it seems to be in the United States. Further, while I think the type of analysis for which I call would be useful and in some sense applicable in other societies (after all, much of my work is based on an appropriation of French and German social thought), explicitly focusing on the United States is intended as both a local and partial struggle.

ON HOW THIS IS MORE THAN JUST ANOTHER U.S. STORY

In presenting this work, I argue that the developments, dynamics, and ruptures of RSSK have a significance that lies well beyond the boundaries of its own field, beyond its immediate parents (the sociology of education and curriculum theory), and even beyond the larger family of the field of education. In sum, I suggest the theoretical and methodological developments of this one small field are illustrative of long-standing and continuing tensions in most varieties of academic social analysis—and perhaps an even wider range of academic work.

On first sight, this argument is fairly unremarkable. As will become apparent, the most publicly recognized socio-political academic battles of the past two decades have affected RSSK no less than any other field. Hence, for example, herein are tales of the feminist confrontation with male-centered Marxist analysis, and of post-structural and postmodern challenges to virtually every progressive intent. More centrally, what follows also pivots on the radical struggle to challenge conventional or mainstream academic tenets. The academic divides along these lines will assuredly be recognizable through that part of the academy which concerns itself with social analysis as well as within

< 9 >

some of the humanities and philosophy. While the possibility of any direct application of the specific debates of RSSK will certainly fade the further one moves from its analytical space, the basic terms of the debates within RSSK are set in the very same molds that have formed the outlines of academic debate in even its more remote cognate relations. In this sense, it is obvious that an analysis of RSSK could inform any of its academic neighbors.

But I would be a fool if I believed this obvious observation was sufficient to persuade readers who consider themselves to be outside of the field of education to follow through to the remainder of this work. Without overly optimistic illusion, I still argue that the analyses of radical sociology of school knowledge need to be recognized more widely for the potentially crucial insights they offer the Academy as a whole, as well as for the insights they offer the development of States. Roughly speaking, the argument that immediately follows can be traced as a conjunction of RSSK with the work of Benavot, et al. (1991), Boli and Ramirez (1986), Boli, Ramirez, and Meyer (1985), Meyer (1980), Meyer, Ramirez, and Soysal (1992), and Wallerstein (1990, 1991).

To the Academy, I suggest that the history of radical sociologies of school knowledge demonstrates the dangers in the inherent tendency toward that prototypical academic delusion that our debates matter to anyone other than ourselves. While I do not follow Nietszche completely and am not willing to simply proclaim the whole academic enterprise absurd, my analysis of RSSK has made me keenly aware of the way in which Nietszche's chastisements of the Academy have not been taken seriously enough even as they are often taken too seriously. Since one of the main objects of analysis in RSSK is educational institutions which have recognized social effects, there is an obvious site of possible application of this one field's knowledge beyond the walls of the Academy—i.e., extant educational systems. Nevertheless, as I hope to demonstrate, the regulative demands of academic production have often led those interested in having their work impact beyond the walls of the Academy to produce knowledge which is virtually socially irrelevant outside of the immediate frontiers of one academic field.

To those busily constructing analyses of modern, postmodern, and post-colonial states, I must point out that the conceptual nexus on which RSSK has been built is central to what we know of current socio-political endeavors. The argument that radical sociologies of school knowledge have a central place in our understanding of current socio-political maneuvers has many, many dimensions to it. Here, I outline seven basic points of departure as follows:

1. That the inhabitable planet has been divided into entities called nation-states, and this fact, in itself, represents the development of a world-cultural system.

< 10 >

2. That within most of the planet's nation-states, formal educational systems have been constructed.
3. That these educational systems are demonstrably quite similar and thereby mark a further advance of a world-culture.
4. That these modern educational systems, in every instance, are demonstrably associated with social inequality.
5. That schooling is demonstrably intertwined in the processes of producing each nation-state's societal inequality.
6. That a basic medium by which schools produce social inequality is knowledge, most obviously embodied in official and hidden curriculum.
7. That underlying the educational production of social inequality is the relationship between power and curriculum.

In this light, it should be clear that understanding the relationship between power and school knowledge is crucial for any nation-state's endeavor to develop equitably. Whether or not any one nation-state cares to worry about social equity is, of course, an open question. But within virtually every international socio-political organization (such as the OECD, the United Nations and its operational arm UNESCO, and even within the International Declaration of Human Rights), the role of education and the place of equity or equal opportunity is central. In this light it should be sociologically evident that an incisive and expansive understanding of how school systems interrelate power and knowledge is crucial to most nations, as explicit policies are constructed to purposively lever that interrelation.

As one very acute and lingering example, is it commonly acknowledged that the Neo-Conservative policies of the Reagan-Thatcher era explicitly traded off the chance for an increase in the production of socio-educational inequality for an ostensible increase in national economic productivity. To the best of my knowledge, the available and relevant academic evidence suggests now, as it did in the early 1980s, that the rationale supporting these policies was at best guess work and more probably empirically dubious. Despite this fact, to the best of my knowledge, particularly within the United States, an enduring and persuasive knowledge base on which one might have built a convincing counter-case did not exist at the ground level—at the level of classrooms, teachers, parents, and schools. And to the best of my knowledge, in terms of the available knowledge about curricular practices and social inequality, educators or policy makers or politicians so inclined to worry about the level of socio-educational inequality in their nations are currently only marginally better off than they were fifteen years ago. Thus, in very real and very serious terms, it seems to me anyone concerned about social inequity should find interest in radical sociologies of school knowledge.

On a more ethereal level, however, I note that virtually every radical

< 11 >

social theorist or philosopher has turned to the processes of education when the pragmatic question of how to advance our social organizations has been addressed. Whether we turn to the central eminence of U.S. philosophy, John Dewey, or call on the so-called classical philosophy of Plato or Aristotle or Aquinas, or turn to a Marxist understanding of the role of knowledge within the productive forces, or listen to the Southern Asia understandings of Tagora or Ghandi, or to modern European theorists such as Habermas or Bourdieu, or the ancient wisdom of many indigenous peoples, such as the Australian Aborigines and Torres Strait Islanders, the Pacific Islanders, the Maoris, or many of the Native American nations, it has been clear to many that the future of our social organizations is embodied in our children. Unless we have a very good understanding of the relationship between power and knowledge within the now global institution of schooling, we would know little of how we, as social beings, raise those children.

And since the nation-states into which the planet has been divided are almost all amalgamations of what once were multiple smaller cultures, smaller groups of people, the question of how the knowledge and cultures of those subsocietal social groups will be altered, muted, and mutated within the growing school systems of the world should be, in my estimation, at the forefront of many national debates. Unfortunately, as far as I can tell, these debates and the work generated in the attempt to understand these debates are not at all well known, well publicized, or even of any concern outside of the social field identified by the relationship between power and curriculum.

< 12 >

two

Constructing the Field

It must be acknowledged that in few of the civilized nations of our time have the higher sciences made less progress than in the United States; and in few have great artists, distinguished poets, or celebrated writers, been more rare.
—de Tocqueville, *Democracy in America*

One can note, in the case of the United States, the absence to a considerable degree of traditional intellectuals.
—Gramsci, *Prison Notebooks*

IN MANY WAYS, THE FIELD I ANALYZE IN THIS PROJECT, the radical sociology of school knowledge in the United States, is peculiarly American. There are many characteristics of the work done in this field which mark the lines of intellectual endeavors of the larger social arena known as the American Academy. Where the American Academy has been seen to present itself as anti-intellectual, apolitical, empiricist, overly practical, and isolationist, radical sociologists of school knowledge as oppositional intellectuals have consciously aspired toward a high degree of intellectualism, anti-empiricism, and overtly strategic political commitment (Hofstader, 1962; Popkewitz, 1991). From this standpoint, there seems to be a spiritual congruence between the dispositions of radical educational scholars and the thoughts of Alexis de Toqueville and Antonio Gramsci. Where American education and sociology have been largely and decidedly ignorant of European intellectual movements, the radical sociologists of school knowledge openly (though not exclusively) built their intellectual positions on European works. And so it goes that I, like many before me, turn toward Europe to describe the intellectual origins of RSSK.

Before turning to my excavation of this field, though, I would like to introduce what I intend this chapter to do. Roughly speaking, I frame this chapter as an analysis of the conceptual origins of what has become something of a signature position in United States's RSSK—namely, Michael Apple's "Parallelist Position." In this position, three social dynamics are presented as essential for radical sociological analyses of curriculum: race, gender, and class. While each of these three dynamics and the interconnections between them are taken as potentially crucial, no single dynamic is to be given analytical primacy prior to any analysis. *Pace* orthodox Marxist positions, the Parallelist Position does not analytically place a priori primacy on economic class relations. In addition to these three social dynamics, three social spheres are nominated as important sites of investigation: the economic, cultural, and political spheres. Arguing here against what is seen as an overly economic Marxist tradition, Apple suggests analyses of culture and the State are also crucial. As with the social dynamics included in this model, the logic governing the social spheres is similarly additive—a priori primacy is given to none, and the interconnections among the three spheres are highlighted as potentially important.[1]

This conceptual matrix is, in a sense, considerably more complex than were the first works which proposed to analyze the relationship between power and curriculum through sociological lenses. Indeed, it is perhaps difficult to see easily how such a position is the consequence of its apparent Marxist ancestry. For instance, one could also note the surface similarity between this conceptual matrix and traditional Weberian analyses of class, status and power. But when viewed within the context of a developing analytical history, this position can be understood as growing out of a series of progressive conceptual moves.

Hence, in this chapter, I intend to narrate the intellectual lineage of the United States's RSSK beginning with Michael F. D. Young's opening essay from *Knowledge and Control*. To tell this story, I shall be using a language of development and progress in terms that mark how this field can be seen to have more or less linearly developed. In this view, the sociology of curriculum can be seen to have dialectically oscillated between "subjective," interpretivist understandings of the socially constructed nature of curriculum and how individuals construct meaning through texts (broadly speaking), and "objective," structural accounts of how curricular practices reproduce social stratification. In this Hegelian rendering of the ever recreated synthesis of past oppositional approaches, progression is seen and progress assumed.

In constructing this story, I shall be demonstrating that since Apple's formulation of the Parallelist Position, the Structural Neo-Marxist research agenda of the radical sociology of curriculum has analytically stagnated. Here, the focus of this chapter is specifically on the analytical logic of this Structural Neo-Marxist agenda. I am not suggesting that this analytical logic impedes the production of research. I am suggesting however, that this line of research is caught within a logic whose consequent claims and conclusions are as predictable as they are limited. Generally, as I shall argue in much more detail below, in its research endeavor the analytical logic of U.S. Structural

< 14 >

Neo-Marxist sociologies of school knowledge faces recurrent conceptual dilemmas which it seemingly cannot escape. First articulated in 1983, twelve years have passed since the public announcement of the Parallelist Position, and no signs have been given that this tradition has moved beyond its initial concerns and intellectual frame (Apple and Weis, 1983a). This point, in itself, should be demonstrated and explained, for it implies that what may have appeared a progression will no longer progress.

It is very important to note that the very possibility of seeing this stagnation lies endogenously within the Neo-Marxist analytical lenses and language of that tradition. In telling a story of a stagnated tradition, I will simultaneously be using the very language which makes claims of stagnation seem plausible. To substantively explain this view, I will consider how central Neo-Marxist concepts limit what is possible for a sociology of school knowledge. As I delineate two major strands within the Structural Neo-Marxist sociology of school knowledge (the structural and the phenomenological), I shall highlight, *inter alia*, two conceptual legacies of this discourse—what I call a lack of interpretive justification and a tendency to confound potential empirical verification.

Problems of interpretation and verifiability are commonly raised in educational research, and that I raise them with respect to the radical sociology of school knowledge is probably not that surprising. In this chapter I will not directly address the debates about these methodological issues per se. Rather, my interest in this chapter is to establish that the research in RSSK is open to these methodological criticisms and to argue that the conceptual framework represented in the Parallelist Position carries serious limitations for attempts to persuasively respond to such methodological problems.

One final caveat should be noted before I turn to surveying the origins of RSSK. In the analysis below I have not attempted to provide an exhaustive account of the research done in this field. Rather my interest is one of trying to frame the conceptual categories which regulated or governed the way in which American scholars imported early European studies in the field. The texts I reference and discuss below have been selected for their illustrative utility in this effort.[2]

THE ORIGINS OF A FIELD

Past attempts to survey the development of this field of inquiry cite, among others, the work of Michael F. D. Young and Basil Bernstein in England and Anyon, Apple, and Giroux in the United States, as prime authors in the field (Whitty, 1985; Wexler, 1987). Within these reviews, Young's (1971c) edited volume *Knowledge and Control* has been seen as the germinal volume in the field of the sociology of curriculum. I too begin my historical survey of RSSK with this declaration.

< 15 >

As his book title suggested, Young saw central concerns for the sociology of education turning around two pivotal positions. On the one hand, building from the work of Dawe, Young maintained that the "defining problem" of the sociology of education was one of social control. Here Young argued that the sociology of education's focus on control lay in the recognition that 1) the "problem of order" or "doctrine of control" has been the cornerstone of sociological inquiry since the eighteenth century; and that 2) twentieth century commonsense conceptions of "science" and "rationality" have embroiled sociology in the representation of "dominant legitimizing categories" (Young, 1971a, pp. 2–5). On the other hand, the second (and perhaps more central) pivotal position among the constellation of the New Sociology's analytical repertoire was the questioning of how sociological analysis related its own practices and proclamations to knowledge. Central here was the notion that knowledge itself is a social construct, a position that has been linked to the works of philosopher Alfred Schutz and sociologists Berger and Luckman (see Esland, 1971; Karabel and Halsey, 1977a). In seeking to understand the ways in which sociological studies of education were implicated in relations of power and control, Young argued that traditional educational sociology had not sufficiently questioned "what counts as educational knowledge."

Subtitled "New Directions for the Sociology of Education," Young presented the collected works in this book as a response to what he and his colleagues saw as the fundamental inadequacies of the sociology of education. In opposition to seemingly taken for granted assumptions implicit in public policy proposals for educational reform, the New Sociology chastised sociology of education for not adequately making explicit these public assumptions and for not questioning their sociological implications for educational practice. Young, for example, criticized what he saw as "government pressure for more and better technologists and scientists," questioning the social construction of what was taken as "science" in public policy. In opposition to a tendency in the sociology of education to take for granted educational problems, the New Sociology sought to reveal an implicitly accepted "order doctrine." Here the New Sociology has been interpreted as rejecting a structural-functionalist sociological view in favor of phenomenological studies that have been seen as an "interpretivist" view (see Karabel and Halsey, 1977a). And in opposition to the sociology of education's lack of attention to the content of education, the New Sociology placed questions of the curriculum and knowledge center stage.

More specifically, among the surveyors of this field, Young's (1971b) opening chapter to *Knowledge and Control*, "An Approach to the Study of Curriculum as Socially Organized Knowledge," has been presented as the benchmark declaration of what the sociology of school knowledge is. In this chapter, a foundation for the sociological study of curriculum was stated

< 16 >

positively, rather than in a series of negative oppositional stances. Paraphrasing Raymond Williams, in part, Young framed the New Sociology's agenda in these terms:

> Sociologists seem to have forgotten . . . that education is not a product like cars and bread, but a selection and organization from the available knowledge at a particular time which involves conscious and unconscious choices. It would seem that it is or should be the central task of the sociology of education to relate these principles of selection and organization that underlie curricula to their institutional and interactional setting in schools and classrooms and to the wider social structure. (p. 24)

Here it was clear that Young sought to connect the patterns of micro-level daily practices of schooling ("principles of selection and organization that underlie curricula") to their mezzo-level institutional setting and to the macro-level societal structure. By questioning the organization of school knowledge (manifest in the curriculum) and attempting to relate it to wider social structures, Young's perspective retraced a central problematic of the sociology of knowledge (a connection he made explicit in a subsection of his essay entitled "The Sociology of Knowledge and the Curriculum") (pp. 26–27).

After favorably citing Alfred Schutz's phenomenological insights into the social construction of knowledge, and stating that this work was not then well known in sociology, Young (1971b) stated that from the perspective of the sociology of knowledge, "(t)he school curriculum becomes just one of the mechanisms through which knowledge is 'socially distributed'" (p. 27). Young then went on to criticize the sociology of knowledge for its lack of impact on the sociology of education, stating that "(t)hree strands, which characterize the more familiar traditions in the sociology of knowledge (i.e. not Schutz), indicate not its lack of potential but why the direction it has taken has made its contribution to the sociology of education so insignificant" (p. 27).

Young's offered three criticisms of the sociology of knowledge: 1) that its research had been mostly concerned with epistemology and the existential nature of knowledge, a program in which "substantive empirical research (had) been eschewed," 2) that since Marx there had been a "neglect of the cognitive dimensions of the categories of thought," and 3) that the process of transmitting knowledge, itself seen as a social construct, had not been studied (p. 27).

With these criticisms and the view that the sociology of knowledge offered strong potential for the sociological study of school knowledge, Young then entered into an interesting evaluation of sociology's founding traditions—those associated with sociology's founding fathers, Marx, Weber, and Durkheim. According to Young, although Marx's theories offered a general account "for the changes in men's (sic) consciousness or categories of thought in terms of the changing means of production and the social relations they

< 17 >

generate" (pp. 27–28), Marxist theories had not addressed education sufficiently and had neglected the process of knowledge acquisition. Correspondingly, Young pointed out that although Marx's claim that education in a capitalist society is a tool of ruling class interest gave some direction to an examination of the relationship between education, elite curricula, and the economy, Marx's general theoretical level did not "point to explanations of the dynamics of particular configurations or different curricula" (p. 28). Among the Marxist theorists Young considered were Gramsci, Perry Anderson, and Raymond Williams.[3] Weber's work on education was taken by Young to be helpful for its comparative framework, but limited by its lack of "an overall framework for linking the principles of selection of content to the social structure" (p. 30). Durkheim's work on education was seen to be "not very helpful" (p. 31), in part due to the standing criticisms of Durkheim's harmonious view of society and focus on social integration. But Durkheim's sociology of religion and its connection to the sociology of knowledge, according to Young, had been employed by Bourdieu and Bernstein in a potentially productive way.

Young's recognition of the value a Durkheimian analysis offered the sociology of school knowledge can be understood simply by juxtaposing how Young had framed the central problematic of his field with Durkheim's main concerns in his sociology of religion. Recall Young claimed that,

> It would seem that it is or should be the central task of the sociology of education to relate these principles of selection and organization that underly curricula to their institutional and interactional setting in schools and classrooms and to the wider social structure. (cited above)

In the terms of a Durkheimian analysis, this can be readily stated as an attempt to conduct relational analyses of the connections between mental structures and social structures.

But Young's understanding of power, and his concern for examining how curricula are determined, favored a more Marxist approach. In discussing his conceptual outline for "an approach to the study of curricula as socially organized knowledge," Young posited the claim that,

> consideration of the assumptions underlying the selection and organization of knowledge by those in positions of power may be a fruitful perspective for raising sociological questions about curricula. We can make this more explicit by starting with the assumption that those in positions of power will attempt to define what is taken as knowledge, how accessible to different groups any knowledge is, and what are the accepted relationships between different knowledge areas and those who have access to them and make them available. (pp. 31–32)

< 18 >

In this view, knowledge was taken as a social construct and society was taken to be differentiated along lines of power relations. Implicit in this view of knowledge was the notion that intersubjectively valued "knowledge" can operate as a property component of social differentiation and stratification. And the view that "those in positions of power will attempt to define what is taken as knowledge" vaguely mirrored Marx's understanding of education in capitalist societies. Yet the connection to economic class was not explicit, and not necessarily implicit, in Young's oft cited formulations of the sociology of school knowledge's basic problematics considered above.

In relation essays by other writers in *Knowledge and Control*, it was clear, however, that the early English New Sociologists considered class a viable category in analyzing "the wider social structure." For example, Nell Keddie's 1971 essay, "Classroom Knowledge," the fifth chapter in *Knowledge and Control*, was a qualitative case study of "streaming" in one English comprehensive school. Examining the social basis of how teachers categorized students into differing streams, Keddie suggested that social class (as defined by the research "subjects") was a latent and implicit category used by teachers to sort students' behavior. Here Keddie focused on the differentiation of middle-class students and working-class students, their disproportionate placements into different streams, teacher and student perceptions of classroom practices and differential treatments of school knowledge within the different streams. Against the then taken-for-granted assumptions that categorized poorly achieving students as "socially deviant" (or "culturally deficit"), Keddie argued that commonsense educational notions such as "ability" were part of a social process which in fact produced social deviance rather than responded to it. Simply put, part of Keddie's argument suggested that once teachers identified students as having certain educational "abilities," they were also relying on perceptions based on social class.

Keddie's emphasis on the socially constructed nature of teachers' knowledge (their categories of thought, such as the notion of "ability"), its implication in schools' organizational differentiation of students into streams, the students' categories of thought, and the correspondence between social class and the kind of knowledge engendered in differential schooling practices, made clear that her concerns lay well within the bounds of Young's conceptual matrix. With this perspective, Keddie had begun to empirically address the three central questions Young (drawing on Bernstein) had posed for the sociology of curriculum: "How stratified are knowledge areas?", "What is the scope of knowledge areas?", "And, how related are the knowledge areas?" (1971b). According to Young, these questions allowed studies to begin to address questions of the relations between the power structures in society and the differentiations of knowledge in curriculum. In Keddie's case, the wider social structure was differentiated according to social class.

< 19 >

But Keddie's essay did not directly address Young's call for examining these principles of selection and organization of school knowledge. As a descriptive account, Keddie's essay was quite illuminating; but Keddie provided no theoretical explanations for the focus on social class (other than saying that the differentiation of schooling corresponded to social class differences).

Predictably, Marxist sociologists of curriculum held strong criticisms of the sociology of school knowledge precisely because of its lack of attention to the principles underlying class differentiations (Sharp and Green, 1975; Sharp, 1980). While sympathetic to Young's (1971a, 1971b) critique of traditional sociology of education, the object of the Marxist critique lay in the New Sociology's turn toward phenomenologically "subjective" studies.

In 1975, Rachel Sharp and Anthony Green criticized the phenomenological studies advanced in *Knowledge and Control* because they felt they had not sufficiently "contextualized" classroom experiences within the "larger" societal structure. Specifically critical of Geoffrey Esland's and Keddie's accounts, Sharp and Green illustrated their position with the example of what had become known as the "self-fulfilling prophecy." At that time many classroom-based studies had noted that once teachers acted on taken-for-granted categories, such as "ability," students behaved in ways that fit the category into which they had been slotted. Sharp and Green weren't critical of this specific aspect of such research. Rather their concern was that by focusing only on the classroom, studies such as Keddie's either assumed, rather than made problematic, the teachers' power to define reality, or ignored teachers' power altogether.

According to Sharp and Green, it was one thing to recognize the power of the ways in which teachers categorize students, but it was another to account for the basis of the categorization. If we assumed that the basis of the categorization lay within individual teachers, then teachers had the power to simply change their views (and all would have been wonderful). But that assumption was problematic, since teachers had *reasons* for categorizing students. In Sharp and Green's words, the approach employed by these phenomenological studies was insufficient because,

> by focusing their attention on the consciousness of social actors they have narrowed the scope of sociological enquiry to a point where the kinds of explanations they can offer for social processes are found seriously wanting. (p. 14)

The reasons on which teachers base categorizations, so the argument went, lie in the wider social structure of society.

To understand and study the processes with which Sharp and Green were concerned, they proposed an alternative perspective.

< 20 >

The perspective we are advocating is one which attempts to situate teachers' world views and practices within the context of social and physical resources and constraints which they may or may not perceive, but which structure their situation and set limits to the freedom of action through the opportunities and facilities made available to them and the constraints and limitations imposed on them. (p. 30)

This view was not meant to imply that all social actions are determined by social structures. On the contrary this perspective understood any individual as acting relatively freely, but still "acting within a context which cannot be intended away by consciousness and which narrows the range of likely ensuing behaviour." (p. 30)

Documenting the theoretical movement toward a Marxist perspective, the "context" Sharp and Green related to their account of classroom practices was often the context of the economic class structure. Overall, Sharp and Green's analysis focused on the development of students' identities within "progressive" classrooms. Similar to Keddie's work, in this analysis students' identities differed according to students' class backgrounds, in relation to a classroom-based process of differentiation, or "social stratification in the classroom." Unlike Keddie's analysis, however, Sharp and Green related classroom practices to class at multiple levels (e.g., understanding the relationships between the headmaster and teachers, between teachers and parents, between teachers and students, etc.).

The contrast between the two analyses is perhaps best seen in an example. One issue raised in Sharp and Green's analysis is related to interpreting teachers' actions. According to Sharp and Green,

> teachers are encapsulated within a context where the problems of management and control require some implicit hierarchical differentiation of pupils in order to solve the problem of order and provide some legitimation for the allocation of scarce resources, i.e. the teacher's time and energies. (p. 127)

Here teachers' actions are clearly not simply interpreted in terms of the conceptions teachers hold in their heads. In the class structure, teachers were seen as members of the proletariat working class because they sell their labor power in exchange for wages. And because the material conditions of their work were under the control of what would now be called a capitalist state apparatus, teacher perceptions could be understood readily in relation to classroom conditions in which they faced large numbers of students (particularly within working-class schools) with few material resources. While this example was only one layer of their analysis, Sharp and Green directly connected their observations of school experience to the "larger" class structure of society at many other levels as well.

There are two things to note about this Marxist account of schooling.

< 21 >

First, while explaining explicitly that they understood class in relation "to the means of production" (the classical Marxist conception), in Sharp and Green's analysis "class" held the status of a somewhat assumed category. Students' class backgrounds were, in many ways, assumed in accordance with commonsense understandings of class location. Second, while rejecting phenomenological interpretations, arguing such a perspective places too much emphasis on the "subjective." Sharp and Green's own research was based on qualitative data collection (interviews and observations). In the U.S. context, in which qualitative research had been virtually equated with "subjective" studies, the juxtaposition of Sharp and Green's theory and methodology presented something of a perceived inconsistency.

Sharp and Green's critique of phenomenological studies also provided an early signal of three trends in this field. The first of these is a central theoretical dimension in U.S. RSSK. Roughly characterized, I would suggest that Sharp and Green's criticisms relied on the binary poles of the "objective" and "subjective" positions in the field. As will be seen below, this binary differentiation has been repeatedly raised in slightly altered homologous forms, such as in the "structure versus agency" terminology. Second, I would also point out that in all of the early studies of the field the primary research mode was qualitative. And third, the field's focus on class as a central category for social analysis, and its affinity toward Marxist analysis, was already apparent. Each of these characteristics can be seen as originating points for trends that continued, with some deviations, in the American field into the 1980s.

THE BOOM YEARS

In the three years beginning with 1975, the year Sharp and Green's book was published, a substantial number of studies were published that were related to RSSK. At least four seriously influential works were published and readily available for academic consumption in the United States First, from England in 1975, Basil Bernstein (1975/1977a) published the third volume of his socio-linguistically based studies, *Class, Codes, and Control*. While his earlier essays on education were well known by this time (with one of them published in *Knowledge and Control* and later reprinted in volume one of *Class, Codes, and Control*), this third volume of his series was his first book which focused entirely and directly on the questions raised in the sociology of school knowledge. Subtitled "Towards a Theory of Educational Transmissions," it was U.S. educational scholars' most direct access point to Bernstein's works. Second, in 1976 the U.S. Neo-Marxists Samuel Bowles and Herbert Gintis (1976) published their *Schooling in Capitalist America*. Third, the English translation of Pierre Bourdieu and Jean-Claude Passeron's (1970) *La Reproduction* (translated from French as *Reproduction in Education, Society, and Culture*) was

< 22 >

published in 1977. And finally, Paul Willis's English ethnography of working-class boys, *Learning to Labor*, was also published in 1977.

Each of these volumes has been taken as a central text in the radical sociology of school knowledge, and each has been discussed at length in many other studies. Since my interest in this chapter is one of trying to articulate how past theory and research in the field contributed to the conceptual formation of U.S. RSSK, my concern is not to provide full, in-depth interpretations of this work. Rather, my concern is to provide a description of how these texts were appropriated into the U.S. context. Consequently, here I would only like to briefly characterize typical readings of their general theoretical frameworks.[4]

To mark a theoretical shift between these works, I will consider them slightly out of their temporal order. That is, only one of these works, *Schooling in Capitalist America*, theoretically focused almost exclusively on economic structures, and in this sense it can be seen to follow on the heels of Sharp and Green's analysis.

Bowles and Gintis's analysis was based on two lines of research. On the one hand this book presented a historical Marxist analysis of education as the major means of reproducing class structure in a capitalist society (the United States). On the other hand, large-scale quantitative sociological analyses were employed to establish what was labeled the "correspondence principle," establishing a correspondence between differentially created habits, dispositions, knowledges (consciousness, in the Marxist language), and class structure. Roughly put, this principle was in part meant to illustrate that working-class students were given schooling which imparted the habits, dispositions, and knowledge which would make them good workers, and middle-class students were given habits, dispositions, and knowledge necessary to take on middle-class occupations.

Bowles and Gintis argued that the capitalist economic structure of society required the reproduction of specific forms of consciousness distributed across a differentiated class structure, and that education was "one of several reproduction mechanisms through which dominant elites seek to achieve this objective" (p. 147). But because capitalist expansion, in a Marxist analysis, involves periods of severe economic crisis (with these cycles due to the inherent "contradictions" of capitalism), as the economic "base" of society changes, so too must the "super-structural" educational system. Thus, in their historical analysis of the U.S. economy and its relation to education, Bowles and Gintis argued, "(t)he three points in U.S. educational history which we have identified all correspond to particularly intense periods of struggle around the expansion of capitalist relations" (p. 234). These three historical points (the antebellum period, the Progressive era, and the unrest of the 1960s), according to Bowles and Gintis, represented points of both economic crises and educational reforms designed to settle the unrest caused by the economic crises.

< 23 >

This analysis was, like many radical critiques of the mid-1970s, constructed as a rejection of the notion that schooling works to allow younger generations an opportunity to earn their position in society, hence rejecting the view of society as a "meritocracy." This aspect of the research in *Schooling* currently seems unremarkable. But the research Bowles and Gintis used to support their arguments is remarkable for a number of other reasons. First, the basis of this work was quite comprehensive in terms of its sample size (compared to classroom-based research). Second, the quantitative sociology in this work brought radical critiques significant "scientific" legitimacy in the Academy. Third, while Bowles and Gintis offered theoretical Marxist definitions of class, their empirical analyses often based class categorization on very traditional sociological parameters, such as measures of fathers' incomes and occupational status positions. In fact, much of the data used by Bowles and Gintis was taken from studies done within the "American status-attainment tradition" of sociology.

Comparing the use of "class" within Sharp and Green's and Bowles and Gintis's analyses sheds considerable light on how class has been conceived in Neo-Marxist sociologies of school knowledge. Both these studies employed notions of class which were strictly based in economics. Here the focus has traditionally been on questions of the "material" conditions of social relations, and how educational experiences correspond to the economic class structure of society.

But there are differences in how these analyses use class categories. On the one hand, for Bowles and Gintis, class has been deployed within the *distribution* of economic factors such as income, wealth, and occupation. The early sociology of curriculum offered by the Australian sociologist of education, P. W. Musgraves (1972), also employs class in this manner. In studies such as these, classes were distinguished through a categorization of the range of economic characteristics people were said to "own." Looking at the whole distribution of these economic characteristics in a society, sociologists differentiated who was lower-, middle-, and upper-class by simply splitting up the range into three categories (or more).

On the other hand, when employing a more orthodox Marxist conception of class (as did Sharp and Green), the focus was not on the amount of income or wealth people had; rather the focus was on what position people held in relation to the labor process within a capitalist society. If one had to sell his or her labor in exchange for wages, and did not "own" any of the "means" of production (other than one's own labor power), s/he would have been considered part of the proletariat; as a group these people were the workingclass. If one owned some means of production (owning a business or factory) and did not have to sell his or her own labor, s/he was considered a member of the capitalist class. The importance of an occupation, in this view,

< 24 >

was not how much status or income it had; rather, it was a matter of an occupation's relation to the labor process.

While there is some "blurring" between these two understandings of economic class (income distribution, occupational status, and the actual working conditions of varying occupations are not entirely distinct after all), the distinction between identifying economic class location through distributional measures and identifying class strictly in relation to the labor process is a crucial Marxist argument. Underlying this distinction is an analogous distinction between mental and manual labor, and an emphasis on the actual ownership of the means of production—a distinction which was to become of central import for later work in the field.

Interestingly, one of the strengths of Bowles and Gintis's argument, its focus on the macro-societal relationship between schooling and the economy, was also seen as one of its weaknesses. An echo of earlier criticisms of mainstream educational sociology was to be heard again as Bowles and Gintis's thesis was repeatedly criticized because of their model's inability to account for the daily practices of schooling. As Apple (1979b) put it,

> (T)he economistic position provides a less adequate appraisal of the way these outcomes (the reproduction of the division of labor, *inter alia*) are *created* by the school. It cannot fully illuminate what the mechanisms of domination are and how they work in the day-to-day activity of school life. (p. 2)

In a similar vein, *Schooling* was also criticized because of its treatment of curriculum. While Bowles and Gintis had focused on unseen aspects of the curriculum in the form of dispositions associated with differentiated curricula (what educational critics had called the "hidden curriculum"), they had not given an adequate account of the overt curriculum (Whitty, 1985, pp. 25–29).

These theoretical concerns were at the heart of Bernstein's and Bourdieu and Jean-Claude Passeron's sociological endeavors. For Bernstein, and Bourdieu and Passeron, schooling could be seen as relatively autonomous from the economy. In these analyses, the relationships between school knowledge, institutional practices, and societal differentiation were a matter of understanding symbolic and cultural reproduction in education. Largely informed by Durkheim, Bernstein and Bourdieu and Passeron advanced highly complex theoretical frameworks linking the micro-level pedagogical practices of schooling to the macro-level realities of social inequality.

Bernstein's socio-linguistic studies had long been well known in multiple fields of social inquiry, and his influence on the early foundations of the sociology of school knowledge was readily apparent in Young's initial conceptualization of the field. But the radical sociology of school knowledge, despite its frequent references to Bernstein, substantively drew very little directly from his theorizing (Wexler, 1987; Whitty, 1985; and Sadovnick, 1991). Generally,

< 25 >

Bernstein's theoretical papers were taken as a reminder that school knowledge and curriculum were not to be taken for granted, and that the sociological study of curriculum could contribute to an understanding of education's role as a mechanism of legitimation and social control. More specifically, Bernstein's attempt to differentiate between fractions of the middle class was also taken as a significant insight (Apple and Wexler, 1978). However, Bernstein's distinctions between different types of symbolic and linguistic codes, and different forms of the "classification and framing" of school knowledge were to receive little direct "application" in the U.S. radical sociology of school knowledge literature until the early 1980s (Beyer, 1983; Sadovnick, 1991).

Bourdieu and Passeron's *Reproduction* received much more direct attention (though usually with a healthy dose of dismissive critique), and their arguments that the knowledge and dispositions distributed by schools could be analyzed as forms of cultural capital, and as class *habitus*, fit readily into the cultural Neo-Marxist ideology-critiques advanced by Apple and Giroux.[5] In addition to Bourdieu and Passeron's specific concepts, two general arguments advanced in *Reproduction* also became widely discussed. The first of these arguments suggested that, for specific fractions of the middle class, schooling offered a mechanism for ensuring their children's position in their family's class location through a logic of reconversion between cultural and economic capital. This argument is premised on the recognition that schools largely operate through specific, but arbitrary, cultural forms which "filter out" those students who have not acquired the specific cultural capitals schools reward. For class segments rich in the cultural capital of the schools, large educational investments (of time, effort, and economic capital) could later be reconverted into economic capital. This reconversion would be due to the further educational and higher occupational access given those who had achieved high levels of education.

The second argument taken from *Reproduction* was a critique of education's role in legitimating social inequality through a "meritocratic" ideology. Because the cultural forms used in schooling are presented as natural or given, so the argument went, those students who did not have the cultural capital of the school (e.g., the lower classes) would misrecognize their lack of educational success as a legitimate basis for their subsequent lower social status. Although similar to Bowles and Gintis's critique, *Reproduction's* critique of "meritocracy" was built on the premise that the cultural exchanges of schooling were relatively autonomous from the direct economic demands of capitalism and that autonomy itself further buttressed the legitimating functions of education. By working as a cultural market, education not only legitimated the reproduction of social inequalities in which it was implicated, it also legitimated itself; or, as Bourdieu and Passeron put it, "(l)egitimation of the established order by the School presupposes social recognition of the

< 26 >

legitimacy of the School" (Bourdieu and Passeron, 1990).[6]

Thus, with the analytical frameworks of Bernstein, and Bourdieu and Passeron, the radical sociology of school knowledge was given theoretical advances to move beyond the economically based arguments of Sharp and Green, and Bowles and Gintis, into a distinctly cultural analysis. As Bernstein contemplated the consequences of his approach in the introduction to *Class, Codes, and Control, Vol. III* (1977a), it was clear he thought this analytical turn provided important insights into the pervasiveness of schooling's mechanisms of reproduction:

> [His] approach does provide some strategies of change of educational institutions—change in alignment of groups, interests and power as the classification and framing change their values. It also indicates what are likely to be new forms of social control and the new attributes of the person which may become candidates for labels. It attempts to reveal the ideological basis of forms of socialization within the family and the ideological basis of apparently 'progressive' pedagogies in the school. To my mind, it raises the basic issue that we can change the social means of the reproduction of class relationships, but not necessarily change the cultural means of such reproduction. It points to the question that although family and school are not themselves major levers of radical change—those lie in economic and political structures—family and education shape mental structures and so forms of feeling and thinking which may militate for or against changes in cultural reproduction. It therefore raises as a major problematic the relationships between social and cultural reproduction. (p. 30)

However, where the cultural turn, and the focus on cultural reproduction, marked a significant advance in the field's theory, there was also a continuity among the Neo-Marxist accounts advanced by Sharp and Green, and Bowles and Gintis, and the Durkheimian accounts advanced by Bernstein and Bourdieu and Passeron.

In each of these four arguments, decidedly structural accounts of the relationship between school knowledge and social structure had been advanced. Where Sharp and Green had been critical of Keddie's phenomenological account, in which no systematic analysis of the social structure was apparent and in which it seemed as if individual people could simply change their thinking to make things better, these structural accounts of social and cultural reproduction advanced theoretical understandings of the social genesis of individual consciousness.

I should note another interesting continuity that flowed through these structural accounts. Each one of them had advanced strong, class-based critiques of "progressive" educational initiatives which were intended, in part, to cash in on the liberal promise that schooling could function to transform social inequalities.[7] Sharp and Green argued that even in "progressive" classrooms the class location of teachers conditioned pedagogical practices which

< 27 >

disadvantaged working-class students. Bowles and Gintis interpreted "progressive" educational reforms as means of insuring the continuance of a capitalist class structure. Bernstein had argued that the then current move for more open pedagogy, what he termed "invisible" pedagogy, carried implicit norms which would mitigate the cultural norms of working-class families and possibly function to the advantage of a fraction of the middle-class, against the working-class (Bernstein, 1977a). And Bourdieu and Passeron (1990) had statistically shown that even as access to universities in France had expanded in the 1960s, with more working- and middle-class students entering university, the differentiation among disciplines and distribution of students within those disciplines according to social class background had simply recreated the class differentiation that "democratization" of the university was supposed to help alleviate (pp. 221–33).

Combined, the economic/culture differences and the structural continuities among these four theories presented something of a paradoxical twist for U.S. radical sociologists of school knowledge. Both *Education and Social Control* and, even more so, *Schooling in Capitalist America* had been roundly criticized for their ostensible "determinism." That is, each of them was taken to imply that individual actions were largely predefined by social structures. For example, in a discussion of Bowles and Gintis's work, Giroux (1981c) suggested,

> (w)hile the correspondence principle is of critical importance in understanding the nature and role of legitimating institutions such as schools, many radicals stretch the principle to the point of caricature and end up with an oversocialized model of schooling. The result is a mechanistic analysis that encloses itself in the dead-end of one-dimensionality; thus little room is left for radicals to explore the contradictions inherent in the schooling process or to analyze the tensions, rejection of values, and the deep disjunctions experienced by many students. (p. 69)

By so strongly arguing that schooling served to reproduce society's class structures, these economic-based analyses failed to consider other dimensions of schooling, according to U.S. sociologists of school knowledge. If schooling served only to reproduce economic class relations, as these theories were taken to suggest, it would have followed that society had never changed significantly. And that seemed obviously problematic. In order to account for both the ways schooling reproduces oppressive conditions, such as class positions, and the ways in which schooling might actually alter societal structures, later arguments went, we needed to also understand the culture of schooling. But neither Bernstein nor Bourdieu and Passeron gave U.S. sociologists of school knowledge much to be happy about. In fact, the structural-cultural theories of Bourdieu and Passeron, like those in *Schooling*, became a prime target in the

< 28 >

U.S. radical rejections of "deterministic" arguments (Apple 1979b, 1982c; Giroux 1983a).

There is a similarity between *Schooling* and *Reproduction* which distinguishes them from the other texts considered above, and which seems to correspond with the strength of their being labeled "deterministic": both of these texts employed large-scale, quantitative statistical methodologies. Herein lies one possible origin for the subsequent trend within the sociology of school knowledge of moving away from quantitative work. Seeing possibilities for change seems to hold an inverse relationship with the scope of one's vision. The larger the context one examines, the less change one sees.

And so it goes that Paul Willis's (1977) *Learning to Labor*, an ethnographic account of young working-class males and their counter-cultural relationship to schooling, was received with great enthusiasm and taken as a sign that there was counter-hegemonic hope on the horizon. Interpreting Willis's study in this way may seem odd considering, as Willis himself put it, "(t)he fact that kids from counter-school culture nevertheless do go forward relatively willingly to wage labor" (p. 206). But a counter-hegemonic interpretation it did receive. Giroux (1983a) offered an example of such an interpretation, and he is worth quoting at length here:

> Willis demonstrates in his study of the "lads" . . . that much of their opposition to the labels, meanings, and values of the official and hidden curriculum is informed by an ideology of resistance, the roots of which are in the shop-floor cultures occupied by their family members and other members of their class. The most powerful example of this mode of resistance is exhibited by the lads in their rejection of the primacy of mental over manual labor. Not only do the lads reject the alleged superiority of mental labor, they also reject its underlying ideology that respect and obedience will be exchanged for knowledge and success. The lads oppose this ideology because the counter-logic embodied in the families, workplaces, and street life that make up *their* culture points to a different and more convincing reality. Thus, one major contribution that has emerged from resistance studies is the insight that mechanisms of reproduction are never complete and are always faced with partially realized elements of opposition. (p. 283, emphasis in original)

Giroux, of course, was not ignoring the reproductive implications of Willis's study, nor was he the only one who interpreted the cultural struggles of the lads in a politically optimistic light (Willis, 1981a, p. 207).

Other, more somber, interpretations were also readily advanced in the U.S. sociology of curriculum. For example, Michael Apple (1982c) emphasized the lads' complicity in their own oppression. As he put it,

> By rejecting the world of the school, by rejecting what the "ear'oles" do, the lads also reject mental labor. They see it as effeminate, as not physical

< 29 >

enough. *The seeds of reproduction lie in this very rejection.* The distinctions made and acted upon by the lads imply a strong dichotomy between mental and manual labor. The seeing of strength in the physical, the dismissing of mental "book learning," provides an important element in the recreation of ideological hegemony of the dominant classes. (p. 98, emphasis in original)

Whether U.S. radical sociologists of school knowledge embarked upon their analyses of Willis's work with optimistic or pessimistic lenses, though, didn't seem to prevent them from reaching some consensus on the political implications of the resistance Willis (and many others) had begun to investigate.

For Giroux (1983a), Willis provided insights which could "point to new ways of constructing a radical pedagogy by developing analyses of the ways in which class and culture combine to offer the outlines for a 'cultural politics'" (p. 284). And for Apple (1982c), the resistance uncovered in such an ethnographic account meant, "that the lived culture of the students themselves may offer potent areas for political work" (p. 131). However ongoing cultural struggles may have contributed to countercultural youth's own oppression, that those struggles were occurring meant organized radical curricular efforts could be undertaken and could, if done well, be met with some successes.

And so it was that, analytically, U.S. RSSK had seen the theoretical pendulum of earlier studies complete a theoretical cycle. Where the sociology of school knowledge had initially advanced a "subjective" phenomenological agenda, and then in opposition taken a turn to more "objective" structural accounts, it had returned once again to "subjective" ethnographic approaches. And, homologously, where it had begun with a relatively optimistic political volunteerism, and had turned decidedly pessimistic with the structural accounts, it had once again found political hopes of transformation through possible cultural politics.

By the late 1970s, two American curricular theorists, Michael Apple and Henry Giroux, had established a strong connection between the original agenda of Bernstein and Young in a bid for a New Sociology of Education in the United States. By this time, of course, Apple and Giroux were not alone as the sole importers of the English New Sociology of Education, but each, by virtue of their prolific productivity and their theoretical arguments, had taken a stance of calling other U.S. educational scholars to the New Frontier. For example, in a review entitled "The New Sociology of Education: Analyzing Cultural and Economic Reproduction," Apple cited the initial problematics raised by Bernstein, Bourdieu, and Young to argue, "(w)hat happens inside the school at a cultural level must be understood before we can understand what happens outside the school at an economic level" (Apple, 1978, p. 495). Apple (1978) further argued that both the "structural" and "interpretive" traditions of the sociology of education could be employed in "the kind of cultural and economic program I am articulating here" (p. 498). In 1979,

< 30 >

Giroux similarly proposed a new agenda of research for curriculum in his, "Toward a New Sociology of Curriculum" (Giroux, 1979).

For both Apple and Giroux, the intellectual tradition on which such an agenda could be based was Marxist. The choice to build from the Marxist tradition was not necessarily a logical consequence of this field's development. As Whitty has pointed out with respect to England, it was rather strange to find the (non-cultural) Marxist structural analysis of Bowles and Gintis being appropriated, since it had been so strongly criticized, and since Bourdieu had been advancing a structural cultural analysis since the mid 1960s.[8] Nevertheless, by the end of the 1970s, the dominant mode of inquiry in the U.S. sociology of school knowledge had become Structural Neo-Marxist analysis.

There are, of course, many possible reasons for this analytical turn, some of which are simply personal and biographical. But even as the U.S. New Sociology of Education had established itself in opposition to the "Old" sociology, it also carried with it, as its main conceptual dilemma, the long-standing sociology of education concern for understanding the relationship between education and economic class (Karabel and Halsey, 1977a; Wexler, 1987; Whitty, 1985). Of course, as Marxist analyses, the conceptual framework for the U.S. New Sociology was quite different than the staple concepts of the mainstream U.S. educational literature.

EXPANDING THE AGENDA

Marxist social theory generally, outside of the fields of education, had seen something of an upsurge in popularity and productivity throughout the 1970s—in almost all of the Anglo- and Western European Academies. With a long-standing analytical concern for understanding the relationship between social structure and individual consciousness, as Young had pointed out, the Neo-Marxist theorizing prevalent in the 1970s had developed a wide array of conceptual lenses through which schooling could be analyzed. In this regard, Apple and Giroux were exactingly justified in their criticisms of the American educational community for its ignorance of this tradition. After all, if anyone had been concerned with understanding how to alter the social structures and institutions of societies toward more equitable and just arrangements, it had been the European (and Asian and North American and Latin American, etc.) Marxists.

The conjunction of the sociology of school knowledge's structural and interpretive agendas was perhaps most clear in Apple's Marxist phenomenology. Apple argued that structural Marxist accounts ought not forget the phenomenological study of ideological formations, and it was through this lens that he suggested that Willis's *Learning to Labor* provided key insights into understanding both the force of ideological hegemony and the cracks opened in the wall of economic determinism. Apple's review of *Learning to Labor*

< 31 >

provides a concise account of the U.S. New Sociology's major conceptual lenses. There Apple (1979a) wrote,

> we should be clear about what Willis has accomplished. First, he has extended our knowledge of *what goes on "within the black box"* of schooling. Second, he has provided a powerful set of metaphors for understanding both *reproduction and contradiction.* Third, he has taken us a very large step beyond simple correspondence theories of the overt and hidden curriculum of schooling by showing the *relative autonomy of the cultural level.* And fourth, he has done all this while at the same time embedding it within the real lives of real people. (p. 111, emphasis added)

From Apple's account we can see that his major conceptual categories were pivoting around the general sociological dichotomy of structure versus agency. The catch phrase "what goes on 'within the black box'" represented the curricular agenda of understanding the daily practices of schooling. A structural concern for understanding reproduction was taken as central and yet pitted against a Marxist view of "contradictions." Cultural forms were neither wholly determined nor free-floating, but (hence) given "relative autonomy" status. And Apple's fourth concern represented the overriding political concern of RSSK to speak with, for, and about a political constituency.

But the conceptual apparatus articulated by the U.S. New Sociology did not remain static. In part connected to its overt political agenda, in its late 1970s and early 1980s theorizing, the U.S. New Sociology began to expand its analytical frame beyond questioning economic and cultural relations. It was at this time that the U.S. New Sociology began to articulate an explicit focus on understanding the role of the State. By drawing the connection between the overt political agenda of the U.S. New Sociology and its focus on understanding the State, I do not mean to imply that its political agenda was the only reason for this conceptual turn; there were at least two direct conceptual reasons involved in this move as well. First, the European Neo-Marxist theorizing on which Apple and Giroux relied had long been concerned with the State. English Marxist theorists such as Raymond Williams, Perry Anderson, and Ralph Miliband had pointed to the role the State played in legitimating capitalism. German critical theorists such as Jürgen Habermas and Claus Offe had also articulated analyses of the state. French Neo-Marxists, such as Louis Althusser and Nicos Poulantzas, had also focused strongly on analyses of the Capitalist State Apparatus. And Gramsci's analysis of hegemony had relied heavily on the notion of an "ideological state apparatus."

The second direct conceptual reason for the U.S. New Sociology's focus on the State was rather simple. When analyzing the ways in which schooling reproduced social structures, it was an obvious empirical fact that public schooling is under the direct control of the State.

< 32 >

And so it was that when Giroux (1981c) began to articulate his analysis of schooling as a mechanism which reproduced a dominant hegemonic ideology, he built his analysis, in part, on a critique of Althusser's analysis of the "Ideological State Apparatus." Giroux's concern for articulating a "dialectical" analysis of schooling, one which was both critical of schooling's reproductive functions and yet opened up avenues for transformation, was evident in his critique of Althusser. As he put it,

> Althusserian models of reproduction provide a broader view of the hegemonic function of school by viewing them as part of the Ideological State Apparatus. While this position does us the service of linking reproduction to the larger imperatives of the state, it deflates its own possibilities by defining ideology as a form of "interpellation" in which subjects simply become bearers of imposed roles ... Lost here is the notion of relative autonomy as well as the possibility of contradictions emerging among the schools, the media, the state, the economy and other institutions. (p. 18)

Here it was clear that one of Giroux's central problematics was trying to understand both the reproductive elements of schooling and its transformative possibilities, as had been the case in his optimistic reception of Willis's *Learning to Labor*. This dual focus was also signalled in Giroux's conceptual choices. Here the concepts of hegemony, state apparatus, and the imperatives of the state were associated with a structural focus on reproduction. Relative autonomy, contradictions, and (implicit in this critique) an activist notion of the subject were linked to the transformative concern of Giroux's New Sociology. Each of these concepts was traced to origins in Marxist theorizing, and each was employed in Giroux's explicit dialectical attempt "to integrate ideology, hegemony, and culture into a successful theory of reproduction and transformation" (p. 18).

Apple's direct analyses of the State became apparent in the transition from his first book, *Ideology and Curriculum*, to his second, *Education and Power*. Where, in 1979, Apple had only begun to articulate State control of schooling in terms of governmental funding, by 1982 the State was a central focus for Apple.[9] As was the case for Giroux, Apple (1982c) was also concerned with recognizing both the reproductive and transformative aspects of schooling. His own explanation of how he came to focus on the State is worth quoting at length here:

> The original stimulation I had received from (Erik Olin) Wright on contradictory processes and institutions that mediate economic pressures and which have their own needs, needs that may not be totally reproductive of the interests of capital, pointed me to an area that provided an ideal counterpart to my focus on the creation of ideological hegemony and the relative autonomy of culture. This was the political sphere, the state, and its own interaction with ideology and hegemony. The state became an

essential ingredient in my analysis as I began to realize that the power, amount, and scope of state regulation of and intervention into the economy and the entire social process tends to increase in part as a function of the "gradual unfolding of the process of capital accumulation," of the need for consensus and popular support of the process, and the accompanying continuous "declassing" of people by reorganizing political and legal discourse around individuals as economic agents, among others. Hence, there was a dynamic interplay between the political and economic sphere which was found in education. While the former was not reducible to the latter—and, like culture, it had a significant degree of relative autonomy— the role the school plays *as a state apparatus* is strongly related to the core problems of accumulation and legitimation faced by the state and a mode of production in general. (pp. 28–29)

Here Apple, too, revealed his concern for understanding the ways in which schooling did not simply reproduce the economic structure of society—with conceptual tools such as relative autonomy and non-"reducible" spheres. It was also clear here that Apple's basic Marxist-structural concern was understanding the workings of capitalism (hence the foci on capital accumulation and modes of production).

From this brief outline of the U.S. New Sociology's theoretical concern for understanding the State, it is evident that the polar tensions between "determinism" and "possibilitarianism," that once marked the shift from a nearly exclusive economic focus to cultural analyses, were once again recreated. When U.S. New Sociologists began focusing on the State, of course, this pendular path already had been taken within Marxist State theorizing (in more than one national context) (e.g., Apple, 1982; Carnoy, 1982; Dale, 1982; Whitty, 1985). From the position of looking back on a decade of debate within Marxist theory, then, it is understandable that the U.S. New Sociologists did not replicate the turns Marxist State theorizing had taken, but were able to initially adapt a theoretical stance with respect to the State that matched the dual stance they had reached with respect to the economy and culture.

But the earlier outline of the U.S. New Sociology conceptual agenda was perhaps a bit misleading. That is, from the label "Marxist phenomenology," and from the argument about accepting the strengths of both "structural" and "interpretive" traditions, one would expect something of an equal-sided dual focus. However, as was clear in Giroux's and (perhaps even more so) Apple's approach to analyzing the State, and as became increasingly clear in the studies done by the U.S. New Sociology, not only was the "structural" side of the U.S. New Sociology's agenda predominated by Marxist categories, so were their "subjective" interpretations.

For example, beginning in 1979, Jean Anyon presented a series of articles which attempted, primarily, to empirically investigate and substantiate the ways in which schools reproduce class differentiations and legitimate social differentiation (see Anyon 1979, 1980, 1981a, 1981b, 1981c, 1983). In substantiating the ideological legitimation said to occur in schools, Anyon presented analyses of textbooks and other evidence relevant to her concern (Anyon, 1980). In these studies, Anyon attempted to document how, historically, the content of texts had been selected, or determined, by dominant social groups in such a way as to legitimate unequal class positions.

While much of this work relied on syntheses of other empirical research, Anyon's most distinctive work came in her ethnographic study of five elementary schools in "contrasting social class communities" (Anyon, 1980). These schools were said to reside in four different classed communities and were correspondingly classified: working-class, middle-class, affluent professional, and executive elite. By focusing on the nature of students' work, Anyon examined ownership relations, relations among people, and relations between people and their work. Employing analyses of the hidden curriculum, Anyon (1980) took her study to support the claim that,

> the hidden curriculum of school work is tacit preparation for relating to the process of production in a particular way ... (and) School experience differed qualitatively by social class. The differences may not only contribute to the development in the children in each social class of certain types of economically significant relationships and not others, but would thereby help *reproduce* this system of relations in society. (p. 90, emphasis in original)

Underlying much of Anyon's interpretations and her focus on students' work and ownership relations were the Classical Marxist dichotomy between mental and manual labor, the identification of classes based on ownership relations, and the assumption that work relations define social groups.

Stating that Anyon had made Marxist assumptions in her famous research is, in a way, stating the obvious. Andy Hargreaves (1982) has already pointed out that Anyon's theoretical assumptions may have been a bit too heavily used in her analysis of data. But what I would like to more specifically indicate here is that the use of Marxist theory in interpreting "qualitative" data translated into broadening the structural side of the New Sociology's theoretical attempt to bridge the structure-agency gap. To be more specific, consider an example taken from Anyon's work.

In describing the hidden curriculum of the school labeled "Affluent Professional," Anyon (1980) included the following passages from her field notes:

Teacher: Tom, you're behind in your SRA this marking period.
Tom: So what!
Teacher: Well, last time you had a hard time catching up.

< 35 >

Tom:	But I have my [music] lesson at 10:00.
Teacher:	Well, that doesn't mean you're going to sit here for twenty minutes.
Tom:	Twenty minutes! OK. (He goes to pick out a SRA booklet and chooses one, puts it back, then takes another, and brings it to her.)
Teacher:	OK, this is the one you want, right?
Tom:	Yes.
Teacher:	OK, I'll put tomorrow's date on it so you can take it home tonight or finish it tomorrow if you want.

Teacher:	(to a child who is wandering around during reading) Kevin, why don't you do *Reading for Concepts*?
Kevin:	No, I don't like *Reading for Concepts*.
Teacher:	Well, what are you going to do?
Kevin:	(pause) I'm going to work on my DAR. (The DAR had sponsored an essay competition on "Life in the American Colonies.") (pp. 82–83)

In interpreting these passages, Anyon introduced these passages by saying, "The following two dialogues illustrate the process of negotiation between student and teacher." Here, Anyon was building her argument that upper-class schools practice a hidden curriculum which allows students to take control over their work (as opposed to working-class schools in which students' work was predefined). To this end, Anyon further pointed out that in this Affluent Professional classroom there were few overt rules and students often freely went to the library on their own. She ended her description of this classroom with the following statements:

> Finally, the children have a fair amount of officially sanctioned say over what happens in the class. For example, they often negotiate what work is to be done. If the teacher wants to move on to the next subject, but the children say they are not ready, they want to work on their present projects some more, she often lets them do it. (p. 83)

This interpretation worked in nicely with Anyon's Marxist-based concern for ownership and students' relations to their work. In her conclusion, Anyon further suggested, "In the *affluent professional school* the children are developing a potential relationship to capital that is instrumental and expressive and involves substantial negotiation ... Although they do not have control over which ideas they develop and express, the creative act in itself affirms and utilizes the human potential for conceptualization and design that is in many cases valued as intrinsically satisfying" (pp. 89–90). In Marxist (humanist)

< 36 >

terms, these students, according to Anyon, are being inculcated as future members of the bourgeoisie—those who would be involved in mental labor.

But this, of course, isn't the only possible interpretation available. From a Foucauldian post-structural perspective, this evidence clearly indicates specific episodes of inculcating self-discipline. And from a feminist perspective, that the children with whom the teacher "negotiated" were both male might indicate, for one thing, the teacher's ambivalent position of authority relative to her male students. While her position as teacher carries authority, her position as woman implies subordination (e.g., Walkerdine, 1990).

The point in presenting possible alternative interpretations of Anyon's data isn't merely to question hers.[10] The point is that her interpretation offers a clear example of two theoretical issues. On the one hand, as an example of U.S. New Sociology, Anyon's argument in this essay exhibited the degree to which the theoretical agenda was structural—despite proclamations about recognizing resistance and agency. On the other hand, because this theory was based in Marxist analysis, Anyon's argument evidences that the primary social structure analyzed was defined by economic class.

These two theoretical foci were also evident in Giroux's and Apple's other works. The Structural Neo-Marxist interest in documenting the material and ideological reproductive dimensions of schooling was found, among other places, in Giroux's studies of rationality and citizenship education and in Apple's analysis of the form of curriculum.

Giroux focused on school knowledge in that he argued rationality in citizenship education was based on technical rationality which reified knowledge and individualized social dilemmas (Giroux, 1983a). This technical rationality, Giroux argued, served to legitimate human powerlessness and thereby served to recreate the political status quo. He stated,

> the citizenship education model ... neither recognizes nor responds to social and structural dysfunctions; instead, social and institutional failings are translated into personal ones. (p. 180)

Relying on Anyon's work for his empirical base, Giroux further argued that,

> school knowledge must be analyzed to determine to what degree its form and content represent the unequal presentations of the cultural capital of minorities of class and color. (p. 197)

Here Giroux presented an interesting theoretical argument about how differentiated school knowledge and the form of rationality embodied by this knowledge could contribute to passive forms of political socialization.

Apple examined the form of science curricular packages to build his argument that the effects of commodified school knowledge on the work of teachers correspond to the subsequent transmission of technical control in the

< 37 >

knowledge students are presented in such curricula. In "Curricular Form and the Logic of Technical Control" Apple laid out an analysis of science curriculum materials which showed how the form of such material could be seen to de-skill, and produce a "possessive individualism" for, teachers and students. Drawing on the traditional Marxist split between mental and manual labor, Apple argued that when curricular packages form the processes of teachers' work, the mental labor of organizing and creating curricula was left in the hands of (class and gender differentiated) experts. In this way the teachers were proletarianized. But they were also the managers of the students.

Connected, in *Education and Power*, with an analysis of how schools produce and reproduce technical knowledge, Apple (1982c) explained how this form of knowledge affects students:

> Those students who are identified as being able to produce ... important technical/administrative knowledge are increasingly 'placed' on the mental side of this dichotomy. This is done internally by the natural workings out of the curricular and guidance program of the school. (p. 50)

Hence, Apple argued that both the students and teacher become embroiled within an individualized labor process which served to produce an array of "contradictory effects." On the one hand, the simplistic form of technical knowledge served to deskill the teacher and sort the students. On the other hand, this left teachers in the managerial mode, placing them in a contradictory class location.

Similarly, possessive individualism was seen to have contradictory effects. As individuals, neither the students nor the teacher may consciously recognize their structural location as members of dominated fractions in society. But the individualism promoted through the form of these curricular materials risked the possibility of allowing both teachers and students to resist the conditions in which they are to work. Though individualism was seen to serve the administrative need for bureaucratic control (state control, that is), it could also lead, said Apple, to the unionization of teachers as they resist such control (pp. 155–59).

In trying to understand how Apple saw the role of school knowledge in the (ostensibly) contradictory processes of schooling, it may be helpful to consider his own direct discussion of school knowledge found in *Education and Power*. In two sections entitled "School Knowledge: Distribution or Production?" and "School Knowledge and Capital Accumulation," Apple's general conceptual framework for understanding the connections between power and school knowledge and his specific claims were explicitly presented (pp. 42–45).

Arguing against human capital theorists (who see school knowledge as distributed bits of skills and fact which can become invested, by students, in

< 38 >

future economic occupations), Apple pointed out that such a distributional view implied that covert values and dispositions were also distributed through the hidden curriculum. This argument mirrors and was explicitly connected with that put forth by Bowles and Gintis in their *Schooling in Capitalist America*. While Apple agreed with this view, he also pointed to another way in which schools reproduce class differentiations.

Appropriating Bourdieu's notion of cultural capital, Apple claimed that schools not only distribute knowledge (cultural capital), they produce it. Stated directly, he wrote that "schools also act as one of the primary modes of production of cultural commodities needed by a corporate society" (p. 45). Citing his arguments from *Ideology and Curriculum*, Apple recapitulated his view that schools act in a manner similar to capitalist economies by producing educational forms of "under and unemployment" (Apple, 1979b, pp. 36–37). Here Apple's concern was with the school's role in producing the technical/administrative knowledge needed, by capital, for capital accumulation.

In producing technical knowledge, schools were said to serve two functions. On the one hand, technical knowledge was directly essential to capital accumulation and therefore contributed to economic growth and productivity. On the other hand, technical knowledge carried implicit mechanisms of control which allowed schools to mirror corporate interests in segmenting the labor force. The important dimension here is that while technical/administrative knowledge operated within the economic and cultural spheres, it also served the State's needs to guarantee capital accumulation as well as its political needs for legitimation.

The three arguments and analyses just outlined document that the U.S. New Sociology was clearly bound within a Structural Neo-Marxist conceptual framework. That is, even while attempting to draw class analyses of schooling into the cultural realm (with explicit connections to cultural Marxisms), these U.S. RSSK employed analytical categories based in a Marxist understanding of social structures. School cultures, in these arguments, were taken to be specifically structured by the unconscious social residue of capitalism (as understood by Marxisms). Where Anyon sought to link economic class and cultural differences in accordance with the mental/manual split, Giroux associated the technical rationality of curriculum with political passivity, and Apple upheld a persistent analysis of schooling as a labor process.

Here I would note an interesting quality of the theoretical framework of these analyses. Perhaps in the critical attempt to enter into "dialectical" reasoning, or in the attempt to understand things relationally, the concepts employed in this Structural Neo-Marxist framework highlight conflicting phenomena. This was most apparent in Giroux's explanation about the need to consider education as part of the State. It was also evident in Apple's examination of "contradictory" processes in schooling practices. As I noted

< 39 >

in my introduction, this form of theorizing provided something of a fail-safe theory.

Consider, as one example, the reproduction versus resistance couplet. Interpretation through such a lens would undoubtedly always find empirical verification. If something wasn't seen as reproductive, it could easily have been labeled resistance. Or, as another example, if school practices didn't clearly meet the needs of capital, they could be interpreted as a result of democratic struggles within the State. Speaking in terms of "contradictions" may have provided more subtlety to the U.S. New Sociology's theory; but it also provided a theory which could never be wrong.

But there was another conceptual move these arguments signalled, as well: the inclusion, as analytical categories, of a limited number of social categories other than economic class. The signs of this move may have seemed minor, but nevertheless they were there. First, I pointed out a possible feminist reading of Anyon's data. And Anyon (1984) herself later conducted some studies of gender differentiation. Second, it should be noted that Giroux did not *only* speak of class when discussing subordinated groups (recall his "minorities of class and color"). And third, Apple raised gender as an analytical category in his discussion of de-skilling teachers.

The origins of this shift would be difficult to fully trace. In tracing the inclusion of a focus on gender, one could point out Angela McRobbie's (1978, 1980) strong feminist critiques of Willis's study. Or, one could point to the influence of Mary O'Brien's (1981) *The Politics of Reproduction*, noting the later publication of O'Brien's (1984) article, "The Commatization of Women: Patriarchal Fetishism in the Sociology of Education," in an educational journal (e.g., Apple, 1991).

In tracing the origins of the New Sociology's inclusion of race as a central category, one could generally note the long-standing history of racism in the United States, and the historical location of the New Sociology in the wake of the Civil Rights movement. (Of course this point could have been made with respect to the Women's Movement as well.) Or, one could note that when the Parallelist position was first articulated as such, it was coauthored with Lois Weis (1985)—whose interest in researching race relations has been consistent and continuing.

I don't mean to be discounting these possible origins of race and gender as analytical categories, as a means of documenting their inclusion in the U.S. New Sociology's agenda. What I do mean to point out in suggesting multiple possible points of origin is a pattern. Of the possible explanations for the use of gender and race as central categories in the analyses of the U.S. New Sociology, which I have just hinted, none obviously lay within the Structural Neo-Marxist theoretical agenda.

This is not meant to imply that there are no reasons within the conceptual

< 40 >

framework of the Structural Neo-Marxist conceptual framework which could account for the inclusion of gender and race. That would probably be overstating the case. However, the reasons for examining gender and race given by the U.S. New Sociologists themselves were many and often seemed remarkably non-Marxist.

There were two ways in which this move to include race and gender seemed plausible. On the one hand, as had been played out in the New Sociology's cultural turn, there was a descriptive effort to generate a comprehensive theory. The homologous logic of inclusion these conceptual maneuvers represent was rather straightforward: what was not disclosed in an economic focus had been addressed through an examination of culture; and what was not disclosed by focusing on economic class could be disclosed by examining other social relations. On the other hand, as had been done with the turn to examining the State, there was also a logic of political activism behind these moves. I'll consider each of these logics in turn.

With the "explanatory" logic, for example, when introducing Gail Kelly and Ann Nihlen's (1982) essay on patriarchy and education in his volume *Cultural and Economic Reproduction in Education*, Apple's explanation for its inclusion was rather direct. He stated, "Schools are deeply involved not 'just' in the contested reproduction of class relations, but in race and gender reproduction as well" (p. 21). From this brief justification, it seems that the concern for understanding reproduction, and the conceptual centrality of the notion "reproduction," carried with it a concern for developing a more comprehensive theory of the ways in which schooling contributed to societal relations of domination. As Apple and Weis (1983b) explained the initial formulation of the Parallelist Position and its three "dynamics" of social life (class, race, and gender),

> Ideological form is not reducible to class. Processes of gender, age, and race enter directly into the ideological moment. It is actually out of the articulation with, clash among, or contradictions among and within, say, class, race, and sex that ideologies are lived in one's day-to-day life. (p. 24)

Here, it seems that the justification for including social dynamics other than economic class was a result of the attempt to understand ideological forms (of consciousness, I presume) as they are lived out in daily life. This justification was, at least, a simulation of the New Sociology's cultural turn and a focus on understanding economic class relations through "lived-experience."

Studying race and gender relations, for Apple and Weis, was not entirely separate from understanding economic class relations; but the attempt to account for phenomenon which were not illuminated by the exclusive focus on class was clear. As they further explained the Parallelist Position,

< 41 >

Each of these dynamics (class, race and gender), and each of these spheres (economics, cultural, politics), has its own internal history *in relation to* the other. Thus, to give an example, it is impossible to completely comprehend class relations in capitalism without seeing how capital used patriarchal social relations in its organization. The current deskilling of women clerical workers through the introduction of word-processing technology and the overall loss of jobs that will result among working class women offers one instance where class and gender interact in the economy. In schools, the fact that elementary-school teachers are mostly women who historically have come from a particular segment of the population again illuminates the dual dynamics of class and gender. The rejection of schooling by many black and brown youths in urban centers, and the sense of pride that many unmarried minority high-school girls have in their ability to bear a child are the result of complex interconnections among the histories of class, race, and gender oppressions and struggles at the level of lived culture. (p. 25)

There are a number of things I would like to note about these justifications. Here, I would point out that the theoretical logic behind these conceptual adaptations is remarkably conventional in its attempt to generate a more complete theory, and that this logic is also a classic example of what Sir Karl Popper (1968) has called *ad hoc* hypotheses. According to Popper's search for falsifiable scientific theorizing, ad hoc hypotheses are auxiliary hypotheses that are added to theoretical frameworks but which do not increase the possibility of falsifying an "original" theory. Typically such auxiliary hypotheses, according to Popper, are adopted simply to account for evidentiary examples for which an original theory cannot account. The term *ad hoc* is used to specifically denote those auxiliary hypotheses which are neither logically consistent with the original theory nor restrict the scope of the original theory.

Note that these moves are supported by way of selected empirical examples. In this light, Andy Hargreaves (1982) may have overstated his charge that, "Apple's objection to correspondence theory ... is not so much that theory's inaccuracy" (p. 111). Clearly in this inclusive logic there was a strong concern for expanding the descriptive powers of the New Sociology's theoretical framework, and this move was largely based on an examination of "real" lived culture. But because the inclusion of race and gender is supported by a response to a previous theory's incapability to account for some phenomena, and mere examples are given to justify the choice of including these two social relations (race and gender), there is no systematic explanation as to why *these* two are included *but not* others.

When one's staple concepts are built from an examination of the social relations of production, there are few analytical reasons, at best, for examining race and gender. I am not arguing that a focus on the control of the means of production, or an examination of a differentiation of labor according to the mental/manual split, could not address gender and race; but

< 42 >

attempts to open these materialist theoretical lenses beyond class relations leave no reason to prespecify any particular set of social relations other than class as descriptively important.[11] Certainly, it is possible (or likely) that, upon empirical investigation, race and gender would emerge as important dimensions that have conditioned economic class relations. A huge number of studies have already pointed this out. But such an analytical approach would certainly also find social relations based on religion, sexual orientation, national and regional origin, or linguistic dialect (and the list could go on) as empirically important social differentiations that have (and will) intersect with economic class relations.

Moreover, the conceptual consequences of the New Sociology's cultural turn cut even deeper than merely the issues involving the choice of gender and race as major theoretical categories. Ironically, by employing a similarly inclusive logic in the New Sociology's theoretical advancement, a serious inconsistency in the field's theorizing was opened up. By employing a cultural lens, which was in part initially included due to its added descriptive potential, and by selecting multiple social dynamics, which thereby opened the Parallelist Position to the objections I just raised above, a central question is raised: Why begin with a Marxist theory at all? Let me explain where I see the inconsistency leading to this question.

Recall that the turn to understanding cultural practices in schooling was justified by arguing that a strict focus on economic relations did not fully illuminate the daily processes of schooling and the ways in which school knowledge reproduced social differences. This argument was based on a rejection of the strong determinism of orthodox Marxism. At the same time, economic class was maintained as a central category of social differentiation. Based on the notion of culture as "lived-experience," the cultural lens further allowed for including other historically contingent dynamics of social differentiation that were deemed significant. But if such a cultural lens is used to identify significant social dynamics, and these dynamics are seen as historically contingent, there is no reason to presume that economic class would always be a significant dynamic of social differentiation. Expanding the question of the relevance of gender and race as major theoretical categories, here I would ask, if one begins with a concern for "lived-experience," why include *any* of the three social dynamics named in the Parallelist Position and not others?

Granting that an economic focus would probably lead to identifying economic class as a significant social dynamic, I see an inconsistency between this lens and the cultural lens. The a priori notion that economic differentiations are central was based on an analysis of the materialist base of social relations. But the claim that this materialist focus isn't fully illuminating in describing "lived-experience," if it were consistently applied, would reject the a priori economic notion as well. With the notion of culture as

< 43 >

"lived-experience," the New Sociology in turn supplanted its a priori focus on economically based social differentiation with an *a posteriori* cultural notion that historically contingent social differentiations ought to be examined. But an *a posteriori* cultural position gives no guarantee that economic class will be a significant category.

The material analysis included economic class by definition (classes are conceptually defined by relations to the means of production, and relations of the means of production empirically identify classes). Hence, to maintain a broad cultural lens (chosen in opposition to an economic lens) and at the same time claim economic class must be a central category of social relations is to maintain an inconsistent conceptual framework. Economic class can only be maintained, a priori, as a central category in the Parallelist Position by placing primacy on economic social relations.

One could anticipate an objection to this analysis coming from a materialist Marxist cultural analyst. That is, many cultural Marxists would claim to hold both a position of economic primacy, and a historically contingent understanding of culture. In fact, this materialist cultural position is what Apple argued for in his earlier *Ideology and Curriculum*. There, Apple argued against deterministic economic analyses which posit a mirror link correspondence between the economy and culture. Instead Apple (1979b) suggested,

> there is a somewhat more flexible position which speaks of determination as a complex nexus of relationships which, in their final moment, are economically rooted, that exert pressures and set limits on cultural practices, including schools. Thus, the cultural sphere is not a "mere reflection" of economic practices. Instead, the influence, the "reflection" or determination, is highly mediated by forms of human action. (p. 4)

Here Apple was drawing on Raymond Williams's (1976) materialist analysis of culture. Apple (1982c) seemed to continue this line of analysis through *Education and Power*, where he favorably commented on the view of ideology offered by Marxist ethnography,

> (Ideology) was not a form of false consciousness "imposed" by an economy. Rather, it was part of a lived culture that was a result of the material conditions of one's day to day practices. (p. 27)

While this materialist analysis of cultural practice would be consistent with placing economic class in a primary analytical position, it still leaves open what other categories would be included in contingent, *a posteriori*, historical or cultural investigation. However, unlike Williams's historical analyses (and I should point out, Apple's own earlier studies), the Parallelist Position predefines what other categories are to be examined.

Further, this materialist cultural position seems to not be the one Apple

< 44 >

had in mind when proposing the Parallelist Position. In fact, Apple argued against placing primacy on economic relations in his recent rearticulation of his framework. According to Apple (1988b),

> I have taken what is commonly known as the *parallelist* position. That is, I have argued that we should not automatically assume the primacy of class relations over those of gender and race. (p. 121, emphasis in original)

Here, Apple explicitly rejected making a priori decisions about what social dynamics would be most significant in any given context. But, again, if this is the position, why predefine any social dynamics?

Thus, in its descriptive endeavor, the Parallelist Position stands as a set of mutually exclusive conceptual presumptions woven into a logically inconsistent theoretical framework. Combined with the ad hoc nature of its development, one which saw categories and concepts added as attempts were made to make up for past theoretical defects without seriously questioning its point of origin, the Parallelist Position amounts to a conceptual screen used to filter out empirical findings of predetermined import.

As radical, however, the U.S. New Sociology's intention of being descriptive was not its only one. Earlier I noted that in addition to a logic of theoretical inclusion, the U.S. New Sociology also employed a logic of political activism in its development. It is by looking through the lens of the New Sociology's transformative interest, through its political lens, that some consistency is brought to the Parallelist Position.

Giroux's arguments about the need to include gender and race in the New Sociology's analyses offered a good example of the logic of political activism I have in mind here. For Giroux (1983a), the issue of adding social dynamics other than class revolved around developing an "adequate" theory of resistance. His explanation is worth quoting at length:

> A second weakness in theories of resistance is the inadequate number of attempts to take into account the issues of gender and race. As Arnot, McRobbie, Walkerdine, and others have pointed out, resistance studies generally ignore women and gender issues to focus instead primarily on males and class when analyzing domination, struggle and schooling. This has meant that women are either disregarded altogether or that when they are included in such studies it is only in terms that echo the sentiments of the male countercultural groups being portrayed. This raises a number of significant problems that future analyses will have to face. On the one hand, such studies have failed to come to grips with the notion of patriarchy as a mode of domination that cuts across various social sites as well as a mode of domination that mediates between men and women within and between different social-class formations. The point here, of course, is that domination is not singularly informed or exhausted by the logic of class oppression; nor does domination take a form that affects men and women in similar ways.

< 45 >

Women, though in different degrees, experience dual forms of domination in both the home and workplace. How the dynamics of these get interconnected, reproduced and mediated in schools represents an important area of continuing research. On the other hand, these studies contain no theoretical room for exploring forms of resistance that are race- and gender-specific, particularly as they mediate the sexual and social divisions of labor in various social sites such as schools. The failure to include women and minorities of color in such studies has resulted in a rather uncritical theoretical tendency to romanticize modes of resistance even when they contain reactionary views about women. The irony here is that a large amount of neo-Marxist work, while allegedly committed to emancipatory concerns, ends up contributing to the reproduction of sexist attitudes and practices, albeit unknowingly. (pp. 104–5)

To paraphrase this explanation, then, Giroux recognized that past "resistance" studies had not examined race and gender directly, and he saw two problems. On the one hand, male centered studies provided an "inadequate" view of domination (one which didn't recognize patriarchy and, I presume, racism). On the other hand, while these studies may have opened emancipatory insights for white males, they also contributed to the further domination of women and people of color.

From this explanation we can see that the two problems Giroux saw with past resistance theories correspond to those I have labeled descriptive and political. I have already pointed out the conceptual problems faced by the U.S. New Sociology in its descriptive moment, but I would like to consider its political intent in a bit more detail.

For Apple (1988b), the political interest in addressing race and gender was closely linked with recognizing that public schooling was part of the State and that political struggles in the State were not only about class. As he has rearticulated his Parallelist Position, he argued,

(G)iving more parallel status to gender and race dynamics complicates matters considerably. The recognition that culture and the State are linked to and relatively autonomous from the economy does little to lessen that complexity. These involved relations—conflicts between (*and* within) race, class, and gender formations, over political, cultural, and economic power, over social and educational goals within the State—are real. . . . Not only must we reject the class reductionism still so pervasive in democratic socialist thought, but we also need to question the notion that only economic struggles 'really' count in the long run. . . . In *political* terms, none of these has a necessarily privileged place. It is the effect of all of these together that matters. Thus, interventions and struggles in each are important. (Apple, 1988b, pp. 124–25, emphasis in original)

As the State was added from a recognition of schooling's transformative potential, so too were gender and race included in the Parallelist Position.

< 46 >

Hence, the concern with understanding how people resist the reproductive functions of schooling here can be seen as the point of origin from which the conceptual categories "gender" and "race" came to be included in the Parallelist Position. Race has long been a concern to U.S. radicals, and its inclusion can adequately be understood as the reflection of a racist society. Gender seems to have appeared from an intersection between a growing feminist movement (within curriculum) and the realization that most of the teachers in the U.S. (within the primary and secondary levels) are women. My point here is simply to emphasize that the inclusion of race and gender as central categories in the Parallelist Position is clearly in response to a concern for resistance and political action.

I would also like to point out that the way in which race and gender came to be included under the conceptual banner of the U.S. New Sociology corresponds to the manner in which culture and the State were added to its theoretical social spheres. Recognizing that its past theories held serious political weaknesses, by offending and ignoring women and people of color, the U.S. New Sociologists responded by simply amending their conceptual framework. On the one hand, politically, this could be seen as being sensitive and open to critique (not to mention wise). On the other hand, however, these actions are indistinguishable from political damage control conducted in the attempt to keep one's position as the spokesman of all the dominated masses. In this light, the question of why other categories are not included can be directly addressed in terms of strategically calculated political losses.

Plausible political explanations for the isolated inclusions of (and only of) gender and race abound. Religion would be excluded because of the fact that the most active religious movements in the United States have been, throughout the 1980s, extremely politically conservative.[12] Sexual orientation would be ignored, in part, because of the fact that the gay and lesbian constituency is relatively small.[13] Similarly, because of sheer numbers, the marginal gains to be had by considering national or regional groups in the United States are minuscule. (And, to mention a possibility not yet considered, alliances with the growing ecological movement in the United States suffers from a history of, perhaps justifiable, political mistrust.) Of course, other political explanations could be advanced with respect to each of these potential constituencies; but the point is simply that in this light, inclusion in the conceptual framework of the U.S. New Sociology as a social dynamic would be based on strategic political rationality.

I should point out that the analysis I have just presented relies on distinctions many radical theorists would find problematic. Specifically, when I drew a distinction between a priori and *a posteriori* reasoning, I had mimicked the traditional distinction between analytical and empirical logic. I am aware that many Critical Theorists would, at best, hesitate to accept this distinction. As

< 47 >

has been pointed out many times in the radical literature, "empirical" facts do not speak for themselves; they are theory-laden. Analytical lenses do shape, even create, what we see. I agree with this position. But by drawing this distinction I mean to highlight that the analytical choices made in the Parallelist Position, through an inconsistent analytical logic, implied the very commitment to economic primacy which was ostensibly rejected, and left the U.S. radical sociologists of school knowledge standing in the shaky political position of nominating which social dynamics ought to be considered important forms of domination.

CONCLUSION

Since the Parallelist Position was first publicly articulated in 1983, its conceptual categories have served as the central concerns of Structural Neo-Marxist sociology of school knowledge. The only significant alteration has been McCarthy's "non-synchronous" attempt to make it less static and responsive to many contexts and multiple subjective positions of oppression (McCarthy and Apple, 1988). Even with this alteration, though, the Parallelist Position has remained, in essence, the benchmark of Structural Neo-Marxist theory for the past eight years (Apple, 1988b).

Set within the major dichotomy of structure versus agent, the recent attempt to speak of "non-synchronous" relations can be taken as a direct response to the homologous macro-micro split. While the three spheres of the parallelist position describe macro-level phenomena (structure), the three dynamics speak of micro-level enactments (agency). That Structural Neo-Marxist theory has remained within this framework is apparent from Apple's (1988b) explanation of the problem faced by such endeavors:

> the problem is . . . how we combine the *structuralist* insights about the relationship between the school and the social and sexual division of labor with a culturalist perspective that places human *agency* and the concrete experiences of people at the center. (p. 119, emphasis added)

But, as is evidenced by the theoretical oscillation between "deterministic" and "possibilitarian" moments, this framework has been built on shifting conceptual ground. Facing something of an educational variation of Heisenberg's uncertainty principle, the Structural Neo-Marxist theoretical framework of the U.S. New Sociology seems to face a continual trade-off. Phrased in one of its possible two directions, the more insight gained into the social structures of educational reproduction (the more one "knows" about social spheres), the less one illuminates the daily practices based on individual agency (the less one knows about social dynamics). Conversely, the more one knows about social dynamics, the less one knows about social structures. This trade-off might also be seen to hold between the New Sociology's dual interests in

< 48 >

proposing a theory that is both descriptive and emancipatory. The more one holds out for a consistent descriptive theory, the less one can maintain transformative appeal. And the more one pushes for transformative appeal, the less one can maintain a consistent descriptive theory.

I introduced this chapter by suggesting that the U.S. RSSK had stagnated. My concern has been to trace the conceptual dilemmas I see as undergirding that stagnation. First, I have cited the field's ad hoc mode of theorizing, which, as Popper has shown, will continue to defy standards of falsifiability. While I recognize that many of the authors in this field would reject such a scientific standard, I will be arguing in Chapters Six and Seven that such a stance provides little persuasive power within a larger field of educational research that at least nominally maintains falsifiability as a scientific norm to be upheld. For now, I simply wish to have established that the U.S. New Sociology in fact has constructed its theory in an ad hoc fashion.

Second, I noted that the conceptual apparatus set up by the U.S. New Sociology has proven vague and difficult to employ and defend. Simply noting Andy Hargreaves's critique provided some evidence of this. Further evidence was taken from Anyon's research. There, what Anyon had interpreted through her Marxist focus on relations to the means of production as "negotiation" and evidence of students' "ownership" of their own work processes is possible evidence of either gendered classroom practices or practices of inculcating self-disciplining.

Finally, I argued that while the political interests of the U.S. New Sociology offered some consistent plausibility to its inclusion of gender and race among its central categories, this conceptual move has translated into a descriptively inconsistent theoretical framework. This theoretical inconsistency, I would further argue, has given the New Sociology potential responses to most specific criticisms. I will address this in more detail in Chapter Five. For now, I take having shown the Parallelist Position's theoretical inconsistencies as also having given reason to question its very foundation. As I have already alluded, I take this to mean shedding the U.S. New Sociology's foundation in its Marxist heritage. Of course, I am not alone in taking this position, but my reasons and subsequent stances are vastly different than those who, like Giroux (1984), have suggested similar renouncements.

By way of conclusion I would like to further highlight two trends that have characterized the research advance in the U.S. New Sociology. The first is rather evident: since Bowles and Gintis's *Schooling in Capitalist America*, most of the research in this field has been primarily qualitative. Indeed, Apple (1986b) himself has noted this trend, and it is apparent in the early works of Anyon, Apple, and Giroux discussed above. The second trend I would like to point out here requires a bit more explanation.

It seems to me that the major dialogue with which the U.S. radical

< 49 >

sociology of school knowledge has been concerned has been among its adherents and allies. More specifically, I have shown that each of the theoretical turns taken in the development of the Parallelist Position has been in response to a criticism either from within the field or from political allies. The turn away from economic-based arguments was hastened by radical investigations of culture and cultural studies of resistance. The inclusion of the State as a central social sphere was sparked by a political interest in theorizing transformation and the empirical insights of other Marxist analyses. The coherence of the addition of gender and race was found within the U.S. New Sociology's political agenda as well. These analytical turns outline what I would call a trend toward internal dialogue.

Hargreaves (1982) also charged the New Sociology with "a failure to engage in dialogue with non-Marxist ethnographic accounts of school classroom life" (p. 120). The response to his criticisms, or rather the lack of response, offers further negative evidence for the trend toward only listening to one's friends and political allies. That is, even though Hargreaves was highly critical of Apple, Anyon, Giroux, Whitty, and Arnot, to my knowledge only Whitty responded in print (see Whitty, 1985). The question I am posing here is not whether U.S. RSSK attempted to present its position to mainstream educational research communities, but whether it has taken mainstream criticisms into account in further developing its theoretical lenses and its research agenda. From this account of the development of the Parallelist Position, it seems that in its early years it did not. Unfortunately, this is a trend that has continued to the present with few exceptions.

In the next chapter, I shall survey some of the research that has been conducted in this field since the initial presentation of the Parallelist Position. In doing so, I shall be continuing to document some of the arguments and issues I have raised here. I should note specifically that I will argue that while the field has significantly altered its early linear development, it has also continued to maintain the two trends I have just highlighted. For all the theoretical diversity brought to the field in the past eight years, the field has continued to empirically rely most heavily on qualitative research and has continued to isolate itself from the larger mainstream educational research community. Perhaps predictably, this later trend is one with which I am not satisfied. However, before justifying my dissatisfaction with the field, more of its story needs to be told.

< 50 >

three

Deconstructing the Field

I N THIS CHAPTER, I EXTEND MY ANALYSIS by examining RSSK that have been published since 1983. To do this, however, I will be altering my analytical framework. My observations about these later radical sociologies of school knowledge will suggest both a consistent productivity of the field and a theoretical fracturing.

By simply providing several examples, I will demonstrate that the 1980s have been wonderfully productive for RSSK. In a way, this observation is related to trends I have already noted in the field's early development. That is, with the field's qualitative analyses and its lively internal debate, a great number of theoretical voices have been made plausible. By combining developments in educational studies with empirical and theoretical insights from disciplines outside of education, radical educational writers have begun to articulate a wide variety of theoretical agendas directly salient in the attempt to sociologically understand the relationship between power and the curriculum. Both its internal debate and its qualitative studies have aided the field's productivity.

In a somewhat different light, I will argue that recent developments in radical curriculum scholarship in the United States also mark a theoretical fracturing of the field of sociology of school knowledge. There are two basic analytical lines along which I see the field fracturing. First, the rise of feminist voices and growing diversity of theoretical agendas among feminisms offer the sociology of the curriculum sophisticated and powerful educational analyses. Second, it would be very hard for any observer of the field to have missed the influx of post-structural and postmodern literature. Given the public attention that post-structural and postmodern critique has attained in the academy, the claim that this field has fractured states the obvious. I would like to make clear that, unlike many (other) defenders of the Enlightenment, this fracturing is not something I regard as threatening or damaging.[1]

Before I finish introducing the basic outline of how I construct the field's recent literature, however, I should make more clear what this analytical framework shall be.

ON THE ANALYTICAL FRAMEWORK

To present my analysis of current literature in the field, I will be focusing on one question as I examine the work: "What are the frontiers of the discourses within/among RSSK?"

This "post-structural" question clearly begins with an assumption of multiplicity. Here it is assumed that any one discourse which I can inscribe as a sociological account of school knowledge is but one among many. While it is possible, for example, to speak of late 1970s United States radical sociology of curriculum as largely influenced by Neo-Marxist literature, the post-structural disposition against monolithic logic would highlight the fact that a good deal of feminist work focusing, in large part, on the experiences of young women was also salient in the late 1970s. There was also, of course, the serious influence of Marxist insight within this feminist literature. But for this guiding question, such an overlap of analytical and political agendas is not to be addressed simply by finding common threads within all radical accounts of school knowledge. Overlap and difference become visible through the questioning of frontiers of multiple discourses.

The notion of frontiers itself, however, carries something of a double meaning. On the one hand, from a European Continental perspective, frontiers denote relatively fixed boundaries or borders between sovereign or separate entities (nation-states, for example). On the other hand, from the European experience of Westward expansion in the United States, the notion of frontier also denotes ever receding limits between the known and the unknown, between the charted and uncharted, between the named and unnamed. From the view of some Native Americans, the "frontier" of the Eastern Invasion connotes an ever receding limit between the claimed and the unclaimed. Each of these denotations inform my use of the term "frontier." In questioning the frontiers between radical curricular discourses, I mean to be asking both what can be named as fixed or stable distinctions among and between discourses and what can be seen as the moving borders between the named and unnamed within and among them.

< 52 >

Combined with a modified Foucauldian notion of discourse, this post-structural guiding question begins analyses of intellectual arguments from a much different point of departure than would a structural inscription. In questioning the frontiers among and between the discourses of RSSK, I am not concerned with authors or agents. Foucault's rhetorical question, "What matter who's speaking?" I take very seriously here.

In Bourdieu's (1988) terms, when analyzing discourses we are faced with a distinction between the "empirical individual" and "the epistemic individual." Recognizing that the individuals' names, the words, used in the scientific discourse of this analysis do not refer to the same things as the people who are known to others by those words, a post-structural analysis of public discourses begins first with the reflexive recognition that the objects of its analysis are constructed by the analysis itself. Of this distinction Bourdieu writes,

> the words of scientific discourse, and especially those designating persons (named individuals) or institutions (such as Collège de France), are exactly the same as those of ordinary discourse, of fiction or history, whereas the referents of these two species of discourse are separated by all the distance which is introduced by the scientific break and by construction. (pp. 21–22)

As representations or signifiers of particular discourses, to refer to a named author in the post-structural sensibility is not to talk about a "real" agent. Here descriptions are built upon inscription.

And so it is that one of the ways in which I shall characterize the field in this chapter is by deploying a rather simple (simplistic) distinction among these recent works. First, I will attempt to survey those sociologies of school knowledge which have most strongly held allegiance to the Neo-Marxist tradition. Next, I will present a selective survey of non-Marxist analyses.

The distinction I draw here is for both analytic and aesthetic reasons. On the one hand, the Marxist pull toward Hegelian dialectics shows a much stronger connection with the Enlightenment analysis currently defended and attacked in debates between Modernists and Postmodernists, as compared to most (not all) of the non-Marxist analyses. On the other hand, by drawing such a distinction, the multiplicities within, and the fragmented nature of my analytical field are accented.

By way of prefacing this chapter, I would also like to say a few words about the limits of this chapter's analysis. Overall, I should point out that the framing and ordering of this chapter intentionally (and additionally) reconstructs the consequences of an imposed post-structural analysis. That is, by pushing to the margins what could be a point of origin, the Parallelist Position, and marking the ways in which temporally subsequent arguments are dispersed and fragmented from that point, this chapter (if done well) shall validate my argument that the field has fractured. Each with its own past, the current alternatives

< 53 >

available to the sociology of school knowledge are so many, and so different, that suggesting there still is a field (known as the sociology of school knowledge) itself seems implausible. In a sense, students of the New Sociology are faced with the ultimate postmodern experience—excessive choice in an over-supplied market of theoretical consumption.

The construction of continuity and the invocation of linear temporality corresponding to the structuralism found in early RSSK are, in a sense, ruptured here. This rupture is, for me, implicit in the question guiding this analysis—my first so-called post-structural guiding question, "What are the frontiers of the RSSK?" Through assumptions of pluralities, partial equivalences and discontinuities, my presentation of the recent RSSK is meant to highlight differing social, political and intellectual histories. Foreshadowing the position I hope to develop throughout this project, resolution of these differences is not sought.

The consequences of constructing this chapter as I intend are numerous; but there are two of which I am quite conscious and which I consider particularly important.

First, the attempt to employ analytical frameworks consistent with those employed in the objects of my two-sided analysis requires an unfortunate imposition of a rather fictitious dichotomy. Policing the boundaries of that dichotomy, the distinction between structural and post-structural, is a forceful enterprise which invites mistakes. Some of the problems with this forced distinction will, for example, be discussed in relation to McCarthy's (1988) "non-synchronous" alteration of the Parallelist Position.

The second consequence of presenting my response to my two initial guiding questions in the fashion of this and the preceding chapter is related to *how* my analysis ruptures the structural sensibilities of time and history. Whilst the structural analysis of Chapter Two recreates a sense of development, understood as taking place within linear time, this chapter is intended, in effect, to stop time. Although I will note differing histories and past allegiances, my simple juxtaposing of recent RSSK is meant to both place post-structural discourses in the reactionary/after position they hold contingently by empirical necessity, and to mimic a tendency I see in the way some so-called post-structural analyses of school knowledge use time and history. That is, despite the frequent post-structural critiques of structural temporal sensibilities, the post-structural positions taken within the sociology of school knowledge seem to me to have not heeded their own advice. This issue shall be raised in relation to the arguments of Cherryholmes (1988).

One last caveat: I would like to point out that my analysis in this chapter shall be limited to examining the theoretical claims advanced in the field. In this sense, like the previous chapter, I take this chapter to be largely limited to a textual analysis. Aside from academically pointing out the value of entering

< 54 >

into such an analysis, I justify this limitation with the promise that I shall attempt to move beyond this self-imposed limit in later chapters of this work.

CURRENT DISCOURSES IN THE FIELD

Recent Marxist articulations in the field

To be sure, rather orthodox Marxist interpretations of schooling and curriculum are still among the U.S. RSSK. In this discourse, the conceptual legacy of "contradictions" is readily apparent. For example, written in broad macro-level strokes, Carnoy and Levin (1985) propose an economically based "model of educational change" strikingly similar to that of Bowles and Gintis:

> The dynamic of the American educational system, we suggest, can best be understood as part of a much wider social conflict arising in the nature of capitalist production, with its inequalities of income and power. These inequalities lead to struggles by subordinate, relatively powerless groups for greater equality, economic security, and social control. (p. 24)

But, with a stronger emphasis on the political sphere than earlier base/superstructure analyses, this view shares a U.S. New Sociology concern. The struggles and conflict resulting from inequalities produced in capitalism, for Martin Carnoy and Henry Levin, are played out in the social arena of the State. In nominally democratic nations such as the United States, these struggles take on a specific character which is contradictory to the workings of Capital. As they put it: "In a politically democratic society, the State provides space for such struggles" (p. 24). Thus, educational reforms in capitalist democracies can be interpreted as resulting from macro-level societal contradictions.

There are two major theoretical considerations I would highlight about this view. First, the notion of "contradiction" is used to create a hermetically sealed interpretive framework:

> In public education ... the social conflict is expressed in the conflict between reforms aimed at reproducing the inequalities required for social efficiency under monopoly capitalism and reforms aimed at equalizing opportunities in pursuit of democratic constitutional ideals. Thus American education is subject to severe internal tension, since it is pulled in the two contradictory directions of inequality and democracy. (p. 24)

Second, while cultural interpretation may offer insight into these struggles for Carnoy and Levin, the cause of these struggles is seen clearly to lie within capitalism:

> (I)t is misleading to carry explanations of culture and ideology too far from the organization of production as *the* underlying social dynamic. If ideology and production are part and parcel of the same structure of social class

< 55 >

relations (as Bowles and Gintis contend), reproduction is no less so. Schools are ideological apparatuses, but they are ideological in the sense that they attempt to reproduce the social relations of production and the class division of labor. (p. 24, emphasis added)

This position is clearly articulated with knowledge of the New Sociology's cultural and political agenda. But that agenda is to be incorporated in the presented fact that the United States is primarily a capitalist society:

Political power and belief systems are subject to conflict, as Giroux argues. The public schools, as a State apparatus, are relatively autonomous from production. But the contradictions in education arise primarily because education is inherently part of the conflict over resources—who will get them and who will control the way they are used. Conflicts in schools are not primarily over the principles of capitalism, but over its practices. It is true that domination can exist without capitalism, but to understand schooling in capitalist countries requires analyzing schools as reproducers of capitalist social relations and the capitalist division of labour. (pp. 24–25)

From this view, historical investigations proceed, pointing out, among other things, the long U.S. history of differential curricula for different social classes. During historical periods in which Capital is seen as strong, the curricular legacy of behavioristic Taylorism is cited as a capitalist push to have schools function for economic efficiency. Working-class students, in this view, are given a curriculum which functions to make them obedient and efficient manual laborers. But when the legitimacy of capital is called into question, the State responds to democratic struggles with an expansion of the educational system—though this expansion too is stratified to continue insuring class differentiation.

More specific applications of an orthodox Marxist approach are also available for those interested in teacher education. Mark Ginsburg (1988), for example, takes the notion of contradiction to apply to multiple levels of educational processes. On the societal level, struggles over ownership and control of the means of production mark central contradictory processes:

(R)elevant is the contradiction that production takes place for profit accumulation by capitalists rather than to satisfy the needs of workers, who constitute the vast majority of people. Moreover, another contradiction arises because of the profit motive to reduce labor costs and increase productivity; this is that while many workers experience deskilling/proletarianization and thus become less expensive workers and more easily replaced by other humans or machines, a few workers undergo reskilling/professionalization as they can be seen to enhance the design or control of the work process. Associated with this latter contradiction is another one between mental and manual forms of labor, that a few people are seen to engage in work of the mind, while the majority are viewed to engage in work of the hand, leg, back, etc. (p. 8)

< 56 >

Familiar Marxist dichotomies mark the walls of this conceptual framework: capitalist/proletariat, de-skilling/re-skilling, proletarianization/professionalization, mental/manual.

> This societal level analysis is readily placed onto multiple levels of education: In the context of schooling and teaching, these contradictions surface in a slightly different form. First there is the contradiction that many educators teach, while few occupy management positions. Second, although schooling may be provided for the masses, that available only on a selective basis is considered higher status. Third, knowledge and skill with "mental work" is contrasted with and given higher value than knowledge and skill associated with "manual work." (p. 8)

Here, the separation of the design of the labor process from "actual" labor plays a significant conceptual role. Differential job roles, differential curricula, and differential knowledge and skills are each, once again, to be mapped along the familiar Marxist lines of analysis.

For teacher education this reading becomes centrally important, since student teachers are to enter into the contradictory class location of teachers, and thus into jobs which require them to continue reproducing the contradictory functions of schooling. Here the work of teachers is examined in terms of their class location:

> From a Marxist, class conflict perspective, the class location of teachers as intellectuals and situated in the middle class(es) is . . . contradictory. Within this viewpoint, teachers' economic functions are seen to include, to varying extents, aspects of both the global functions of capital and the function of the collective labourer; thus teachers share, in part, the class relational experience of both the bourgeoisie and the proletariat. Generally, similar to workers, teachers do not own or control means of production (or even the means of "educational production") and work for wages or salary. However, similar to the bourgeoisie, they live (some would argue barely) off the wealth created by productive workers and to some degree operate as managers/socializers of future workers. (p. 9)

From this perspective, the histories, processes, professionalization rhetoric, and ideologies of teacher education programs are analyzed.

Where Carnoy and Levin (1985) argue against extreme acceptances of the cultural turn, Ginsburg's (1988) continuation of the U.S. New Sociology's legacy is clear. In analyses of the deskilling processes governing teaching and teacher education, in the turn to focusing specifically on teacher education, and in analyses of the potentially legitimating ideologies of teacher education, the early U.S. New Sociologies of Apple, Giroux and Anyon are continued.

For Ginsburg, the centrality of the concept of "contradiction" partially

< 57 >

lay in the political potential such a view offers, and is built from the same insights as the U.S. New Sociology's Structural Neo-Marxist framework. As he puts it,

> The approach adopted here posits a notion of relative autonomy of the cultural level and provides space for human agency, that is, people's relatively autonomous acts of resistance, contestation and struggle. Thus my approach is informed by Giddens's concept of "duality of structure"—that the "logic" of macro political economic and ideological spheres both constrains and enables human action and consciousness, while at the same time this context is reproduced, challenged, or sometimes transformed by human thought and action. Moreover, because human agency is a factor and because social formations (at the societal and world system levels) contain contradictions, the potential for social transformation or change "however trivial or minor" is "inherent in all moments of reproduction." (p. 4)

Continuation of the Structural Neo-Marxist framework seems evident in this quote: relative autonomy, cultural analysis, resistance, contestation, and the Giddensian dual conjunction of structure and agency all mark analytical turns of the radical educational endeavor.

From within such Marxist ideological analyses of contradiction, the radical political agenda is articulated in terms of a discourse which calls forth educators to take on the role of transformative intellectuals. Building on the dichotomous lenses of his Marxism, Ginsburg sees two possible roles for teachers that are set against each other in his language of contradiction:

> they (teachers) might be conceived as part of a buffer group, protecting the upper or dominant class(es) from challenges by the lower or subordinated class(es) . . . (or) Alternatively, they might operate as activist intellectuals working with subordinated groups to bring about fundamental changes in schools and society. (pp. 8-9)

From this Marxist perspective, the role of the teacher as a potential transformative agent becomes both a central conceptual concern and sign of what is to be taken as sufficiently radical.

In this discourse, the concern for imagining teachers as transformative agents is built, in part, from Critical Theory's archeological excavation of its Greek philosophical heritage and Marx's eleventh thesis on Feuerbach. Where Marx tells us that the point of philosophy is not merely to interpret the world but to change it, and where for the Greeks theory was not divorced from practice, the call for transformative intellectuals is cast in the rubric of *Praxis*. Further conscious links with the discursive traditions of Western communism and socialism are used to entitle the call for transformative educators. Labeled "What is to be Done? Critical Praxis by Educators of Teachers," Ginsburg's closing chapter, for example, clearly calls upon the legacy of *Praxis* and Lenin.

< 58 >

This call for transformative educational agents is, in some ways, predictable. The distinctive logic of this discourse sets the frontier between itself and mainstream educational discourse by its call for action. Reiterating the Gramscian logic Apple uses to close his first volume, *Ideology and Curriculum*, Ginsburg (1988) rejects the possibility of a "neutral" intellectual and sets his discourse against non-action. In his words,

> From Gramsci's analysis, the implications of not speaking out and not acting are clear. Not only do we facilitate our colleagues' and our students' organic links with current and emerging dominant groups ... but we thus hasten the day for our own assimilation and conquest. (p. 216)

Having, then, no choice but to act on the side of the dominated, the attempt to answer the question, "What is to be done?" becomes a question of delineating an appropriate transformative educational agenda. As Ginsburg calls for interventions in debates over teacher education reforms, for interventions in developing curriculum and pedagogy in preservice teacher education programs, and for becoming activist intellectuals, the calling to a radical educational agenda is marked by distinctions students of the New Sociologies have learned to easily recognize.

Another characteristic of Ginsburg's discourse also marks the frontiers of the Structural Neo-Marxist sociologies of school knowledge. First, when identifying agents of change, Ginsburg employs a strategy of maximizing the potential for transformation with a move toward universalization. Here the audience of this proselytizing is expanded with the phrase "educators of teachers." About this expansion, Ginsburg is explicit:

> As educators of teachers, I include people in universities who teach generic and subject-specific teaching methods courses, educational psychology and social foundations of education courses, and arts and sciences courses comprising prospective teachers' major and other coursework. Most, if not all, university faculty, are thus, educators of teachers. The label applies to all educators—administrators and teachers—whom preservice teachers encounter during field observations and other assignments as well as during student teaching. (p. 203)

This move to expand the oppositional masses corresponds to the early Structural Neo-Marxist inclusion of race and gender among its dynamics of ideological analysis. When Carnoy and Levin (1985) and Ginsburg (1988) speak of the (ostensibly democratic) struggles of women and people of color (and both analyses do), this discourse reveals its constitutive political strategy.

But even as Ginsburg plays out continuities within the Structural Neo-Marxist discourse, he also pushes the frontiers of its discourse into its most proactive variation. In explicitly concentrating on what is to be done, this

< 59 >

discourse relies on and continues an argument made, in part, by one of the first generation U.S. New Sociologists, Henry Giroux, to distinguish between merely critical and truly transformative intellectuals. Here, in its examination and explicit evaluation of the role of the intellectual, the discourse of the transformative intellectual can be seen as lying on the border between the Structural Neo-Marxist agenda of the U.S. New Sociology and a newer, more proactive structural discourse. As Aronowitz and Giroux (1985) produce categorizations of intellectuals, differentiated according to the degree to which the dominant hegemonic ideology of society is fought, the evaluative implications of this proactive discourse are explicit (pp. 23–45).

So it is that within the Structural Neo-Marxist sociologies of school knowledge, self-imposed discontinuities are presented in the call for transformative intellectuals. As Aronowitz and Giroux categorize four types of intellectuals, they make evident distinctions which form discursive identities. Here four ideal-types of intellectuals are presented: transformative, critical, accommodating and hegemonic. Distinguishing among these four types is accomplished along two dimensions. The prime dimension separates the radical from the mainstream. The second dimension separates the free-floating intellectual from the socially committed.

The distinction between the mainstream and the radical separates the transformative and critical intellectuals from the accommodating and the hegemonic. Together the transformative and critical intellectuals are "ideologically alternative to existing institutions and modes of thought," and "critical of inequality and injustice" (p. 37). Accommodating and hegemonic intellectuals either (respectively) "function primarily to mediate uncritically ideas and social practices that serve to reproduce the status quo," or "self-consciously define themselves through the forms of moral and intellectual leadership they provide for dominant groups and class" (p 39). Here the dichotomies of radical self-identification are clear: allegiance with dominated groups versus allegiance with the dominant; critical of versus reproducers of the status quo.

The distinction between the committed and free-floating intellectual separates the transformative from the critical, and the hegemonic from the accommodating. Whereas the transformative intellectual unites "the language of critique" and "the language of possibility" to engage in overt political struggles, "working to create the ideological and material conditions in both schools and the larger society that give students the opportunity to become agents of civic courage," the critical intellectuals "do not see themselves as connected either to specific social formations or as performing a general social function that is expressly political in nature" (p. 37). According to Stanley Aronowitz and Giroux, the source of this difference lies in the critical intellectuals' "isolated posture" in which "they try to define their relationship to

< 60 >

the rest of society as free-floating" (p. 37). Contrary to this posture, which is identified with Karl Mannheim's (1936) resolution of the paradox of ideology, Aronowitz and Giroux (1985) advocate the position, attributed to Sartre, that "only the committed intellectual can arrive at assertions that serve human emancipation" (pp. 37-9)

Identified with the devalued "free-floating" posture are a host of intellectual positions held by nontransformative intellectuals:

> Often this retreat from politics is justified on the basis of arguments that posit the impossibility of politics for reasons as ideologically diverse as the claim that we live in a totally administered society, or history is in the hand of a technology out of control, or the simple refusal to believe that human agencies exist that have any effect on history. (p. 37)

Here "post-structural" analyses of the disciplining of modernity, pessimistic analyses of technology, and theories of social reproduction which do not highlight agency are all rejected.

Also rejected are "enlightenment conceptions" such as objectivity. Explicitly tied to accommodating intellectuals, who are seen to share with critical intellectuals the "free-floating" posture, professionalism and scientific objectivity are presented as being opposed to correct, expressed politics: "Another more subtle variation is the intellectual who disdains politics by proclaiming professionalism as a value system, one which often entails the spurious concept of scientific objectivity" (p. 39). Arguing that objectivity and truth are forms of ideology associated with one historical period (the Enlightenment), Aronowitz and Giroux clearly reject claims to scientific objectivity as contradictory to the task of making the pedagogical more political.

Structural feminist discourses

It is not only within a Marxist agenda that structural sensibilities are current within RSSK. A strong structural feminist agenda has been available to U.S. sociologists of school knowledge since, at least, the early 1970s. As its recent contributions make clear, structural feminist analyses of curriculum build on a strong and unique tradition of scholarship. Given my earlier centering of the almost exclusively male-authored New Sociology and its subsequent "developments," there are two general points I would like to make before I attempt to outline recent structural feminist contributions relevant to RSSK: first, unlike the U.S. New Sociology's ostensible allegiance with the U.S. "working-class," structural feminist discourse is historically endogenous to the Women's Movement; and second, independent from the New Sociology, feminist scholarship has been successful on its own in forging a strong voice within educational research for about two decades.

To clarify these points, I simply reiterate what many others have already

< 61 >

pointed out. Where it is questionable whether New Sociology critical intellectuals were ever connected with class struggles (both because of the class location of academics and because of the obvious lack of class struggle within the United States), feminist scholars working to further political agendas within the Women's Movement embody the social struggles about which they write (e.g., Wexler, 1987). Despite the New Sociology's tendency to speak for all the oppressed masses, it seems evident to me that feminists have done a fine job of speaking for themselves. Attempts to read feminist work "into" the tradition of the New Sociology risk forgetting the history of feminist educational scholarship in the United States (and in much of the rest of the Anglo-educational research community), erasing the self-reliant contributions of past feminist research, and reenacting the all too familiar sham of having men speak for (the assumed to be supportive) women (e.g., Lather, 1991; Nicholson, 1991).

It is with these concerns in mind that the position of structural feminist discourse in relation to RSSK becomes problematic. That is, since it is not clear that "the field" has found a way of speaking across the differences upon which many feminisms are based, I would not want to suggest that feminist interpretations of curriculum are necessarily part of the field of the sociology of school knowledge; but feminist arguments seem to me clearly relevant to the concerns of RSSK. On the one hand, more than a few feminist educational writers have expressed skepticism about the sociology of education generally and the New Sociology more specifically (e.g., Acker, Megarry, Nisbet, and Hoyle, 1987; O'Brien, 1984). Based on this skepticism, many feminisms would distinguish themselves from the field. On the other hand, given that feminist analyses of school knowledge have long examined the micro-macro connections between the daily practices of school knowledge and "larger" relations of gender differentiation, it seems clear that their theoretical insights would at least be of interest to the field (e.g., Frazier and Sadker, 1973; Stacey, Bereaud, Daniels, 1974). It is in the recognition of feminist educational analyses' unique history, tradition, and identities that one sign of fracturing among the sociologies of school knowledge becomes apparent.

Structural feminist discourse on school knowledge centers on gender differentiations and the role schools play in structuring gender differences (e.g., Anyon, 1984; Arnot, 1984; Connell, Ashenden, Kessler, Dowsett, 1982; Kelly and Nihlen, 1982; Maher, 1985; Taylor, 1989). Understanding gender as a social/cultural structuring process, these works often speak of patriarchy and at times employ many of the same conceptual lenses as the Structural Neo-Marxist analyses: reproduction, resistance, contradiction. But there are also additional concerns in understanding the connections between family and school life, and the public sphere and the private. Here I'd like simply to outline some of the concerns these works address.

< 62 >

For structural feminisms built in tandem with the Structural Neo-Marxist discourse, the intersection between class differences and gender differences is crucial. This work examines the ways in which a sexual division of labour, reproduced by schools and school knowledge, results in young women appropriating particular occupational trajectories and social roles. For example, Anyon (1984) focuses on differences, according to class, in the ways young women accommodate and resist both schools and "what is expected of them as girls." Here, governed by the dichotomous structure-agency logic, Anyon documents the ways in which young women actively participate in processes of sexual differentiation within the conceptual apparatus employed by the New Sociology. Tomboyishness, using "excessive" femininity, and non-compliance are all cited as strategies of simultaneous accommodation and resistance. For Anyon, "most girls are not passive victims of sex role stereotypes and expectations but are active participants in their own development" (p. 44). The processes of gender differentiation in this account are primarily revealed through examining the tacit behavioral mechanisms of the classroom, the hidden curriculum. With the concern for understanding the structural reproduction of gender differences, there is the familiar concern for recognizing the role of human agency.

Distinct from the New Sociology and with a central focus on the reproduction of patriarchy, Gail Kelly and Pam Nihlen (1982) point out that there are multiple social practices which contribute to sexual inequality in schools and society. Authority patterns among school personnel demonstrate that most schools are primarily staffed by women but under the authority of men. Patterns of subject matter staff segregation in post-primary schooling show a correspondence between high status disciplines and professions (science, math, and the applied sciences) and male dominance. Examining formal curricular materials in these areas shows that women are largely absent; and, even when included in these formal documents, women are usually not in "public" roles but relegated to the "private" domain. To the extent that these patterns tacitly convey images of proper but unequal roles for men and women, they can be seen as part of a hidden patriarchal curriculum.

Additionally, Kelly and Nihlen continue, many schooling practices overtly contribute to gender differences. After all, much of what is described in the above-mentioned processes moves beyond the tacit. Moreover, counseling practices which differentially identify acceptable future occupations are seen to leave a limited set of options open to women. Deciding what occupations are appropriate for women is often a very conscious matter on the part of guidance counselors, parents, and students.

Lastly, Kelly and Nihlen point to a need for more research on the distribution of knowledge within the classroom. While some research has shown, according to these two structural feminists, that the types and amount of rein-

< 63 >

forcement teachers give children differ according to gender (with class and race variances), much more direct study of gender-based variations of classroom practices is needed. As they put it,

> The few studies that we have on classroom knowledge distribution by gender suggest that teachers do not take female students seriously and that within the classroom girls' academic performance is systematically devaluated. This implies that the school is not "for keeps" for the female. While fragmentary data suggest such conclusions, we have far too little hard data. (p. 173)

It should be noted that this statement was published in 1983. Since that time a fair amount of data has been reported which would provide some general answers to the questions Kelly and Nihlen raise. To my knowledge, within radical educational research there still remains a dearth of "hard" evidence regarding daily classroom practices and within classroom differences according to gender (e.g., Delamont, 1989).

The structural feminisms found in the arguments of Anyon and Kelly and Nihlen are in many ways similar to the discourse of Structural Neo-Marxist research. With commonly shared touchstones expressed in a focus on class-based gender differences or in a call for "hard" evidence (possibly meaning generalizable or less open to a refusal to admit its validity), structural feminisms are often expressed in a language most sociologists would see as their own. However, this is certainly not true of all structural feminisms.

Here I would like to focus in particular on one specific strand of this kind of structural feminist discourse that is, for me, provocative, compelling, and poignant. I have in mind, as one example, Madeleine Grumet's (1988) structural feminism which in part builds its theoretical lenses from the theories of Nancy Chodorow (1978) and Dorothy Dinnerstein (1976). Built from the phenomenological grounding of motherhood, the gap between Structural Neo-Marxist discourse and this feminism could not be wider.

With its grounding in women's experience of biological reproduction, this discourse is based on experiences a male could never wholly share (unless some amazing biological changes occur). As a man and son, I must acknowledge the hesitation with which I approach this discourse. Grumet (1988) introduces her text, making her potentially universal intent explicit:

> The project of this text is to draw that (bodily) knowledge of women's experience of reproduction and nurturance into the epistemological systems and curricular forms that constitute the discourse and practice of public education. It is an argument drawn from the experience in my own life that is most personal and at the same time most general as it links me to those who share my sex and gender and those who also acknowledge reproductive responsibility for the species. (pp. 3–4)

< 64 >

Acknowledging "reproductive responsibility" is, Grumet argues, something all humans could potentially do. Even if we do not have children ourselves, the shared experience of biological reproduction is universally human. As Grumet suggests,

> Male or female, heterosexual, homosexual, bisexual, monogamous, chaste, or multipartnered, we each experience our sexuality and attachments within a set of conditions that contain the possibility of procreation. Our identities incorporate our position relative to this possibility ... Even if we choose not to be a parent we are not exempt from the reproductive process, for we have each been a child of our parents. (p. 6)[2]

Hence, while the word "reproduction" may be the same word as is found in other RSSK, in this feminist discourse, the metaphor is, as Grumet points out, quite literal (p. 4).

There are many aspects of schooling Grumet analyzes through this theoretical lens. Curriculum and pedagogy are of central concern; but for illustrative purposes, I would like to focus on Grumet's approach to studying the daily lives of teachers. Associated with the fact that most pre-tertiary teachers are women, many structural feminist accounts of schooling share this focus.

Part of Grumet's analysis builds on a historical analysis of the feminization of teaching in which the impersonal bureaucratic forms of compulsory schooling are seen as contradictory to the nurturance of women's experiences as mothers. Psychoanalytically, Grumet suggests that as women came into teaching, they were also faced with circumstances which resulted in a denial of their femininity, thereby ensuring the continuance of patriarchy:

> The feminization of teaching became a form of denial as the female teachers in the common schools demanded order in the name of sweetness, compelled moral rectitude in the name of recitation, citizenship in the name of silence, and asexuality in the name of manners. (p. 44)

This contradiction is also seen to have been accompanied by many other historical trends that shape the culture of schooling:

> (T)he contradictions that evolved in the nineteenth century between the doctrine of maternal love and the practice of a harsh and regimented authority, between women's dominance in numbers and our exclusion from leadership, between the overwhelming presence of women in classrooms and the continuing identification of men as the only persons with the capacity to know, are still present in the culture of schooling. (pp. 44–45)[3]

While this historical analysis aides in understanding the roots of the culture of schooling, says Grumet, "it cannot tell us how the experiences symbolized by these signs were integrated into the daily lives and understandings of the women who lived them" (p. 45).

And so it is that Grumet turns to an analysis of gender in her attempt to understand the logic of how women have contributed to their own oppression:

> This is the logic we need to understand, for women, through our work as mothers, as students, and as teachers, have contributed our labor and our children to institutional and social organizations that have extended our own subordination. (p. 45)

Understanding the logic of teachers' daily practices, for Grumet, lies in understanding gender as referenced by "that sexual identity as it is experienced, acknowledged, and owned by the individual" (p. 45). Questioning gender by way of questioning that which seems "natural," Grumet argues that, "(a)n analysis of teaching cannot ignore teaching's association with femininity" (p. 46).

Continuing her focus on that historical period in which women "took over the classroom," the nineteenth century, Grumet offers an illustrative analysis of the daily lives of teachers based on what may seem unlikely sources. Drawing on the literature of D. H. Lawrence and the images of teaching he drew in his *The Rainbow*, Grumet calls into question the idealized images of teaching found in the diaries of Cyrus Pierce, the principal of the first normal school in the United States. Here the "historical" document, the diary, is presented as demonstrably fictitious, and the fiction, Lawrence's depiction of Ursula's loss (rejection) of femininity as she entered teaching in an industrialized society, is seen as a most realistic description of one teacher's daily experiences.[4] Where Ursula was enticed into teaching with the ideal of bringing her maternal love to children, as a teacher she complied and employed the cold authority of the industrialized, patriarchal school.

Grumet aptly suggests that this process was quite likely to have been the case for many women who entered teaching in the nineteenth century. While being held to a class-specific moral standard of femininity they would inevitably fail to meet, the practices of schooling which contribute to class, ethnic, and racial inequalities can be understood as the teachers' own attempts to deal with self-failure. Grumet's (1988) words more readily explain than mine:

> The predictable incapacity of the loving teacher to save society through the example of her own submissiveness led to an inevitable failure—a failure of moral fiber, a failure of femininity, a failure of professionalism. It is no wonder that those recalcitrant students who were reluctant worshippers at the alter of maternal love (otherwise known as the tedious and strict classroom of the common school) were branded as deficient, if not pathological, in order the share this burden of blame. (p. 52)

Hence, the historical ideal that women could bring a maternal nurturance into the common school classroom is revealed as "sheer sentimentality." But in identifying what has been lost in schooling, Grumet also points toward what could be: "(T)eaching rests waiting for us to reclaim it and transform it into the work of women" (p. 58). It is in this endeavor to identify what could be that structural feminisms have articulated a feminist pedagogy.

The development and analysis of a feminist pedagogy has been central in the work, for example, of Frances Maher (1985). For Maher, the content and form of discourse within the classroom is of central concern. Part of Maher's analysis consists of a critique of traditional pedagogy. Maher argues that the traditional pedagogical style of the classroom supports masculine "assertive speech," "competitive 'devil advocate' interchanges," and "impersonal and abstract styles." Contrary to traditional patriarchal pedagogy, Maher advocates a pedagogy grounded in women's experiences of connectedness and caring. For Maher this "interactive and democratic pedagogy is appropriate for all oppressed groups seeking consciousness of their own past and future aims and identities. Men, too, can learn to think and learn 'like women'" (p. 46). Hence, the audience of structural feminist pedagogy discourse is potentially universal.

From this (very brief) outline, it is clear that the sites of interests in structural feminist educational discourses are many, from macro-level explanations of societal sex differences to micro-level examinations of teachers' daily lives and classroom practices. But it is also clear that the differences between the theoretical discourse of structural feminisms in education and the Structural Neo-Marxist educational agenda represent a rupture within RSSK.

Most apparent in the discourse of Grumet and other biologically minded structural feminisms, the basis of theoretical understandings is radically (in a literal, etymological sense) different than that of the Structural Neo-Marxist New Sociology. Here the experiences of women—as girls, adults, mothers, students, and teachers—are the basis of the knowledge built within this discourse. Where Marxist Ideology-Critiques of education, grounded in the experience of the "labor process," examine the hidden curriculum as duplicitous in the reproduction of capitalism, structural feminist accounts of schooling focus on patriarchy and are grounded in the knowledge of women's experiences. Where structural feminisms point out that Marxist theory has excluded women, structural feminisms grounded in the experiences of motherhood consciously and convincingly exclude and decenter men. Here the frontier between some structural feminist discourses and the Structural Neo-Marxist U.S. New Sociology is ruptured, and the image of a fixed boundary, a gap one may or may not cross over but that will not itself move, appears as a fair inscription.

< 67 >

On the post-structural frontiers of the Neo-Marxist agenda

Where fixed frontiers divide some discourses of RSSK, other frontiers appear more flexible. For example, while still within a Neo-Marxist discourse, Cameron McCarthy's (1990) proposal for a "nonsynchronous" modification of Apple's Parallelist Position can be seen as pushing the structural boundaries of the New Sociology toward a post-structural analysis. To explain this characterization of McCarthy's proposal, I should first outline what McCarthy suggests his proposal offers.

From its origin, McCarthy's research agenda is fundamentally different than that of the U.S. New Sociology: McCarthy's primary concern is to understand the relations between race and curriculum. Noting the obvious empirical reality of racial inequality in U.S. education, McCarthy's explicit reason for this focus is both direct and cutting:

> To put the matter forthrightly, . . . both mainstream and radical educational researchers have tended to undertheorize and marginalize phenomena associated with racial inequality. Of course, this is not to deny the fact that there is a growing "interest" in race in the curriculum and educational literature. But as we shall see, current mainstream and radical curriculum and educational theories do not adequately address or account for the persistence of racial inequality in schooling. (p. 2)

Similar to feminisms, McCarthy's overall theoretical point of departure obviously lies outside Neo-Marxism's traditional focus on economic class.

But even with this central and seemingly singular focus, McCarthy is critical of theoretical attempts to address education through simple structural lenses. As he puts it,

> In significant ways, . . . both mainstream and radical conceptualizations of racial inequality are "essentialist" in that they effectively eliminate the "noise" of multidimensionality, historical variability and subjectivity from their explanations of educational differences. Current approaches to racial inequality tend to rely too heavily on linear, single-causal models or explanations. (p. 6)

Hence, with an eye toward multiple dynamics of educational inequality, and the ways in which such dynamics intersect, McCarthy chooses to build on Apple's Parallelist Position.

In the sense that he is concerned with highlighting the complexities of racial interactions, McCarthy's choice to begin with the Parallelist Position is readily understandable and logically consistent. Here, McCarthy is partially supportive of the flexibility and nuance of the Parallelist Position and applauds the potential of this theoretical position for constructing more complete understandings of educational practices. This support, however, is also accompanied by McCarthy's own concerns.

McCarthy offers two major criticisms of the Parallelist Position in building the case for his own nonsynchronous proposal. First, emphasizing that attempts to understand "consciousness" or ideological practices necessitates understanding the everyday actions of individual people, McCarthy is critical of the level of abstraction offered in the Parallelist Position. As he puts it,

> While the (Parallelist) model does serve to make us stop and think about a broader range of dynamics and spheres than before, it is difficult to account for the various twists and turns of social and political life at the microlevel if our application of theory is inappropriately "pitched" at too high level of abstraction. (p. 82)

McCarthy's concern here is straightforward. By focusing on macro-societal levels of difference, the Parallelist Position—despite its proclaimed heritage in the sociology of school knowledge—is potentially too general to be useful in micro-level analysis.

McCarthy's second criticism is a little less direct. Here he suggests that the inclusion of race, gender, and class among the position's dynamics potentially leads to an "additive" interpretation.[5] Within radical social criticism, this claim circulates around concerns for understanding the ways in which individuals might experience multiple dimensions of power relations simultaneously. Without a theoretical account of qualitatively different forms of oppression, so such an argument would go, it is difficult, for example, to account for the ways in which black women might experience vastly different forms of oppression as women, or as *black* women (or, in some circumstances, as *underclass* black women).

In additive models, according to this critique, the only way in which we can understand such complex situations is in terms of double and triple oppressions—which may not always be accurate. As McCarthy explains,

> No attempt is made here (in one ostensibly additive model) to represent the *qualitatively* different experiences of patriarchy that black women encounter in their daily lives, both in the context of the domestic sphere and within the teaching profession itself. In this essentially incremental model of oppression, patriarchal and class forms of oppression unproblematically reproduce each other. (p. 82, emphasis in original)

The problem with such a theoretical approach lies in the recognition that, in specific contexts, different forms of oppression sometimes do not work in tandem, but might better be understood as working through contradictions and tensions relative to each other.

When specifically applied to the Parallelist Position, this "additive" critique points out the way in which its dynamics might be seen as symmetrical. In McCarthy's words:

the parallelist position does not fully address the "mix" of contingencies, interests, needs, differential assets and capacities in the local setting such as the school. Dynamics of race, class, and gender are conceptualized as having individual and uninterrupted effects. (p. 83)

Hence, McCarthy opens the need for an even more nuanced and subtle theoretical language—for the language of "nonsynchrony."

McCarthy's specific language of "nonsynchrony" is drawn from the work of the socialist feminist Emily Hicks (1981), and many of his criticisms of the Parallelist Position mirror Hicks's criticisms of Marxist feminisms. As his critique of the Parallelist Position implies, the point of talking about nonsynchronous relations is, according to McCarthy (1990), to more fully explicate the complexities of local social settings. In his words:

By invoking the concept of nonsynchrony, I wish to advance the position that individuals or groups, in their relation to economic, political and cultural institutions such as schools, do *not* share identical consciousness and express the same interests, needs or desires "at the same point in time." (p. 83, emphasis in original)

McCarthy sees utility in this theoretical approach not only in analyzing daily practices of individuals, but on the institutional level as well: "Hicks' emphasis on nonsynchrony helps to lay the basis for an alternative approach to thinking about these social relations and dynamics at the institutional level" (p. 83). Thus, for McCarthy, the basis of his theoretical approach is seen as emanating from a concern for understanding the complexities of local practices and institutional formations. In a sense, rather than pushing down from the macro to the micro, McCarthy has offered a theory built, at least in large part, from the bottom up.

There are many aspects of McCarthy's effort which show explicit and implicit signs of a post-structural influence. In his focus on the local, and on questions of contradictory social dynamics, McCarthy works against structural presuppositions of smoothly functioning modes of reproduction. In his rejection of 'essentialist' theorizing and in his recognition of multiplicities, McCarthy deploys familiar signifiers of post-structuralism. But there are many aspects of McCarthy's theory which make it difficult for me to proclaim his work post-structural and serve as my justification for suggesting that the language of nonsynchrony merely pushes the frontiers of structuralism toward the post-structural.

For example, I would classify this work as structural for two reasons: First, McCarthy's nonsynchrony carries, by presumption, a strong appeal to the tripartite structures of race, gender, and class. Second, McCarthy's analysis imposes, in ad hoc fashion, "four types of relations that govern the nonsynchronous interactions of raced, classed and gendered minority and majority actors in

< 70 >

the school setting" (p. 84), which are conceptually embedded within traditional Marxist analyses of commodity exchange. That is, McCarthy's relations of "competition, exploitation, domination, and cultural selection" are clearly the residue of structural analyses of economic, cultural, and social exchange.

Given these points, I am skeptical that the nonsynchronous position as articulated by McCarthy has been pushed to its logical consequences sufficiently to warrant the label "post-structural." As with the Parallelist Position, if the call for beginning from subjectivities and specific local analyses were to be strictly followed, one wonders why race, gender, and class are given a priori primacy over other social dynamics. Similarly, while McCarthy deploys his four analytical "types of relations" in historical and social analyses, it is never clear on what basis McCarthy has named these four and not others. Given the clear similarities between past Structural Neo-Marxist analyses and McCarthy's analytical frame, I would speculate that McCarthy's discourse is fundamentally guided by its structural heritage. Of course, I recognize this could be a matter for debate.[6]

Into the post-structural frontier

In a fashion that seems to push even further toward the post-structural frontier, Phil Wexler (1982) has also articulated a post-structural critique of the New Sociology in his call for a "social analysis" of education.

When examining the development of Wexler's analysis, it is evident that post-structural analysis in education has been long coming. Wexler's work began turning toward post-structural theory early in the 1980s. One might speculate that Wexler's relatively early interest in this type of theorizing could be attributed to his intellectual background as a social psychologist. Such a discipline is more acutely aware of the individual versus social dichotomy than others.

Published in 1982, Wexler's article, "Structure, Text, and Subject," begins by noting that the New Sociology of education had, by then, employed three central categories to counter liberal views of schooling: the hidden curriculum, ideology, and socialization. In his words these categories oppose liberal views of schooling in that:

> Hidden curriculum asserts the primacy of social relations over knowledge and technology. The concept of ideology relativizes knowledge in a social context where cultural relativism and cognitive relativism ... sustain rationales for sociopolitical inaction. (And) ... socialization (displaces) the older individual voluntarism. (p. 276)

Using class as his main social category, Wexler synthetically argued that the sociology of curriculum demonstrated that school knowledge 1) reflects class interest; 2) is the unequal representation of the experience of social

< 71 >

classes; 3) is an organizational representation of different class languages; and 4) develops as cultural representation in response to the needs of capitalism; synthesizing the works of Anyon, Bourdieu, Bernstien, and Apple, respectively.

But Wexler was not entirely happy with the successes of the New Sociology. Such work, according to Wexler, still employed a reflectionist analysis: "Critical qualified representational analysis is still representation" (p. 276). This meant that ideology critique hid uncertainty and disjunction, and that, "the language of structural reproduction discourages interest in transformative activity as practice" (p. 291).

To alter this nontransformative mode of analysis, Wexler suggested that radical curriculum theory "requires a mode of analysis which makes the tenuousness of the object apparent, not by contextualizing it, but by deconstructing it" (p. 279). For Wexler such an analysis lay in the deconstruction of "structure," the social analysis of "texts," and in a critical analysis of the "subject." Clearly the connection with then current Structural Neo-Marxist theorizing was strong. But the added interest of analyzing the "subject" proved to open a line of critique which the sociology of school knowledge has not yet moved beyond.

In critizing the New Sociology's analysis of the subject, Wexler asked for something more than the hopeful possibility of resistance. He writes,

> The activity of the subject (in Structural Neo-Marxism) is seen as an enactment of a script written to meet the needs of the system . . . In the model of socialization, whether as transmission of social values and roles, or as textual positioning, the subject becomes the object of a social or cultural system. (pp. 291–92)

And further, when discussing how structural analysis had dealt with this problem (i.e., Willis or Giroux): "the concept of resistance, like the categories of mediation and contradiction, when used as an addenda, only qualifies the model. It does not go far enough to challenge the assumptions of the subject as object" (p. 292).

Here, Wexler turns to a language of openness and disjuncture. Borrowing eclectically from Marxist cultural critique (Adorno and Horkheimer), Marxist literary analysis (Eagleton), semiotic analysis (Eco), and what has become known as post-structural analysis (Foucault and Deleuze), Wexler suggests that a critical sociology of school knowledge ought to recognize the subject as decentered and multiple. In this view,

> the social apparatus creates not only the inmate, who is paradigmatic of object-subject socialization theory, but also the spectator and the human commodity. And in its contradictoriness, the apparatus also produces the contradictory decentered divided subject. (p. 293)

< 72 >

While the specific implications of this analytical language may seem difficult to grasp, it clearly does signify a shift in the mode of analysis. For Wexler, at this point, there was a keen interest in analyzing both commodity production and consumption.[7]

Wexler suggests that the whole process of cultural commodity production offers sites for collective action. That is, as each commodity is produced there are points of appropriation, organizational production, distribution and appropriation by the subject. These points offer specific arenas of possible collective action on the part of oppressed people. Even market competition offers a site of transformation, for Wexler, in the sense that although market competition moves toward stabilization and monopoly (in a capitalistic context), competition itself continually opens new markets.[8]

Although it appears that Wexler was shedding a great deal of the New Sociology's structural interest, it is important to recognize that when he spoke of collective action, he most often referred to class as a category. In this sense, I take Wexler to have moved out of explicit structural theorizing while also maintaining his structural Marxist heritage. Wexler's (1987) move to a poststructural analysis, however, extended with the publication of *Social Analysis of Education*. It is to this work I now turn.

While perhaps the most interesting chapter in *Social Analysis of Education* is Wexler's reflective analysis of the historical developments of "the rise and fall of the New sociology of education," my concern here is to discuss how Wexler more fully develops the implications of his textual analysis for the study of school knowledge. Although Wexler rearticulates (reprints, in fact) much of what he had said in 1982, some further arguments can be found in his book.

In his final chapter, entitled "Education," Wexler claims that "a poststructural language of exile can help free social analysts of education from an incorporated academically established ... critical social theory on the one hand, and a socially inauthentic identification with 'the working class' or with the triadic oppressed groups of 'class, race and gender,' on the other" (p. 181). The point here responds to Wexler's criticism of the New Sociology. That criticism essentially charges self-identification with oppressed groups, by academic radicals, as inauthentic or false. The language of exile reminds academic authors that the languages produced in the academy are decontextualized with respect to schools. In this vein Wexler states,

> Re-contextualized study of knowledge production in schools includes the interactional processes of the institution, the professional identity of teachers, and most importantly: analysis of political practice and possibility in school, as a preface to educational politics. (p. 182)

To be frank, it is difficult for me to understand the implications of Wexler's arguments for the sociology of school knowledge; but the overall

< 73 >

argument suggests that the New Sociology, because of its own romantic individualism and reflectionist language, has failed to recognize that schooling and
education has passed into a new era: an era of collective symbolic production.
This means that when studying the knowledge and self-identification of
students in schools, sociologists of school knowledge need to recognize that
schools are institutional class sites where "class culturally-specific identity
work takes place" (p. 310). In this context, one in which a symbolic economy
is prime, the sociology of education requires a "revision of the intersection of
class and institutional analyses . . . [where] . . . the micro-economy of self-
production will define everyday educational process" (p. 314). In this view,
the interests of a sociology of curriculum have shifted from studies of distribution and production to studies of the contradictions among and between relations of production *and* consumption.

Another (self-proclaimed) post-structuralist curriculum theorist, Cleo
Cherryholmes (1988), has contributed to public debates about the usefulness
of post-structural analysis for studying curriculum. For Cherryholmes, the
language of post-structuralism is a language of critique which allows us to
name multiple "discourses" of power. An important insight here, and one
appropriated from Foucault, is that power is ubiquitous, continually circulat-
ing through our social practices. In contrast to a more conventional notion of
power, in which certain people have or possess power, this view suggests that
power is enacted always by everyone (p. 35; see also Gore, 1993). Broadly
speaking, Cherryholmes's project is a deconstructive one in which he attempts
to lay out a set of theoretical lenses through which curricular materials and
research on curriculum can be "read," and with which the discursive formations of power in curriculum can be named.

While Cherryholmes's arguments may be of great interest for curricular
theory, his work has a decidedly non-sociological character and is conducted
almost exclusively within and about textual analysis (meaning written texts).
As he defines his major theoretical concepts (discourse, practice, speech acts,
text, discourse-practice), for example, such an emphasis is clear. With
'discourse' distinguished from 'discourse-practice' and the inclusion of analytical philosophy's 'speech act,' there is a clear imbalance between concerns for
what is said versus what is done. But his tendency to flatten all things social
into relative "texts" is apparent throughout Cherryholmes's own text.

There is an irony here in that there is a disjunction within Cherryholmes's
text itself. Where Cherryholmes criticizes structuralism for its ostensible lack
of historical perspective, and where he makes repeated claims that post-
structuralism places "texts" and "discourses" within historical contexts,
Cherryholmes himself presents no systematic or extended socio-historical
analysis. With the Derridian view that "nothing lies outside the text," in
Cherryholmes's text the words "time" and "space" are employed with

< 74 >

reference (meaning) to neither. Intended as an introductory text on the use of post-structuralism in educational research, this focus is understandable, yet the irony remains, leaving the utility of Cherryholmes's claims in doubt.

While Wexler and Cherryholmes have begun to open up the levels and sites of a post-structural analysis of curriculum, the use of post-structural critique has gained more currency within a unique discourse relevant to RSSK, a discourse I call (and which is, at times, self-named) post-structural feminist educational research. It is in this discourse that the value and promise of post-structuralism is apparent.

A POST-STRUCTURAL FEMINIST AGENDA

The use of post-structural (and postmodern) discourses within feminism generally has been a matter of significant and heated published debate, (e.g., Nicholson, 1991; Fraser, 1989; de Lauretis, 1986; Spivak, 1988; Hirsch and Keller, 1990). The specific intervention of post-structural feminisms in the RSSK has been no less controversial. Without attempting to understand the entirety of that debate, and without attempting to reconcile the significant and important points of departure marked by post-structural feminist critique, I attempt here simply to trace a few of the arguments raised by post-structural feminist interventions which are relevant to my concerns.

Building directly upon her experience of teaching a special topics course at the University of Wisconsin–Madison, Elizabeth Ellsworth (1989) contextually articulates one post-structural feminist critique of the radical educational discourses known as critical pedagogy. As Ellsworth points out, this course, "Media and Anti-Racist Pedagogies" (C&I 607), took place within societal and local contexts of rising racial tensions, manifested by publicized racist acts, and was intentionally/explicitly designed to build potential political actions against racism. In her introduction, Ellsworth enacts both a feminist appeal to the "personal and political" and a post-structural disposition which privileges local analyses. Basing her critique of critical pedagogy discourses on her own interpretation of her course, her dual enactments are revealed as she qualifies her meaning of the word "critique":

> By "critique" I do not mean a systematic analysis of the specific articles or individual authors' positions that make up this literature, for the purposes of articulating a "theory" of critical pedagogy capable of being evaluated for its internal consistency, elegance, powers of prediction, and so on. Rather, I have chosen to ground the following critique in my interpretations of my experiences in C&I 607. That is, I have attempted to place key discourses in the literature on critical pedagogy *in relation to* my interpretation of my experience in C&I 607—by asking which interpretations and "sense making" do those discourses facilitate, which do they silence and marginalize, and what interests do they appear to serve? (p. 298)

< 75 >

In this rejection of Grand Theory; in this problematization of internal consistency, elegance, and predictive power; in the embracing of the specific and local; and in questioning what is marginalized by discursive formations Ellsworth's enactments of post-structural dispositions are clear. And in her self-reflectivity, in her focus on local pedagogical practices, and in her questioning of male-authored critical pedagogy, Ellsworth's feminism is also unquestionable.

Much of Ellsworth's critique is concerned with showing that, despite the political claims of critical pedagogy to oppose repression and domination, the discourses of critical pedagogy carry with them their own repressive "myths," and that her class's attempts to employ this discourse were politically unproductive and even harmful. As she puts it,

> when participants in our class attempted to put into practice prescriptions offered in the literature concerning empowerment, student voice, and dialogue, we produced results that were not only unhelpful, but actually exacerbated the very conditions we were trying to work against, including Eurocentrism, racism, sexism, classism, and "banking education." (p. 298)

In the context of a university classroom whose students differed widely in their ethnicity, class membership or background, religion, gender, etc., Ellsworth suggests the problems of the critical pedagogy discourses become clear. Even with a class agreement "that racism was a problem on campus that required political action" (p. 303), the conjunction of diversity and the discourses of critical pedagogy proved problematic.

According to Ellsworth, the problems of critical pedagogy discourse are evident in the post-structural and feminist critiques of rationalist assumptions. Suggesting that critical pedagogy is built on such assumptions, Ellsworth is skeptical of rationalism. As she puts it: "educators who have constructed classroom practices dependent upon analytical critical judgement can no longer regard the enforcement of rationalism as a self-evident political act against relations of domination" (p. 304). Drawing on a wide disciplinary base, Ellsworth calls forth post-structural critiques of rationalism to argue,

> While poststructuralism, like rationalism, is a tool that can be used to dominate, it has also facilitated a devastating critique of the violence of rationalism against its Others. It has demonstrated that as a discursive practice, rationalism's regulated and systematic use of elements of language constitutes rational competence "as a series of exclusions—of women, people of color, of nature as historic agent, of the true value of art." In contrast, poststructuralist thought is not bound to reason, but to discourse, literally narratives about the world that are admittedly *partial*. Indeed, one of the crucial features of discourse is the intimate tie between knowledge and interest, the latter being understood as a "standpoint" from which to grasp "reality." (p. 304)

< 76 >

Hence, when constructing her critique of critical pedagogies, Ellsworth is also advocating a situated/partial post-structuralism.

The markers of this position lie, to some extent in the space opened by rejection, by negation. Labeled "A Pedagogy of the Unknowable," Ellsworth (1989) presents her position as being based on accepting what can't be known:

> No one affinity group could ever "know" the experiences and knowledges of other affinity groups or the social positions that were not their own. Nor can social subjects who are split between the conscious and the unconscious, and cut across by multiple, intersecting, and contradictory subject positions, ever fully "know" their own experiences. (p. 318)

Consistent with many other post-structural feminisms, this position values the space and opportunity opened by "confronting unknowability" (p. 321). As Ellsworth concludes:

> My moving about between the positions of privileged speaking subject and Inappropriate/d Other cannot be predicted, prescribed, or understood by any theoretical framework or methodological practice. It is in this sense that a practice grounded in the unknowable is profoundly contextual (historical) and interdependent (social). This reformulation of pedagogy and knowledge removes the critical pedagogue from two key discursive positions s/he has constructed for her/himself in the literature—namely, origin of what can be known and origin of what should be done. (p. 332)

In this text, however shifting and movable, there is constructed a consistent appeal to specific contexts. For all its questioning of consistency, Ellsworth's discourse maintains an amazing consistency throughout. The post-structural focus on the local and the feminist appeal to the personal signifies a homologous correspondence others could see as consistent. Each discourse (the post-structural and the feminist) questions abstracted, generalized theory. Each discourse rejects prediction. And each discourse finds opportunity in theoretical uncertainty, and assurance in practice. In Ellsworth's critique, the personalized interpretation, the unpredictability of her future, and the theoretical uncertainty enacted all lie within the regulative discourses of both feminist politics and post-structuralism.

The conjunction of a feminist politics and post-structural discourse has also been advanced in the work of Patti Lather (1991).[9] Lather's work entails numerous arguments and theoretical positions—many of which are similar to those found in Ellsworth's critique. Providing an overview of Lather's project is beyond my grasp here, but I would like to discuss her work in relation to a dimension of post-structural feminist works in education that I have not yet highlighted. That is, I would like to consider a correspondence between the conjunction of post-structuralism and feminism and what I see as its exceptionally high degree of self-awareness and self-reflexivity. Here I would like to

< 77 >

in/describe this discourse's sensitivity to its own "performity." While it has been common in critical theoretical discourses to pledge allegiance to self-awareness and reflectivity for at least a century or so, the importance of recognizing theoretical proclamations as performance becomes critical in reading this conjunction of a feminist concern for "the personal as political" and the post-structural awareness of "subtexts."

There are many points in Lather's work where it is clear her discourse works on multiple textual levels, with each relating to the other as a form of reflective self-awareness. But it is in Lather's rereading of Ellsworth that the performity of the post-structural feminist agenda reveals multiple questions of sociological import.

To understand something of the context in which Lather enters a re-reading of Ellsworth's critique, it is important to note that this post-structural feminist critique of critical pedagogy received more than a few rather harsh responses from critical pedagogy loyalists (Ellsworth, 1990). Lather's rereading is itself a direct response to attacks on Ellsworth's critique put forth by Giroux (1988) and Peter McLaren (1988)—two of the leading proponents of critical pedagogy.

For Lather (1991), her rereading of Ellsworth (and her respondents) is positioned as an attempt, "(t)o explore the problems and possibilities that this emerging body of work on postmodernism and education raises for emancipatory education" (p. 43). In this light, Lather emphasizes Ellsworth's grounding in her (Ellsworth's) own experience and suggests that "Ellsworth's essay and reactions to it exemplify the complexities of what it means to do praxis-oriented intellectual work in a post-foundational context" (p. 44). In such a context, Lather articulates concerns which revolve around a recurrent radical anxiety about post-structural analysis. Roughly put, a question Ellsworth's essay raises (according to Lather and the Others) is whether or not post-structural analysis undermines the foundation of a radical political agenda.

Here Lather highlights political problems post-structural analyses bring to radical politics. As she puts it:

> postmodernism positions emancipatory reason as vulnerable to interrogation. Tracing collusion of intellectuals with emancipatory desires in the very cultural dominants they are opposing via the intersection of liberatory intentions and the "will to power" that underscores the privileged positions of knowing and changing, the discourses of emancipation are located as much within Foucault's "regimes of truth" as not. Additionally, rather than separating the "true" from the "false," postmodernism destabilizes assumptions of interpretive validity and shifts emphasis to the contexts in which meanings are produced. (p. 44)

Clearly, for both the "broad" leftist agenda of critical pedagogy and the feminist politics of Lather and Ellsworth, this is a concern and risk worth contemplating.

< 78 >

Lather's response to this tension is to highlight the multiplicity of readings such a text as Ellsworth's is likely to encounter. Focusing specifically on McLaren and Giroux's responses, Lather centers on two concerns Ellsworth's critics raise: 1) that the deployment of post-structural analysis can be associated with a "separatist" political paralysis, and 2) that by critiquing critical pedagogy discourses Ellsworth engaged directly in academic struggles against the authors of these "emancipatory" discourses. In turn, Lather offers two of her own readings.

The first reading Lather presents highlights "the textual practices that she [Ellsworth] uses to locate her intervention" (pp. 45–46). Here Lather points out the way in which Ellsworth's text can be seen as a post-structural intervention into the terrain of feminist pedagogy (not a feminist intervention into critical pedagogy). As a post-structural attempt to clear its own "semiotic" space, Lather questions Ellsworth's political wisdom by arguing that,

> Her seizing of a moral high-ground and her demonizing of critical pedagogy's "repressive myths" perpetuates monolithic categories of dominant/dominated, thereby intensifying the conflictive nature of the semiotic environment. (pp. 46–47)

For Lather, this problem could be avoided with an added layer of analysis in which Ellsworth's text would "deconstruct" its own strategies. I presume Lather is suggesting that if a text makes its "semiotic" subtext explicit, it can relativize its own authority and moral valuations.

The second reading Lather offers of Ellsworth's texts (and its critics) is positioned as "a construction of both how her work evokes ways to work with rather than be paralyzed by the loss of Cartesian stability and unity ... and what the material consequences of her project might be" (p. 46). By invoking the post-structural perspective, so this argument suggests, the position of the theorist as "one who knows" (with Cartesian certainty) is displaced and decentered. In Lather's words: "To multiply the ways in which we can interrupt the relations of dominance requires deconstructing such vanguardism" (p. 47). Hence, by seeing Ellsworth's text as an intervention in the articulation of critical pedagogy, the post-structural self-critique is presented as a check on the potentially dominating effects of such consciously transformative theory.

In this light, Lather questions McLaren's and Giroux's accusations of Ellsworth's "discrediting" and "careerism" intents by simply reversing the direction of the academic mudslinging. In her comments on Giroux's response the quality and strategy of this move are evident:

> I read his (Giroux's) statements about "careerism" and the undermining of "the very nature of social criticism itself" as ironically repositioning himself and the other (largely male) architects of critical pedagogy at the center of her discourse. (p. 48)[10]

< 79 >

Aside from the obviously petty quality of this exchange, there is an important theoretical point being made here, which makes both the separatism worries of Giroux and McLaren and the decentering strategy of the post-structural feminists plausible.

Earlier I suggested that Lather's text presents a quality of performity which is relatively unique to post-structural feminist discourse in education. In this exchange with authors of critical pedagogies, this quality is exhibited directly. Let me outline one interpretation of this exchange to explain what I mean.

Considering both the text and subtext of each public stance taken, Ellsworth's original critique can be seen to express its post-structuralism and its feminism in both its text and subtext. Textually, the adherence to a post-structural feminism is explicit—with authoritative references to both traditions as well as to a growing conjunctive lineal heritage. Subtextually, in grounding her work in personal experience, in refusing to offer generalizable proclamations, in refusing to speak beyond her experiences, Ellsworth enacts the political (partial) position from which she speaks.

In counterpoint, when Giroux and McLaren raise the worry of separatism and political paralysis, in a language similar to that which was initially critiqued, they subtextually create the paradox Ellsworth initially opened up. That is, because the response is cast as a general (abstracted) concern over the issues of post-structural analysis in political projects (in general), and because they choose to attack such criticism on the grounds that it is, at least in part, an enactment of academic politics, these critical pedagogues blind themselves to their own subtext; hence they have simply given the post-structural feminist critique further evidence of the rightness of the original criticisms. By making their concerns ones of general politics and post-structuralism (the only real option they have since they are not going to question a feminist politics they claim to support), the critical pedagogues subtextually reenact the abstracted, generalizing qualities post-structural feminists have criticized in the first place. In essence, by focusing on questions of post-structuralism, the critical pedagogues have ignored Ellsworth's feminism. And by presuming Ellsworth's critique was theoretical, the critical pedagogues continue the abstractions Ellsworth explicitly and implicitly rejected in her contextualism.

Here Lather's comments on Ellsworth's strategy of making her own semiotic space could not be more correct. The only way for critical pedagogues to adequately respond to Ellsworth's critique is to accept her terrain and grant her difference. From the position of a respondent, it is no wonder Giroux and McLaren (and many other white male leftists) see this as separatist. As a political act, they cannot build a response which would meet the requirements of this post-structural feminist critique except on the terms it presents. That they haven't accepted those terms is evidence for Lather's claim that the critical pedagogues seek to reposition themselves in the center of the debate. No

< 80 >

matter what the content of their claims, without tending to the subtextual effects of their arguments, the critical pedagogues fight a losing battle. Furthermore, the only way to change their subtext is, in part, to become skeptical about their text.

Understanding this as a political struggle (both academic and otherwise), from the perspective I hold as something of a bystander, I simply feel compelled to point out a recent song lyric: "It's Woman's Day." If there is any text which subtextually enforces the stubborn defiance of its textual politics, it is the post-structural feminist discourse advanced by Ellsworth. The strategic brilliance of this strategy I attribute to the awareness which this post-structural feminism brings to its own performance as a political text, to its subtextual/textual continuity, to its performity.

CONCLUSION

I introduced this chapter by suggesting that a survey of contemporary discourses relevant to RSSK would reveal fracturing. As I discussed the theories I've surveyed, I attempted to mark some of the points of that fracturing along the way: the divide between structural feminists and structural Neo-Marxists; Wexler's radical critique and departure from his Neo-Marxist heritage; and Ellsworth's clear articulation of the silencing she associates with one birthright of the Structural Neo-Marxist discourse—critical pedagogy. These broad distinctions and points of disjunction I take to be clear. Hence, I reinforce them under tidy subsection headings.

But these broad differences carry with them a host of more detailed cultural distinctions enacted in the implicit and explicit valuations of each discursive strand. The Structural Neo-Marxist discourse's foci on "wider social conflict" and "inequities of income and power," and the obvious concern for analyzing class struggles, simultaneously distinguish this discourse from both the mainstream "liberal" educational discourse and less "materially" focused radical analyses. Even as the Structural Neo-Marxist discourse is pushed into the realm of defining transformative intellectuals, the call for politically committed intellectuals serving the interests of human emancipation stirs images of known Communist patriarchs such as Lenin, Gramsci, Engels, and Marx himself. No matter how true or faithful to classical texts of Marx, each (relatively) unique conceptual flag of this discourse further signifies a stance quickly identifiable as Neo-Marxist.

Similarly, the structural feminisms discussed above carry their own signifiers of a unique analytical stance. Beyond the blurred frontiers between attempts to "marry" Marxism and feminism, the concerns of a feminist analysis are as distinctive as they are socially identifiable. Centrally focused on gender, sexism, and patriarchy, these structural feminist discourses are clearly identifiable as positioned in double opposition to both mainstream

< 81 >

educational discourse and Neo-Marxisms. In redefining "reproduction," in placing primacy on the personal, in making public the private, in inverting fact and fiction, and in asserting concrete connectedness above abstract certainty, these structural feminisms create an analytical space and a stance which is truly their own.

As the frontiers of post-structural analyses push into the radical spaces of the New Sociology, further fissures are revealed. As McCarthy initiates a post-structural focus on subjectivities and the qualitative uniqueness of multiple oppressions, the language of nonsynchrony potentially fractures the macro-level structures of his Neo-Marxist ancestry. While his choice of privileging race as a structural dimension is never in question, the logical consequences of nonsynchrony would leave open social analysis along multiple other dimensions. As with the *ad hoc* addition of race and gender in the Parallelist Position, it is never clear that recognizing nonsynchrony would necessarily result in focusing on race. In the current U.S. educational reality, of course, focusing on race is readily justifiable; however, in the language of nonsynchrony, this choice is not a logical necessity, but a historically contingent response.

Class, gender, and race. These have become common signifiers in the radical theoretical agenda in the sociology of school knowledge, and each carries its own history, politics, and social logic. Current radical agendas fight toward unmasking, analyzing, and transforming the societal inequities that exist along each of these dimensions. Each of these political struggles has historically worked both in opposition to, and in tandem with, their Others. Over the past decade, however, in the multiple theoretical agendas of RSSK, it would be difficult to say any one agenda has emerged as prominent. Unlike the earlier New Sociology of education, current sociologies of school knowledge seem to share no singular political/analytical concern.

Singularity in opposition to the status quo has long been sought among radical Americans, and messengers calling for unity are as common now as they have ever been among oppositional Americans (e.g., Aronowitz and Giroux, 1985). But it is precisely that singularity which post-structural analysis defies. Anxieties of separatism, worries over lost political strength, and political distrust of an analysis which highlights such ruptures are all understandable in a postmodern world. The political "Catch-22" critical pedagogues face in attempts to respond to post-structural feminisms I see simply as a sign of the times.

That I, with an eye toward difference, would find a fractured world among the sociologies of school knowledge may seem yet another imposition of an analytical lens. But as Charles Lemert (1991) points out about the use of post-modern theory in sociological analysis:

< 82 >

> Postmodernism, if it means anything at all, means to say that since the
> midcentury the world has broken into its political and cultural parts. The very
> idea of the world revolving on a true axis has proven finite. The axial princi-
> ples of the twentieth-century world—European culture, British administra-
> tion, American capitalism, Soviet politics—have come apart as a matter of
> *fact*, not of theory. The multiple identities and local politics of which [Steven]
> Seidman speaks are not just another way; they are what is left. (p. 167)

So too I argue about the current state of RSSK. My choice of analytical lens in
this chapter is of course not innocent, but it is a choice based on my own
empirical observations of the theories I find in RSSK.

These are not only "theories" in an ethereal sense, either. As social facts
the varying stances taken within sociologies of school knowledge correspond
to a host of other observable facts. For example, even within the small world
of educational research, fracturing is apparent. Within the American
Educational Research Association, rising numbers of Special Interest Groups
reveal newly sanctioned differences. Alongside "merely professional" special
interests are groups identifiable as socio-political concerns, some more singular
than others. "Hispanic," "Lesbian and Gay Studies," "Research in Bilingual
Education," "Peace Education," "Research Focus on Black Education,"
"Research Focus on Education in the Caribbean and Africa," "Research on
Education of Deaf People," and even "Research on the Intellectually
Talented," all entitle groups with agendas readily associated with clear and
specific concerns whose political implications are not opaque. And groups
such as "Critical Examination of Race, Ethnicity, Class, and Gender in
Education," or "Critical Issues in Curriculum" stand as reminders that there
still remain some specialized forces of oppositional unity as one choice within
the larger array of educational research options.[11]

The fracturing within educational research I take to correspond to an
obvious reality of a larger fracturing of U.S. education generally. With the
neoconservative (and others) agenda of advancing models of educational
"choice," with the push to fund school vouchers, with the "restructuring" call
to make schools smaller, signs of dispersions abound in the world of U.S.
education. That I find a similar dispersion even among radicals ought to
surprise no one.

The arguments I have reinscribed in this chapter, in the attempt to fairly
rearticulate some of the many theoretical positions relevant to RSSK, represent only a small portion of the theoretical options available to students of
the field. There are many other studies I could have taken as representative of
my constructed epistemic positions. But the point in constructing these positions, as I said earlier, was not to present an all-encompassing portrait of the
field. If Foucault is correct, if the micro practices of power work within
regimes of truth, then it doesn't matter who the biological author of any

< 83 >

specific practice is. And since these regimes of truth are pervasive, any cross-section would serve the purpose of opening up, revealing its regulating tendencies. Indeed, if the harbingers of postmodernity are right, then in any one voice the signs of changing times would be heard.

But if Bourdieu is also correct, if individual actions are constructed within the "structured and structuring structures" of habitus, then selecting works from an already highly selective field would not reveal a great divergence from the contemporary structures of RSSK, however malleable that field may be. It is based on this last insight that, like Wexler, I would point out that the works I have been reinscribing are members of a very small segment of a much larger Academy, which in turn is only a small part of only one society, which in turn cannot be understood except in relation to its place within a global sphere. And so it is, having attempted to highlight the differences and discontinuities among the discourses in RSSK, I would now like to reconsider their relations to each other in terms of the dispositions and positions they share, placing them in relation to a wider context in which they function.

< 84 >

four

Reconstructing the Field, Partially

T O THIS POINT I HAVE CONSTRUCTED two very different views of my field. In the first chapter, I attempted to structurally analyze the origins of U.S. RSSK through a specific examination of Michael Apple's Parallelist Position. There I was concerned with demonstrating that growth and progress in the theoretical propositions of my field are evident in an intellectual lineage of Apple's analytical position. As I offered my own critique, in Chapter Two, I simultaneously attempted to reconstruct the dialectical progression made possible within my structural frame.

In the third chapter, as with my post-structural frame, progression and continuity gave way to rupture, disjunction, and difference. Constructing (only) four distinct discursive strands of research relevant to my field, I attempted to highlight two dimensions along which fracturing can be seen (the structural/post-structural and the Marxist/feminist). I should point out here that while I constructed only four discursive strands in Chapter Three, I could have more strongly emphasized the differences within the strands I discussed and thereby expanded the number of discourses even more. Pointing out unique historical, intellectual, and political traditions; emphasizing separate and distinct conceptual foundations; and highlighting some of the difficulties these discourses face in attempts to communicate with each other were all ways in which to undermine the structural sensibilities I see in earlier sociologies of school knowledge. It would be difficult to see how the various current radical sociologies of school knowledge could progressively build on each other in the same manner by which the Structural Neo-Marxist U.S. New Sociology progressively developed from its partial English origin. Even though I can find ways to make plausible the debates between critical pedagogues and post-structural feminists, for example, my post-structural sensibilities do not offer me the luxurious illusion that I could ever resolve those debates.

These comments are not meant to imply that any resolution of debates among radical educational scholars needs to be sought, nor that such a mythical resolution would be "good." In fact, my preference is to not seek a resolution; I prefer to construct these debates as social facts and to attempt to place them within a relational analysis of the social contexts in which they take place. If forced, I would define my position in double opposition to the conceptual categories I have constructed in the two previous chapters.

Against the structural disposition to seek dialectical unity and progress in theoretical syntheses, I would point out that the singular history constructed within my analysis of the Parallelist Position is itself a selective representation of the discourses that have questioned the relationships between school knowledge and power. As Ellsworth's critique of critical pedagogy suggests, the intellectual histories and contributions of feminists have been marginalized, at best, in such structural reconstructions. To present the Parallelist Position as a theoretical framework upon which one can construct a (more) adequate analysis of curriculum and power would be to impose a conceptual lens, as McCarthy argues, that would ignore the discontinuities and "internal" conflicts individuals live out in their multiple subjectivities. Empirically, "finding" uninterrupted effects between dynamics of class and gender, for example, might be a good way to "oppose" a singular dominant hegemony, but it is also a good way to ignore the fact that class struggles and gender struggles have not always been consistent with each other. At the risk of imposing my own subjective experience, I do not think, for example, that it is a safe assumption to presume feminists and Marxists can consistently be allies.

Against the post-structural disposition to find difference and discontinuity among author-less discourses, I seek to question each of these discourses in relation to specific social contexts. It is to this task that I turn in this chapter. Here I seek to understand how radical sociologies of school knowledge can be socially identified and understood in relation to mainstream educational research. Given my previous claims that a unity is not to be sought among the various discourses relevant to my field, I should emphasize that while I shall be seeking to understand these discourses in relation to social contexts, I do not presume that the contexts I analyze are simply "out there" in reality. Rather, for example, I take the very idea of a "mainstream" in educational research to be at least partially constructed out of the question I have imposed.

< 86 >

ON THE CHAPTER'S FRAME

To raise the question of the relationship between radical sociologies of school knowledge and mainstream educational research, I seek to begin placing my understanding of these discourses within what Bourdieu refers to as a social field. My concern is to begin outlining positions relevant to U.S. RSSK relative to their "larger" social field of U.S. educational research. To do so is to radically change my perspective on the discourses I have been discussing.

Where I have occasionally, in prior chapters, made reference to connections between theoretical proclamations and social, political, and historical movements, my analysis to this point has been predominantly conducted on a textual level. With the possible exceptions of the political struggles highlighted by post-structural feminist discourse, and my reference to a fragmentation within educational research, most of the social conditions I have spoken about could be seen as taking place "outside" of the Academy. These prior exceptions to my textual focus were to some degree necessary, but they were also raised in anticipation of the sociological frame I seek to highlight in this chapter. Here my concern is to specifically question struggles within one academic arena.

Against the irenic image of the "scientific community" so often presented in liberal assumptions about the intrinsic success of "true ideas," here I assume that within the field of educational "science" there are continual social struggles over the consecration of what is to be known as legitimate science. Against structural Leftist accounts of academic struggles which presume that ideologically correct research carries an intrinsic connection to political struggles outside the academy, I would argue, following Bourdieu, that academic struggles over scientific legitimacy are primarily to be understood within the "specificity of the scientific field." In this logic, analyzing the social spaces in which educational intellectuals work is a task of understanding the correspondences among intellectual positions/stances and relations of power within specific socio-historical contexts. Here I take intellectual arguments as manifest expressions of cultural struggles within multiple social spaces, within habitus and fields.

This perspective is in some ways similar to that of Philip Wexler in his critique of the New Sociology. However, where Wexler insightfully argues that the proclamations of the 1970s New Sociology of Education represent the actions of new-middle class academics in a futile and romantic attempt to identify themselves with a social movement of which these academics could never be part (and maybe never had been), I would suggest that the habitus of one strata of an upwardly mobile lower-middle class had achieved its aspirations in advancing into the academy only to find itself struggling on the terrain of a cultural field which itself was at the time feigning a rupture. The

< 87 >

constructions of the New Sociology of Education, then, are both signifiers of cultural struggles within the educational academic field and representations of the regime of truth practiced by its adherents.

My analysis in this chapter is largely informed by the sociological perspective of Bourdieu. However, rather than attempt an intensive sociological investigation of the discourses relevant to my field, their relative positions of power within the Academy, and of the more specific arena of educational science, and all the possible correspondences between these discourses and the potentially infinite social contexts with which they are related, my concern here is singular. I seek to highlight those distinctions and dispositions in the radical discourses I have thus far outlined which can be seen as partially equivalent relative to what these radical discourses take to be mainstream educational research.

In this endeavor, I am continually reminded of Bourdieu's insistence that sociological inquiry requires a strong measure of epistemological vigilance. Specifically, I recognize that seeking partially equivalent dispositions among radical educational discourses, of course, runs the risk of presenting an illusion of unity among vastly differing agendas. By doing so, I must emphasize however, that I take similarities among radical discourses to be an effect of the similar positions they hold within a particular social space. This is not to deny that these similar dispositions have their own specificities. It is however to recognize that when analyzing these "radical" discourses relative to "mainstream" positions, I have both attempted to build on conceptual categories that lie within radical discourses and imposed my own. It is my hope that these preliminary comments, made by necessity on a general level, will become more clear over the course of what I present below.

My main task in this chapter is to identify social identities within and of my field. To do this I shall consider how the conceptual categories of my field's theoretical propositions can be seen as mental structures which correspond to multiple contexts within the social structures that intersect in and overlap with the field.

Roughly put, I shall do this at two levels. As an introduction to the perspective I am using, I first draw out conceptual similarities among the radical discourses. On the one hand, I point to some similarities between feminist and Marxist or non-feminist discourses which can be attributed to shared structural or post-structural commitments. On the other hand, across both the post-structural rupture and the Marxist/feminist split, I suggest that there are also conceptual similarities between Structural Neo-Marxist and post-structural feminist discourses. In drawing out these similarities, questions regarding the persuasive strategies of these positions seem evident. That is, when focusing on the conceptual categories of these discourses, it seems they present arguments designed to ensure their own marginality. I suggest that while this

< 88 >

may seem strange under idealistic assumptions that these are merely theoretical struggles to advance "true" ideas, under sociological assumptions, these shared conceptual categories can be understood as similar strategies to distinguish positions in academic space.

Building on this introductory level, I then turn to the more specific endeavor of identifying my field's relation to "mainstream" U.S. educational research. Here, I shall reframe my perspective and find theoretical (social) dispositions shared across these varied radical discourses. Even with all the differences I outlined in Chapter Three, I argue that it is possible to identify shared theoretical dispositions within these discourses in relation to how they address what they each take to be mainstream research. These shared dispositions will be identified both within the discourses and, through a detailed analysis of one exceptional critique of the field, as dispositions taken in opposition to mainstream research. I argue further that these conceptual similarities are not simply theoretical frameworks, but manifestations of a social identity shared among these radical educational discourses. Thus, my main concern in this chapter is to analyze how these varied discourses identify themselves, what the logic of their social struggles might be, and how they can be viewed as manifest mental structures within the social structures of the U.S. educational research "community."

ACROSS THE FRONTIERS AMONG THE DISCOURSES

Analytic homologies

Focusing on the theoretical constructs of the discursive strands relevant to my field, there are a number of analytical homologies that can be drawn between these "distinct" positions. For example, within the structural discourses discussed above, it is possible to see recurrent patterns despite the vast gap that lies between the Neo-Marxist and feminist agendas. In their more orthodox variants, both the Structural Neo-Marxist discourse and the structural feminist rely on fundamental conceptual dichotomies upon which class and gender relations are based. For the Marxists there is the question of relations to the means of production and the mental versus manual dichotomy (the bourgeoisie versus proletariat). For the feminists, perhaps more apparent in the biologically based arguments of theorists such as Madeleine Grumet (1988), there is the question of relations to biological reproduction and the dichotomy of epistemological control versus connectedness (male versus female). Each of these structural discourses relies strongly on the notion of contradiction and each imposes a foundational epistemology. For the Marxist discourses, the base-superstructure distinction signals their material foundations, and for the feminists, the sex-gender distinction signals the potential of a biological foundation. Moreover, in each of these agendas, large-scale societal theories are generated, pushing toward virtual universalization.

< 89 >

Within the more specific focus on education, these structural common-places expand. Here I wish to simply point out that in both these structural educational agendas there is a strong emphasis placed on teachers. For the Marxists, this focus is clearly consistent with their transformative intent and their attempt to locate/build a class of agents of change. In the organization of educational systems, teachers are seen to be in closest proximity to the working class, and in this sense, the Structural Neo-Marxist turn toward critical pedagogy is understandable. For structural feminists, a similar trans-formative intent is clear, and the social reality that most pre-tertiary teach-ers are women, combined with the historical construction of teaching as "women's work," offers plausibility to the feminist focus on teachers and pedagogy. After all, for many feminists, teaching is their work: analyzing teaching manifests the conjunction of the personal and political.

By pointing out these similarities, I should emphasize, I am not suggesting that all Structural Marxist discourses, nor all structural feminist theories, accept these positions. I am suggesting, however, that within a structural frame these conceptual commonplaces are always and already present as the terms of the debates are taken up.

Similarly, between the post-structural and the post-structural feminist agendas, there are conceptual homologies as well. Rejecting the universaliza-tion of structural approaches, both the post-structural and post-structural feminist discourses share concerns for locating their claims in relation to specific contexts and historically contingent social movements. Disrupting harmonious structural sensibilities, these post-structural frameworks rely on metaphors of disjunction, multiplicity, and difference. In each, there is the endeavor to deconstruct dichotomies. Interpreting the social world as texts, these post-structural endeavors offer "readings" grounded in subjective experi-ence or in relation to historical formations.

Within the specific focus on education, these post-structural discourses diverge. Where Cherryholmes (1988) and Wexler (1987) offer readings of research, theory, and curriculum, rather generalized endeavors, Ellsworth (1990) and Lather (1991) enact their feminist structure in their shared focus on their own pedagogy and in Lather's appeal to transformative research in a postmodern age. To the extent that Wexler returns to his Marxist heritage and focuses on class relations, he too engages in a specific grounding which Cherryholmes seems to have given up entirely. In this light, one wonders if Cherryholmes's deconstructive analysis is an anomaly among radical discourses, or simply not radical. Furthermore, if there are agents of transformation among these post-structural discourses, it is the theorists themselves. Making this struggle explicit, both Lather and Wexler have questioned the role of their theoretical agendas as part of the Academy.

Finding these homologous analytical frames between the frontier which

< 90 >

separates feminist from Marxist and non-feminist post-structural discourses can, of course, be attributed to a "shared" structuralism or post-structuralism. At this level, there still seems to be a gap between the structural and post-structural discourses left open. But there also seems, to me, to be reason to question whether this divide sociologically represents a gap. When reframed on yet another level, there are homologous analytical strategies which move across the apparent rupture imposed by post-structuralism.

Here I would draw a similarity between two of the most dissimilar discursive strands I outlined earlier. In the second chapter, I presented an analysis and critique of Michael Apple's Parallelist Position. There, to emphasize the degree to which its conceptual framework had constructed empirical claims within structuralist sensibilities, I named the Parallelist Position "Structural Neo-Marxist." Later, in Chapter Three, after documenting the maintenance of the Structural Neo-Marxist discourse, I presented the arguments of Elizabeth Ellsworth as one example of recent post-structural feminist discourses relevant to my field. There, I sought to highlight the wide gaps between these discourses. In fact, given that these two discourses lie on opposite sides of both the lines of my field's current fracturing (the post-structural versus structural and the Marxist versus feminist), it would be difficult to find any two discourses which could be further apart in the field.

Yet, I would like to point out that relative to what each of these vastly different discourses takes to be the mainstream, they share a similar strategy of cultural distinction. As much as I think that it is an accurate label to have called Apple's position "Structural Neo-Marxist," within the Parallelist Position there is a conjunction of the phenomenological interest to describe subjective experiences and a material Marxist (objective) structuralism. In this sense, Apple's work can be seen as a phenomenological Marxist variant of Structural Neo-Marxism. It is in this light that the textual strategies of the Parallelist Position seem remarkably similar to Ellsworth's post-structural feminism.

When approached by critical pedagogues, Ellsworth's position represents something of a political "Catch-22." Given their political allegiance to feminists, critical pedagogues could only argue with Ellsworth's post-structuralism. In responding to Ellsworth's position as if it was only post-structural critical pedagogues could enter into a level of philosophical generality that was rejected in the first place. Apple's conjunction of phenomenology and Marxism could be seen to pose the same problem for liberal mainstream educators who agree that economics-related educational inequalities are unjust. Accepting the structural (economic) side of Apple's position (and of course shedding the "Marxist" label) leaves only the subjective side open to critique. But if, in criticizing the subjectivist side of Apple's argument, a mainstream respondent proposed a need for more "neutral" or "objective"

< 91 >

knowledge claims, s/he would be taking the exact position rejected by the field's intellectual dispositions.

Given these analytical similarities, an interesting problem arises. If these theoretical arguments pose such difficulties for (some of) their audiences, what are the rhetorical consequences? To whom would these arguments be persuasive?

On a "purely" analytical level, I would argue that the strategy employed in Apple's and Ellsworth's discourses virtually guarantees that these discourses will only be persuasive to those who already agree with the structural claims that economic and gender differentiations in U.S. society represent unjust inequalities, and are willing to accept their "subjectivities." Of course, the debates within Marxisms and feminisms associated with these positions further suggest that these discourses are not even persuasive to everyone who shares their structural insights. Consequently, I take the radical discourses available to my field to be only marginally persuasive to what is already a marginal community. From a perspective which takes these arguments to be mostly about intellectual debate (idealistically) and persuasion, these strategies really don't seem to make much sense. On this level, these positions seem designed only to guarantee their own defeat.

Post-structural ruptures and all, it seems to me that the intellectual dispositions which structure my field, however transformative in intent, lock themselves into analytical practices which are, almost by definition, marginal. Of course, finding comfort on the margin is what being radical is sometimes all about. But I would like to push this analysis further to show how it is that the dispositions and analytical claims of the field have been understood as practices of cultural distinction within the U.S. educational academy. On a level of analysis which questions their sense of practice, seeking to understand the logic of their cultural struggles, a much different conclusion could be drawn about the logic of these radical discourses. Examined sociologically, the intellectual positions of the field are not only plausible but also quite effective for distinguishing a position in the academic field.

Distinctions within educational academic space

It is possible to begin to understand the various distinctions these discourses make between and among themselves as part of the cultural struggles to establish "individual" space within the Academy relative to multiple specific contexts. In a very local space, Bourdieu (1984) suggests that many cultural struggles operate as mechanisms by which social actors distinguish themselves from those who hold the most proximate positions within a larger social space (p. 246). In a sense, these are struggles among actors who share a similar local space relative to larger contexts—something like internal neighborhood

< 92 >

conflicts. In this vein, one could examine the debates between critical peda- gogues and post-structural feminisms as a struggle between discourses which share a similarly marginal space within the educational academy.

In something of a "wider" space, the distinctions drawn in other radical discourses seem to occur in a space which may be closer to the educational academic center. For example, as Grumet (1988) employs her psychoanalytic frame and her biologically based epistemology to argue against the Structural Neo-Marxist agenda and to argue for a focus on gender relations, she distin- guishes her position relative to two discourses which may be positioned a bit closer to the educational mainstream. On the one hand, the Structural Neo- Marxism she critiques lies outside the mainstream in large part by the singular virtue of its Marxism. On the other hand, the sex-role socialization theory she distinguishes herself from may be on the frontier of the mainstream by virtue of its relatively recent acceptance into educational discourse. As another example, as Cherryholmes (1988) analyzes "traditional" curricular discourses (such as Tyler's rationale, Schwab's "practical 4," and Bloom's taxonomies), he enters into a struggle in which his post-structuralism functions to distinguish himself from "mainstream" curriculum discourse. (Of course, since these are curricular debates and not Educational Psychology debates, he has not "really" entered center court.)

I should point out that I offer these examples only hypothetically. I am not claiming that I "know" the relative position of each of these discourses within the U.S. educational academy. But I would like to consider these examples to make a few points about this type of social analysis. First, to say that two discourses share a similarly local social space and that they struggle with their closest neighbors does not negate the multiple other contexts in which any one of the discourses is located. Where I do see critical pedagogues and post-structural feminists engaging in a local struggle, I also see that each of these discourses holds strong alliances and distinctions entirely indepen- dently of each other. Second, I would also like to note that time and history become important dimensions in this analysis. For example, while I see sex- role socialization theory as well within the "mainstream," I also recognize that this is a relatively recent occurrence and that relative to other "traditions" its place within the mainstream has less firm historical roots. Lastly, by pointing to very "local" and "wider" contexts, I have attempted to show that analyzing cultural struggles can be done at multiple "levels." I draw these examples simply as a way of suggesting the massive complexity of where this analysis could lead. If I attempted to frame all these possible multiple contexts, I would face a monumental task. To do so would require, at a minimum, a full-scale "mapping" of the entire social space of the educational academy.

As I mentioned earlier, my frame in this chapter is much more focused than the picture my analytical frame could reveal. My concern here is to

< 93 >

question only one relation: the relation between the discourses I see as relevant to my field and what they take to be "mainstream" educational research. From this perspective (or "on this level"), even with the apparent differences between these discourses, even more conceptual similarities than the ones I have already suggested can be seen as shared across these discourses' differences. Three partially equivalent theoretical dispositions are widely shared across these discourses: each casts its critique within the framework of an "alternative" ("new" or "oppositional") theoretical agenda, each relates its own knowledge claims to specific social positions, and each holds a skepticism or all out rejection of scientific objectivity. I will consider each of these dispositions separately, in the next section. But before I turn to describing these partially equivalent theoretical dispositions, I would like to add a few sociological caveats.

I would like to emphasize that I take these conceptual similarities to be homologous theoretical dispositions. In other words, the conceptual similarities I see among the discourses I have examined represent social stances taken in opposition to mainstream educational research. There is an important analytical turn taken here that I would like to underscore.

To be sure, I am suggesting that these vastly different discourses carry similar analytical tendencies. However, because I take these shared theoretical dispositions as stances taken within a particular social field, U.S. educational research, I am not suggesting that the differences and discontinuities between, among, and within these discourses can now be ignored. I do not take these similarities to be a "common" philosophical language. Nor do I assume that the similarities I see represent a "common" political agenda. The point in naming these "partially equivalent dispositions" lies in the attempt to reveal similarities among social positions relative to one context that would not be relevant in another context.

While I am quite aware that the context I am examining, "these discourses' relation to the mainstream," is of my own construction, I am arguing that given that context, the similarities among these discourses are apparent.

AGAINST THE MAINSTREAM CURRENT

There are two ways in which I would like to demonstrate that these radical sociologies of school knowledge hold partially equivalent theoretical dispositions. First, it is possible to see that within each discursive strand I have identified there is a tendency toward these dispositions. To demonstrate this below I consider each disposition separately and explain how distinctions within each strand exemplify these dispositions. In a sense, these partially equivalent dispositions represent what can be seen as the social identity of my field. Second, to give further evidence that these dispositions reveal the frontier that separates radical discourses and "the mainstream," I consider one recent

< 94 >

analysis in the field, Daniel Liston's (1988b) critique of Structural Neo-Marxist sociologies of school knowledge, which has not only drawn from analyses of both sides of the divide, but simultaneously claims allegiance to Marxist analyses and rejects each of these theoretical dispositions. As an exception which shows the rule, I take Liston's arguments to be quite revealing in the attempt to understand the frontiers of RSSK.

But first, wherein do I see these discourses sharing partially equivalent theoretical dispositions?

A disposition toward new theory

There are many distinctions employed within each of these discourses which reveal a disposition toward new theory. The New Sociologies' reliance on the notion of differing "paradigms," their predisposition of placing themselves on the "new" side of the old/new distinction, seems obvious. In the course of naming their project's allegiance with critical social science (as distinguished from the empirical/analytic and the hermeneutic), the New Sociologies manifest this distinction with the further implication that critical social science represents today's "revolutionary" science as opposed to the mainstream's "normal" science.

The specific qualities of Structural Neo-Marxist discourses are apparent in further, more detailed, distinctions employed in their critiques. Against "liberal" mainstream foci on social harmony and meritocracy, the Neo-Marxists choose to focus on social conflict and structured inequities. Against ethereal theory which placidly flows above the masses, Neo-Marxists place their identities in relation to material reality and in the bodily connections to labor. Recall in Chapter Three, Ginsburg's appeal to the knowledge and skill associated with the "work of the hand, leg, back, etc." With the Gramscian notion of the organic intellectual, a common signifier of these theorists' identities, we are given the image of a serious and angry intellectual whose pen is held in a calloused hand. The theories of such a habitus are intentionally and explicitly revolutionary and new.

For structural feminists the mainstream is seen as distinctly public and male. Fighting a history of exclusion (literal exclusion in much mainstream sociological research which only surveyed men), these structural feminists turn toward examinations of sex differentiations and gender as they build new theoretical lenses for their alternative agenda. Against traditionally male dominated research, the structural call for further research, and a new focus, on the experiences of women and girls is explicit. With each structural distinction, signifiers of women's experience are revalued and placed within a constellation of dispositions, and a "feminist" habitus is constructed.

In each of the post-structural variants, even while there is an explicit renouncement of Grand Theory, the focus on introducing a new theoretical agenda which has moved "beyond" past endeavors is marked simply by their labels: post-structural, postmodern, post-analytic, deconstruction.

To be sure, none of these discursive strands shares the same new frontier, but each in its own way has pushed the theoretical frontier of the field in which it situates its struggle. Be it the "Third Wave" feminism of which Ellsworth (1990) speaks, "Neo-Marxism," Cherryholmes's (1988) "Critical Pragmatics," or Wexler's (1987) "Social Analyses" of a "semiotic society," the search for new theories, and a break with the mainstream past, continues within each discursive agenda.

A disposition toward socially situated knowledge

More often explicitly than not, each of these theories also has distinguished itself from the mainstream in relation to how it "grounds" its knowledge claims. Typically, mainstream educational research is taken to be based on the notion that true knowledge is universal. Rather than presume knowledge to be transhistorical or universal, each of these radical discourses locates knowledge in social positions or subjectivities. This proposition is, of course, not a new idea for social theory, nor is it unique to radical discourses. Each of the discourses I've named as relevant to radical sociologies of school knowledge, to varying degrees, takes this position a step further to argue that the knowledge of dominated people is both valid and privileged relative to the knowledge of dominant groups.

In the Structural Neo-Marxist discourses, this position was most explicit in Aronowitz and Giroux's (1985) assertion that "only the committed intellectual can arrive at assertions that serve human emancipation." It was also implicit in Ginsburg's (1988) critique of the questionable value of high status knowledge. In the structural feminist discourses, this disposition was most apparent in Grumet's (1988) assertion that the knowledge of childbirth should serve as the basis for a universal understanding of social reproduction. However the overall claim that sociologies need to focus on the experiences of women and girls in order to understand gender formations also implies privileging the knowledge of women (the group seen to be dominated in gender differentiations).

The post-structural rejection of generalizations and Grand Theory can, in part, be understood as an enterprise which whole-heartedly and explicitly takes the view that knowledge claims are valid only to the extent that they are grounded in specific social positions. When connected with specific transformative political (structural) agendas, the post-structural critique of knowledge explicitly privileges dominated knowledge. As I argued earlier, if taken to its logical result, McCarthy's (1988) "non-synchrony" suggests that adequate knowledge of power relations must be grounded in specific subjectivities. Wexler's arguments that sociologies of school knowledge need to focus on the

< 96 >

processes of self-produced social identities and his call for examining social movements, rely on privileging the knowledge of dominated/struggling social groups. Similarly, Ellsworth's (1990) subtextual defiance and defense of her own reading, and her explicit rejection of critical pedagogy's rationalism reveal a disposition that privileges what she has described as socially marginalized knowledge. And Lather's (1991) entire project of constructing an emancipatory research agenda which is consistent with her feminist politics can be seen as fundamentally based on the attempt to privilege dominated social knowledge.

A disposition against scientific objectivity

Perhaps the most obvious of the dispositions I have identified in these radical educational discourses is the disposition against scientific objectivity. Implicitly, the notion of objectivity is immediately called into question by the disposition toward seeing knowledge as relative to specific social positions. However, there are also some explicit claims which reveal this disposition.

The Structural Neo-Marxist rejection of scientific objectivity was explicit in Aronowitz and Giroux's (1985) comment on "the spurious concept of scientific objectivity," to name just one example. For some feminist discourses, both structural and post-structural, the project of science itself is seen as a manifestation of masculine control (this is an explicit part of the epistemological argument on which Grumet, (1988) relies). For post-structural discourses, the project of science is cast as a historical construct of modernity which has marginalized, disciplined, and oppressed Others. Wexler's (1987) critique of science is revealed in his trenchant attack on "representational" language. Ellsworth's (1990) rejection of rationalism is based on historical memory of science's marginalizing effects. Likewise, Lather's (1991) reconstruction of research is cast as a response to a "post-positivist" era. According to many of these post-structural discourses, scientific objectivity is a thing of the past.

On the frontier of the mainstream

I would like to make the relation between these radical discourses and mainstream educational research more clear. To do this, I would like to examine some of the arguments put forth by one of the field's critics, Daniel Liston. It is in Liston's critique that the frontier between mainstream educational research and radical sociologies of school knowledge is directly addressed. And it is in Liston's agenda that each of the field's partially equivalent dispositions is questioned.

Unlike the other recent moves to make radical sociologies of school knowledge more proactive, and thereby move further from the mainstream, Liston's empiricist Structural Neo-Marxist agenda seems to lie along the frontier between the radical and mainstream. In his theoretical examinations of

< 97 >

the explanatory and ethical bases of RSSK, Daniel Liston, one of the second generation of U.S. radical educational scholars, not only accepts objectivity as a scientific goal, but specifically calls on the past New Sociologies to objectively assess the claims that they have advanced.

Liston's overall criticisms of the New Sociology are cast along three fronts, calling for rigorous empirical assessment, clearly stated and substantiated evaluations, and morally defensible prescriptions (Liston, 1984; 1985; 1986; 1988a; 1988b). However it is Liston's empiricist position which seems most unique among radical educators and in which the frontier between the New Sociology and the mainstream educational community seems most apparent. As Liston (1988b) sees it,

> While many radicals tend to agree that evaluative and prescriptive claims should be ethically sound and reasonable, too few explicitly maintain that explanations ought to be logically coherent and empirically assessable. The part of my project that has met the greatest amount of skepticism has been my emphasis on the importance of explanatory adequacy, especially the value of evidential appeals. Supposedly for some radicals (and non-radicals) empirical assessments constitute the stuff of which positivism is made ... Evidential requests are viewed as suspect ... There is a strong anti-empirical strand within the radical tradition. (p. 18)

For Liston, this anti-empirical tendency within radical educational research is associated with the radical response to enduring questions of social science, such as issues of how one assesses explanations or clarifies the role of values in explanations. While all educational researchers face these issues, according to Liston,

> there are writers in the radical tradition who have approached these difficulties from a particular orientation. Their response appears to be a result of a rejection of mainstream models of inquiry (frequently characterized as positivist) and a belief in the power of radical concepts. (p. 19)

In this view, then, a defining characteristic of the radical educational frontier is an anti-empirical stance taken in opposition to the mainstream.

The central element of the radical rejection of mainstream (positivistic) educational science, according to Liston, is its critical treatment of the relationship between fact and value. Where "positivism" is taken to propose that only value-free (i.e., purely factual) claims are open to empirical assessment, Liston argues, radical educational scholars have taken a position which claims that fact and value cannot be separated. As he succinctly puts it, "If 'positivism' purportedly separates fact from value, then the radical tradition has wed the two together" (p. 21).

But even while holding this position, Liston argues, there remains a need for empirical assessment:

< 98 >

> Notwithstanding the radical conjunction of social theory and ethical beliefs, explanations require a degree of evidential warrant . . . It is neither positivist nor unreasonable to ask for empirical evidence. (pp. 21-22)

Accepting, or at least not explicitly rejecting, the inseparability of fact and value, Liston maintains,

> that any reasonable and useful form of social inquiry must be thoroughly empirical . . . Cogent explanations are those that are constrained by and answerable to a body of evidence. (p. 22)

Given the radical agenda to engage in social critique, which presumably would be about some sort of empirical, social reality, Liston's charge may seem a bit odd. After all, few radical social theorists would probably resist being told that their theories ought to make some general reference to social reality. But as he attempts to more fully articulate what he sees as "cogent explanations" and the role evidence would play in assessing those explanations, Liston makes it a bit more clear that he rests his criticism that radical educational scholarship has been anti-empirical upon a set of very particular notions of what it means to provide "cogent explanations" which are "answerable to a body of evidence." It is Liston's specific conceptions of empirical assessment, what he frames as a "realist epistemology," that are probably associated with the skepticism he sees in radical responses to his arguments.

In Liston's acceptance of a "realist epistemology," each of the three partially equivalent dispositions of RSSK are called into question. The tendency to advance new theoretical claims is tempered by the call for empirical substantiation. The notion that knowledge is based fundamentally on partial and specific social positions is explicitly rejected. And Liston's ethic of impartiality is built on a commitment to scientific objectivity the New Sociology's critique of Positivism explicitly rejected.

It should be noted that while Liston is highly critical of Marxist curricular analyses, his allegiance to them is explicit. In the preface to *Capitalist Schools?* he states, "I wrote this book believing that the Marxist framework, and more generally the radical tradition, has something valuable to say about schooling" (p. 18). It is also evident from Liston's own words that he hopes both to reach beyond a Marxist audience and that he has pushed the frontiers of radical educational discourses:

> My hope, perhaps unrealistic, is that this work will engage both Marxists and non-Marxists alike. . . . While some individuals have read my arguments and found it difficult to overlook the sins of Marxism . . . others look at my claims and see nothing but a pernicious "positivism." (p. 8)

I should also note that while I take Liston's theoretical arguments as evidence of the frontier that lies between mainstream educational research and RSSK, his analysis is largely limited to what I have named the Structural Neo-Marxist discourse of my field. This being the case, one may wonder how this evidence is relevant to the other discourses I relate to my field. Specifically, here I face the question, what does this have to do with feminist, post-structural, and post-structural feminist educational discourses?

Having argued that I find partially equivalent dispositions in the conceptual positions of these discourses, I take the conceptual issues raised by Liston's arguments to directly relate to non-Marxist discourses to the extent they adhere to a rejection of scientific objectivity, an acceptance of epistemic privilege, and a reliance on "alternative" or "new" theory. But, as implied in my sociological frame, this claim is not limited merely to conceptual questions. Taking the conceptual arguments of the discourses relevant to my field as representations of mental structures, I wish to suggest that the authors of these discourses can be seen to share homologous dispositions within the social structures of U.S. educational research.

SOCIAL PRACTICES IN A FIELD

The notion that intellectual dispositions and theoretical positions develop within the context of a scholarly community, and are thereby not simply the "invention" of a singular genius, would probably surprise only a few stalwart individuals. In this sense, my suggestion that the dispositions I have found among the discourses relevant to my field can be understood as related to the social context in which they were constructed is something of a mundane truism. But making the mundane exotic is often a very revealing enterprise.

Each of these intellectual discourses has been constructed in specific socio-historic contexts. However the context in which I found similarities across the differences of these discourses is one which seems to have remained relatively stable over the two decades in which these theories have emerged. Certainly, many things have changed in the U.S. educational Academy in the past twenty years, but it has remained a scientific field throughout. And there are institutionalized characteristics of this Academy which shed some light on how these discourses could be so similar while so loudly proclaiming their difference.

On a general level, the conceptual dispositions upon which these radical discourses have been constructed are understandable simply by considering what it means to be doing "oppositional" intellectual work in U.S. education. Consider the field's disposition toward presenting alternative or new theories. If one is attempting to open an alternative agenda within a scientific community which consecrates its highest social value on "discoveries," or "originality," it is no surprise to find radical scholars continually presenting their work as "new." Consider also the field's disposition toward claiming epistemic privilege. If one

< 100 >

is attempting to challenge and transform relations of domination or unequal power relations, and if one is in the business of creating knowledge claims, it makes some sense that this project would entail privileging knowledge that is seen to be disadvantaged, dominated, marginalized, or oppositional. Consider the rejection of objective science. If one is self-defined as radical, and thereby seeks to cut to the root of the problem, to the root of the status quo, it makes sense that in a field dominated by scientific objectivity the radicals would attempt to undermine that basis of the field.

What do these intellectual "choices" tell us? Initially, it seems obvious that these dispositions represent, as Bourdieu (1984) inscribes the cultural practices of the French working classes, "the choice of the necessary." In a context in which radicals have very little to do with structuring the options open to them, these intellectual constructions hardly represent acts of intentional free will. (Exit the romantic image of the revolutionary autonomous actor). This point, of course, is not new, and only serves as a reminder that radicals may choose to transform the world, but the world they transform is not of their own choosing.

Within this institutional context, each of these theories was constructed within its own local space. For example, it is necessary to understand that Apple's arguments were cast largely within the educational discipline of curriculum (not sociology or the sociology of education) and had been developed during the 1970s. As Wexler (1987) has pointed out, the U.S. curriculum field in the 1970s was, like many other academic disciplines, living in the wake of the 1960s radical university politics. It was in this context that Apple began to forge his space in the field of educational research. Where in the second chapter I questioned, for analytical reasons, why the New Sociology employed a Marxist framework in the first place, here, in my sociological view, this choice makes some sense. Placed within a disciplinary field which held virtually no tradition of radical political analysis, at a time when Marxist theories were the social representatives of radical political movements, it makes socio-historic sense that Apple built on a Neo-Marxist tradition.

Beyond these general issues and analytical puzzles, however, more detailed theoretical "choices" begin to seem more plausible as multiple social contexts are related to the philosophical and political texts.

Earlier I noted that when the conceptual frameworks of these radical discourses were considered "purely" in terms of their intellectual persuasiveness, they seemed to not make much sense. That is, when questioning how some of their potential audiences were addressed, it seemed that these theories were designed to keep their readers at bay. Where I suggested that Apple's arguments might throw "liberal" mainstream researchers into confusion or force them into taking positions already rejected by Apple, I found a similar dynamic between Ellsworth's arguments and her critical pedagogy audience.

But in relation to their multiple academic audiences, in an institutional context which rewards, regulates, and requires "authority" and "originality," each theoretical choice made by these theorists can be understood as following the logic of social practices which carve a distinctive space within the Academy.

Simplistically, as an example, consider Apple's conjunction of phenomenology and Marxism. On the one hand, distinguishing himself from "mainstream" research, Apple asserts the radical politics of Neo-Marxism. On the other hand, in distinguishing himself from overly deterministic "vulgar" Marxists, Apple asserts his phenomenology. Each of these audiences Apple confronts represents a different epistemic position in the social space of the Academy; and it makes sense that the mode of distinction might be different depending on the context. For Ellsworth, the picture, of course, is different. On the one hand, building on a tradition of feminism that has consistently struggled with the multiple political tensions, and the potentially divisive "double oppressions" faced by multiplicatively positioned women, her poststructuralism makes both theoretical and practical sense. On the other hand, when working specifically in an educational Academy in which "critical" men have not always recognized their own complicity in patriarchy, her double rejection/distinction from critical pedagogy's Structural Neo-Marxism also carries some practical sense.

For each of the authors, theories, and discursive strands I have analyzed in this project, similar socio-historical analyses could be constructed to understand how each conceptual framework has been developed. For each, such an analysis would be much more complicated than the very brief suggestive examples I have employed. But that would be to enter into a much more complicated matter than is necessary here. For now I would simply like to summarize some of what I take to be the main points of this chapter.

SUMMARY

In this chapter I have argued that despite the vast theoretical differences which separate the discourses that are relevant to my field, similarities among and across these discourses can be found. In constructing this argument, however, I have neither sought nor found some sort of common philosophical or political ground. Rather, I have argued that the shared theoretical dispositions of my field are better understood as representing stances taken from homologous "radical" spaces within the U.S. educational research community. The shared dispositions I have presented were a tendency toward "new" theory, an adherence to the notion of "epistemic privilege" and a rejection of "traditional" conceptions of scientific objectivity.

My major concern in this chapter was to document the social identity and shared dispositions which the discourses of my field have constructed in

< 102 >

their oppositions to mainstream U.S. educational research. In this sense my view here has been internal. Recognizing that on philosophical and political levels each of the discursive strands I have analyzed represents a unique and distinct analytical agenda, I have argued that on a sociological level shared dispositions can be found. In relation to the two previous chapters, then, this chapter begins what I would call a sociological turn. I have argued that in addition to the philosophical and political agendas of my field, these discourses are sociologically related to multiple social contexts, most notably to their relative positions within the social space known as U.S. educational research. What appear as conceptual contradictions or self-marginalizing rhetorics on the philosophical and political levels can be better understood as a successful logic of the social struggle to open space within the Academy.

In the course of this chapter it also has become evident that to undertake a full sociological analysis of my field and its position within U.S. educational research is beyond the scope of this project. Indeed to undertake such an analysis would require a substantial theoretical and empirical project of massive proportions. Consequently, most of the claims in this chapter are merely suggestive of what might be possible within the kind of sociological frame I have begun to deploy here. However, such a study is not simply beyond the scope of this project, it is also not necessary and would in many ways be beside the point. My main concern in the overall project is to question how my field relates to mainstream research, and that would be only a small part of a full sociological study.

While in this chapter I focused internally, questioning how the discourses relevant to my field construct themselves, in the next chapter my focus is much more external. There, returning to many of the issues and levels of analysis I have thus far employed in the first three chapters, I skeptically question how my field has engaged mainstream educational research, analyzing the potential philosophical reception, political consequences, and sociological implications of the New Sociology's critique of Positivism and I ask a deceptively simply question, "Was the critique of Positivism a mistake?"

five

Was the Critique of Positivism a Mistake?

IN THE PREVIOUS CHAPTER I suggested that the discourses of U.S. radical sociologies of school knowledge, however unique and fragmented, share theoretical dispositions through which they have constructed themselves in a manner which virtually guarantees self-marginalization. I have also suggested, in broad strokes, that this phenomenon can be understood in relation to how these radical discourses have distinguished themselves from what they have taken to be "mainstream" educational research.

In this chapter I would like to return to my initial point of departure to examine in more detail how the U.S. New Sociology of Education distinguished itself from mainstream U.S. educational research through its critique of Positivism. Returning to the critique of Positivism may seem rather odd to those familiar with post-structural educational research. According to many of these radical educational theorists, we have entered a "post-positivist" era. Positivism in other intellectual enterprises, so the story goes, is dead. Philosophers long ago came to see (logical) Positivism as untenable. Psychologists have turned toward "constructivist" theories. Sociologists, among radicals anyway, long ago turned away from Positivism. And cultural/social anthropologists were never too fond of Positivism anyway. Having lived through nearly two decades of radical educational theorists bringing the insights of trans-Atlantic philosophical debates to bear on educational research, contemporary radical educational theorists have announced the end of the Positivist Era in educational research (Lather, 1991).

This proclamation, *prima facie*, seems questionable on a number of levels. Certainly one could raise, as I have, skeptical questions about how much mainstream educational research has really changed over the past two decades. This issue, of course, could simply be a matter of time—radical work could gain ascendancy and we could be actually in a "post-positivist" era (at least it's a logical possibility); but this latter proposition is ultimately not that important (whatever era we are in, the sociologies of school knowledge still have their problems). There are other important reasons for questioning the announcement of the end of educational Positivism. First, such a call presupposes that early educational critics of Positivism correctly identified mainstream educational research as positivistic *and* that Positivism truly had a hold on educational research. There are, after all, more than a few defenders of Positivism still around (e.g., Phillips, 1987). Second, harkening the coming of a "Post-Positivist" era implies that the issues of the old debate have been settled, that early critics were decisive and conclusive. As the title of this chapter suggests, there is good reason for returning to the original critiques of Positivism on which "post-positivists" rely.

This chapter considers the relation constructed between radical critiques in the sociology of school knowledge and the works these radicals consider "mainstream" within the radical educational critique of Positivism. To do this, I propose to examine these relations on three levels, heuristically termed the philosophical, the political, and the sociological. Hence three sections follow; and each subsequent section will employ varying analytical languages. Let me explain.

The first of these three sections will examine the (ostensibly) philosophical substantive debates between radical educational research agendas and their Others (i.e., mainstream/positivist agendas). Of specific philosophical concern are the issues of science's ostensibly inherent support of status quo social relations, epistemic privilege, and incommensurate paradigms. These "philosophic" notions I take to correspond to the theoretical dispositions within the discourses of RSSK; the disposition against scientific objectivity, the adherence to viewing knowledge as socially situated, and the disposition toward new theory, respectively. However while I shall attempt to outline how some theorists have approached these issues, and in that sense employ philosophic analyses, my interest is not one of seeking to define a philosophical position. The central focus of this "philosophical" section pivots on the question of how mainstream philosophers might make sense of the radical positions.

The second section, the "political," questions the politico-strategic issues of the critique of Positivism. Here questions of correctly identifying one's

< 106 >

enemies and the practical consequences of misrepresentation are raised, and in that sense I shall employ strategic analyses. Finally, in double opposition to the limited views presented in both the foregoing sections, I propose a socio-logical analysis of the critique of Positivism as one cultural struggle within the academic field of educational research. Sociologically, I argue, we can question how it is that RSSK in the United States has maintained the very principles of legitimation it claimed to oppose, in relations to both educational research generally and in terms of its relation to itself.

Thus, where in Chapters Two and Three I explicitly addressed philosoph-ical and political concerns before initiating in Chapter Four the sociological analysis of these discourses as part of one academic field, here I take similar turns focusing only on one of the major arguments of one of the discursive strands salient to the field.

PHILOSOPHICAL QUESTIONS

The late 1960s and early 1970s were ripe times for philosophical criticisms of sociological theory generally and educational research specifically. Concerned with the ways in which traditional educational research had continually managed to not impact any significant "progressive" change in educational thought and practices, the New Sociologists declared their territory by deploy-ing three hallmark arguments.[1]

Primary among the New Sociology's arsenal was the notion that knowl-edge is a social construct. While this was hardly a new idea, Berger and Luckmann (1966) served as its contemporary articulation. Historically, Kuhn (1962) provided the notion that differing scientific discourses could be incom-mensurate and therefore translation among different "paradigms" was seen to be impossible. From time to time, "normal science" had to be displaced; and traditional educational science's time "had come." Finally, philosophical support came from Habermas (1971) whose work was taken to show that empirical/analytical science served the interests of control and was, therefore, oppressive. Taken together, the New Sociologists, among many others, synthesized an argument condemning traditional educational research.

Labeled "Positivism," traditional educational research was taken to often rely on the ostensibly epistemological assumptions that 1) knowledge claims objectively reflect reality in a mirror-like fashion; and 2) that knowl-edge and fact are analytically distinct from belief and value. The "Positivism" of traditional educational research was also criticized as a mode of social analysis because it 1) ignored the ostensibly fundamental distinc-tion separating human sciences from physical sciences; 2) sought to emulate the prediction and control characteristic of the physical sciences within social analyses; 3) employed a methodological individualism which trans-lated its epistemological assumptions into psychologized social phenomena

< 107 >

(and endless checklists of mindlessly minute observable behaviors); and (thereby) 4) mistakenly assumed socially created characteristics to be inherent in individual people. In all, traditional educational research, which was taken to have followed this culture of Positivism, was seen clearly to be supporting the *status quo*.

There are three corollary ideas which have been associated with this critique and that are clearly related to the theoretical dispositions I have identified with RSSK more generally. These corollary ideas are 1) that empirical/analytical knowledge and science serve the interest of control, thereby making positivistic science oppressive; 2) that a socially subordinate perspective holds "epistemic privilege"; and 3) that the incommensurability argument means critical social science would not be understood by those in the positivistic "paradigm." While these arguments may be familiar to most readers of radical educational theory, it is not entirely obvious how they can be considered corollary to the critique of Positivism outlined above. These arguments were in fact deployed in the New Sociology's critique of Positivism. To make these two points more explicit, I shall consider each notion in turn, tracing the arguments supporting each notion and explaining how I see them as corollary to the critique of Positivism.

Positivistic science as oppressive

The conception of positivistic science as oppressive was constructed from two separate arguments. The first of these two arguments came directly from the critique of Positivism, and follows from the understanding that when the objective of science is one of explanation and prediction (as was the case in Positivism), scientific language relies on formalized arguments within a closed system or restricted universe of knowledge claims. Following Habermas, radical educational theorists argued that a strict (positivistic) science would serve specific, and particular, interests. In one example of this logic, Michael Apple (1974) constructed this argument as follows:

> Educational research has indeed drawn its mode from behavioristic sociology and psychology, fields that have sought to pattern themselves after strict sciences and that are increasingly under attack for providing support for corporate and bureaucratic interests under the guise of neutrality. Educational research, thus, has adopted the cognitive interests that cohere with these research traditions, those of bringing as many aspects of human activity as possible under technical control and assuring that educators can have surety in dealing with the complex process of human action. Yet, in the search for certainty of outcome in schools, there is a tendency both to eliminate (or at least not give substantial support to) those portions of students' conduct that may somehow threaten the taken-for-granted regularities of the educational setting and to dissolve the elements of argumentation and conflict that enable substantive educational change to evolve. (p. 22–23)

< 108 >

This portion of Apple's argument, however, only sought to establish that the technical nature of positivistic educational sciences served the interests of control by limiting what was taken as a viable, or legitimate, educational question. Hence there was a tendency, so the argument went (in this case), to eliminate those student actions which were "threatening." The form of this "legitimacy" argument has reappeared in applications to many other educational settings as well.

The second argument supporting the first corollary notion relied on the "contextualization" for which Apple has repeatedly called. In one context, in considering how students are labeled, Apple (1979b) suggested,

> Because of the schools' economic role in differentially distributing a hidden curriculum to different economic, cultural, racial, and sexual groups, linguistic, cultural, and class differences from the "normal" will be maximally focused upon and will be labeled as deviant. Technical knowledge will then be used as an intricate filter to stratify students according to their "ability" to contribute to its production. . . . (and)
>
> It is in the combination between the school's use of "neutral" perspectives embodying the interests of technical control and certainty, and the way schools serve the interests of economic and cultural reproduction, that the schools carry out their varied functions. Technical perspectives . . . complement the needs of an unequal society for the maximization of the production of technical knowledge, the distribution of an acritical and positivistic perspective and the production of agents with the appropriate norms and values to roughly fill the requirements of the ongoing division of labour in society. (p. 153)

Here we had the explicit conjunction of the two arguments supporting the view that positivistic science was to be considered oppressive. In each of these cases, Apple was concerned with how positivistic science specifically influenced how students were treated or managed within educational settings; but the structure of this argument has been applied to many other educational areas, such as in analyses of the form and content of curriculum, and in examinations of the management of teachers' professional life. It has become a familiar argument in radical circles.

I take this argument to be corollary to the New Sociology's critique of Positivism because of its direct reliance on that critique. In schematic form, the "positivistic science as oppressive" argument would roughly look as follows:

1. Given that positivistic science (equated here with Habermas's empirical/analytic science) is based on the interests of control; and

2. given that educational science emulates positivistic science; and

< 109 >

3. given that we are in a society based on oppressive social relations (in this case economically based on class, etc.);

4. it follows that the educational use of such science serves the social interests of (maintaining) those oppressive relations.

This view is logically drawn explicitly from the understanding that when applied to social phenomena, Positivism seeks to emulate the control and prediction ostensibly characteristic of the natural sciences. But its other connections with the critique of Positivism also suggest that it can be taken as corollary.

On the "epistemological" level (outside of the realm of the social sciences), this argument is also buttressed by the views that knowledge (and science) is a social construct (the view opposed to Positivism's ostensible view of knowledge as the mirror of nature) and that facts and value are not distinct (the view opposed to "Positivism's" imposed fact/value dichotomy). Apple's analysis of the functions of labeling in educational settings is a direct articulation of the notions that positivistic science tends toward a methodological individualism which takes socially constructed characteristics to be inherent in individuals.

Epistemic privilege

The notion of knowledge as a social construct almost immediately leads to the position that whatever people take as knowledge depends on their relative position with a social setting. In an analysis which understands society as a hierarchical social structure—for example, one in which some have more power than others—the question, "whose knowledge is more accurate?" becomes central. It is in this philosophical context that the proposition known as "epistemic privilege" has been constructed. For example, the idea that people in oppressed conditions have a more accurate knowledge of the mechanisms of their oppression has been linked to Lukács (1971), where Lukács argued that the proletariat's knowledge of capitalism was "more" objective than bourgeois knowledge of capitalism. The issue of epistemic privilege has gained attention, within the past decade, in a variety of feminist theories, for example where Harding (1986, 1991) has argued that feminist knowledge is "less distorted" than non-feminist knowledge. If only with this shared epistemological heritage, the New Sociology's critique of Positivism also raises questions about whose knowledge is to be considered valid.

At first glance, however, my suggestion that an adherence to epistemic privilege was corollary to the New Sociology's critique of Positivism seems disputable. This claim relies on two relatively clear propositions: 1) that the New Sociology's critique of Positivism actually did adhere to epistemic privilege; and 2) that epistemic privilege was corollary to the critique. But neither

< 110 >

of these propositions is obvious and both need to be defended. On the one hand, demonstrating an adherence to epistemic privilege runs against the fact that *explicit* pronouncements of epistemic privilege were rarely made (if at all) in the New Sociology's critique of Positivism. On the other hand, the claim that epistemic privilege was corollary to this critique is not clearly defensible on logical grounds (as was the case with the notion that positivistic science is oppressive).

As was tangentially referred to above, the New Sociology's critique of Positivism charged that positivistic science functions to give legitimacy to oppressive or unjustified educational practices. When stated bluntly this appears to be a rather straightforward claim; but, when it is analyzed more carefully, this proposition is actually quite complicated.

In most cases the "legitimacy" argument began from the epistemological premise that Positivism aspired to neutrality and objective (strongly interpreted) knowledge, and an empirical observation that neutrality was generally taken as legitimate. Many additional propositions, however, can be found in the structure of the overall argument. Whether these other propositions were taken as premises or demonstrated as conclusions depended on the specific author's construction. These others propositions included 1) a claim that Positivism was publicly presumed to be neutral and legitimate; 2) a claim that positivistic logic corresponded to commonsense understandings of educational practice; 3) a claim that these commonsense understandings were taken to be neutral by their association with Positivism's presumed neutrality; 4) a claim that the educational practices associated with these commonsense understandings were unjust; and 5) the conclusion that Positivism legitimated unjust educational practices which failed to serve the (more truly legitimate) interests of emancipation.

Henry Giroux's (1981d) expressed critique of Positivism, found in his essay "Schooling and the Culture of Positivism," provided a good example of this legitimacy argument. By examining this critique it is possible to see two things. First, it will become clear that the legitimacy argument is quite complicated when approached with an analytical logic. Second, it is possible to see that the legitimacy argument itself implied an adherence to epistemic privilege.

There are two general points that should be made about Giroux's critique. First, Giroux based his argument on a distinction between formal Positivism (that held in academic circles) and a "culture of Positivism." Here Giroux was explicitly arguing that the logic of Positivism was in fact generally accepted— hence the phrase "culture of Positivism." We can see, then, that this distinction is the crux of Giroux's general argument. For while there may have been severe disagreement within the academy about the validity of various intellectual forms of Positivism or even an academic consensus that Positivism ought to be considered untenable, within the broader social context of schooling, unexamined positivistic beliefs could still have been seen as a cultural fact. Second, in this specific case, Giroux was concerned with demonstrating that the culture of Positivism corresponded to what he saw as a damaging understanding of "theory." While Giroux's concern about theory is of significant substantive import, to me it was not a central feature of most legitimacy arguments in the New Sociology and is only of specific concern here as a contingent fact. Hence, presently I will not question Giroux's claims on these matters.

Giroux's overall critique was offered in two stages: first, Giroux presented a general theoretical analysis of the critique of Positivism as it was constructed among radical social theorists; and second, Giroux applied this critique to the educational arguments and practices surrounding the then contemporary "loss of interest in history" (as a subject matter debate). In a fashion familiar to many radical critiques, Giroux argued that while traditional or conservative educational critics had correctly identified a problem (in this case the "death of history"), educational debates between conservatives and liberals had failed to adequately understand the cause of the problem (in this case the culture of Positivism) and had taken indefensible positions which unjustly served the interests of a conservative hegemonic ideology.

The formulation of Giroux's general analysis of the culture of Positivism identified its underlying assumptions as those typically associated with the natural sciences. As he put it,

> The major assumptions that underlie the culture of Positivism are drawn from the logic and method of inquiry associated with the natural sciences. Based upon the logic of scientific methodology with its interest in explanation, prediction, and technical control, the principle of rationality in the natural sciences was seen as vastly superior to the hermeneutic principles underlying the speculative social sciences. Modes of rationality that relied upon or supported interpretative procedures rated little scientific status from those defending the assumptions and methods of natural sciences. (p. 42)

Here Giroux explicitly suggested that within the culture of Positivism, social science generally emulated the natural sciences because of a presumably higher scientific status. This quote is interesting not only because of the claim about social science imitating natural science, but also because, in raising the issue of the status of specific scientific endeavors, Giroux was also calling into question the legitimacy of positivistic science. As will become apparent, Giroux not only questioned unjust educational practices, but also the positivistic science he saw as ideologically linked to them (pp. 43–44). Hence, the view here was of a set of interrelated positions including epistemological claims, ethical claims, questions about the role of scientific theory and the role of the intellectual, and the over-riding agenda of political commitment.

Approaching this argument with an analytical logic would be difficult, to say the least. For example, Giroux suggested, "The central assumption by which the culture of Positivism rationalizes its position of theory and knowledge is the notion of objectivity, the separation of values from knowledge and methodological inquiry alike." But in another he claimed, "the existing perspective on theory provides the background for knowledge is (*sic*) value free" (p. 43). If one were looking for unidirectional relationships, as is the tendency in analytical philosophy, this would be a rather complicated matter. That is, to capture the sense in which Giroux talks about this *one* relationship between positivist notions of theory and objectivity, it would be necessary to make at least three claims instead of two:

1. that a view of theory which is limited to questions of technique buttresses epistemological assumptions which take "objectivity" to be "value-free";
2. that a value-free notion of "objectivity" relegates the role of theory to deal with only technical questions; and
3. that these connections between positivistic theory and value-free notions of objectivity mutually reinforce each other, thereby forming a closed positivist unity.

Of course one could dissect these three claims into smaller propositions—making more of them. But keep in mind that these propositions are only referring to one relationship, that between theory and one epistemological issue.

When viewed in its entirety, Giroux's critique of the culture of Positivism included claims about the relationship between ethics and social theory, ethics and the role of the intellectual, epistemology and theory, theory and politics, and so on (. . . and on). Giroux discussed these other relationships in a way similar to the theory-objectivity relationship. Clearly attempting to analytically formulate the overall critique would require a great deal of work—if only in terms of the numbers of propositions which would have to be specified.

But such an analytical attempt could itself be seen as contradictory to the overall claim being made. After all one of the major points Giroux was making questioned the degree to which specific claims had been separated from each other—most obvious in his comment about ethics. Wouldn't translating this argument into minutely specified analytical propositions simply reenact the very separation Giroux argued against? And wasn't the separation characteristic of the culture of Positivism responsible for simply hiding the ethical, social and political questions Giroux was most concerned with bringing into educational discourse?

Clearly, these questions were salient for Giroux. First, Giroux saw the culture of Positivism as dangerous (p. 45). Second, at the same time, the culture of Positivism was seen as concealing (p. 45). Given the view that positivistic rationality was separating out questions which were of central concern,

< 113 >

and given the view that this process of separation leads to concealment, it makes sense to see that Giroux employed the Marxist language of "ideology" when attempting to characterize the culture of Positivism as a unity.

In ascribing the culture of Positivism as an ideology, Giroux advanced two identifiably Marxist propositions. The first of these was the notion that in his stratified society a specific ideology was linked to ruling interests. Echoing Marx's well-known claim that "the ideas of the ruling class are in every epoch the ruling ideas," Giroux argued the assumptions of the culture of Positivism could be (indeed should be) understood "as part of the dominant ideology" (p. 44). As part of the dominant ideology, Giroux presented its influence as particularly omnipresent. Here, there was a correspondence between a general view of dominant ideologies and a specific view of Positivism. On the one hand, a Marxist analysis would suggest that any dominant ideology functions ubiquitously. No matter what the specific epoch (e.g., feudal or capitalist), dominant ideologies were seen as pervasive and widespread throughout society. On the other hand, in the specific critique of his society, Giroux saw the presumed neutrality of Positivism to be particularly pernicious. In his own words,

> Instead of defining itself as an historically produced perspective, the culture of Positivism asserts its superiority through its alleged suprahistorical and supracultural posture. Theory and method are held to be historically neutral. (p. 44)

Viewed as an ideology, from a Marxist perspective, Giroux could speak about the culture of Positivism without enlisting the tendency to analytically separate questions of method from questions of ethics.[2] Here, the Marxist view of ruling ideas being widespread and diffuse corresponded to Giroux's "dialectical" view of the relationships among various elements of the culture of Positivism.

The second identifiably Marxist position within Giroux's argument was the notion that while "hiding" questions of ethics, the culture of Positivism supported a mass "false consciousness." Here Giroux's words were unforgiving. In addition to Positivism's tendency to universalize itself—thereby "erasing history"—the concealing nature of the culture of Positivism carried other worries.

> As the fundamental false consciousness of our time, the positivist mode of rationality operates so as to undermine the values of history and the importance of historical consciousness in other significant ways. First, it fosters an undialectical and one-dimensional view of the world; second, it denies the world of politics and lacks a vision of the future; third, it denies the possibility that human beings can constitute their own reality and alter and change that reality in the face of domination. (p. 45)

< 114 >

The possibility of speaking simultaneously in descriptive and prescriptive terms was explicit in Marxist social analyses of the time. Seeing the culture of Positivism as a false consciousness directly corresponded to Giroux's proclaimed interest in raising critical questions about the ethical and political implications of educational research.

Giroux's general critique of the culture of Positivism dealt with many issues in addition to those just considered, such as arguing that a dominant ideology ought not to be seen as simply reproductive and that an activist conception of human agency opened possibilities for political transformation. In that portion of Giroux's argument I have just discussed, however, he had already proposed some of the general claims of the "legitimacy" argument with which I am concerned. That is, on the societal level, Giroux had suggested that Positivism was publicly presumed to be neutral and legitimate, and that Positivism legitimated unjust social relations (otherwise known as "the status quo"). Of course, these claims remained on a very general level. The more specific educational claims of the legitimacy argument were to be found in Giroux's application of his general critique to the curricular debate over "the death of history."

Having framed his analysis in a Neo-Marxist ideology-critique, the course of Giroux's critique was set. Initially, there was a presumption that the debates of history (as a subject matter) were to be understood through an analysis of "the ruling ideas." This was evident in how Giroux introduced his application:

> I now want to examine how the culture of positivism has influenced the process of schooling, particularly in relation to the way educators have defined the history "crisis" and its relationship to educational theory and practice at the classroom level. I will begin by analyzing how the nature of the loss of interest has been defined by leading members of the educational establishment. (p. 47)

As a subsection of society, education could itself be seen as a stratified community with certain interests representing the view of the elite.

But these "leaders" were not in agreement; and, on the surface of their discussion they would not appear to have been united. Conservative leaders held the perspective that the loss of interest in history was a result of the liberal push to make all things practical. Liberal educators were concerned over the fragmentation they saw as the consequence of overspecialization. Predictably, Giroux did not take these arguments simply at their words. There were assumptions to be examined here.

Underneath their disagreements, Giroux saw commonality among the members of education's ruling class. As he put it,

> American educators have defined the "loss of interest" in history as an academic rather than political problem. . . . these responses view the loss of interest in history as a purely academic problem. Severed from the socio-

< 115 >

economic context in which they operate, schools, in both of these views, appear to exist above and beyond the imperatives of power and ideology. ... These positions, in fact represent part of the very problem they define. The loss of interest in history on schools is due less to the changes in course structure and offerings, though these have some effect, than to the growing effects of the culture of positivism on the process of schooling itself, and in this case, particularly the social studies field. (pp. 47–48)

Because neither of the dominant positions in education had sufficiently grasped the political and ethical implications of their positions, and because both had cast their arguments in "purely" academic terms, the analogous link to the critique of the culture of Positivism was plausible and perhaps even evident.

The analogy to the critique of Positivism was further developed when more specifically applied to the field of curriculum. Viewing the curriculum field as made up of differing paradigms, Giroux invoked the Kuhnian vision of scientific struggle (p. 49). Viewing Positivism as the dominant paradigm in the field, Giroux linked the cognitive interests of control and prediction with those dominant members of the curriculum field:

> As I have pointed out, within the United States the social sciences have been modeled largely against the prevailing assumptions and methods of the natural sciences. In spite of recent attacks on this mainstream perspective, the idea of social science conceived after the model of the natural sciences exerts a strong influence on contemporary educational thought and practice. Historically, the curriculum field, in general, has increasingly endeavored to become a science. (p. 49)

Giroux saw evidence of the pressure for curriculum to become a (positivistic) science in many of the field's trends. Drawing on analyses of the curriculum field which identified two dominant groups, Giroux argued that the influence of Positivism was ominous (p. 48). Here the image of curriculum as being immersed in the culture of Positivism was nearly complete. But one issue was yet left unaddressed.

The dominant paradigm was not some amorphous entity; a paradigm referred to specific people. As Giroux put it,

> As Kuhn has written, "a paradigm governs, in the first instance, not a subject matter but a group of practitioners." ... The concept of a paradigm is important not merely because it guides practitioners in their work, it also illustrates that paradigms are related to the nexus of social and political values in the larger society. (p. 49)

Within a Marxist view of a society dominated by an ideological false consciousness, recognizing the political and social values of the research done in one

< 116 >

field becomes a matter of knowing a person's history. Educational workers did not simply act on dominant ideologies; when born into a context infused with ideology, educational workers *embodied* false consciousness (p. 49).

In this application of his general critique of the culture of Positivism, Giroux placed the specific educational claims of the legitimacy argument center stage. Commonsense in the curriculum field was seen as generally positivistic. The vision of a scientific curriculum was linked to the legitimating neutrality of natural science. By relegating curricular questions about the role of one subject matter to technical and academic issues, the curriculum field could be seen as employing assumptions which supported the (unjust) dominant ideology. Questions about the political and ethical implications of the "loss of interest in history" had been made invisible.

Alongside a number of other arguments, Giroux's critique of the culture of Positivism advanced one of the most complete legitimacy arguments to be found in educational literature. Although I've discussed only a small portion of Giroux's entire essay, the quotes I've extracted from his argument exhibit the broad range (but not all) of the educational issues questioned by the legitimacy argument. Educational research, policy arguments, and more specific educational practices were all questioned. By identifying an underlying culture of Positivism, Giroux had ruptured the legitimacy of virtually the entire educational enterprise.

As I mentioned earlier, there were two points in excavating Giroux's critique at length. First, the details of Giroux's analysis brought into view the extent and breadth of the legitimacy argument. The extensive nature of this critique itself made translating the argument, in linear logical terms, a massive proposition. The dialectical nature of the claims made in the legitimacy argument geometrically expanded this task. Further, the task of translating the critique into separate claims itself was problematic. In these senses, my representation of Giroux's critique was meant to stand as one example of why it would be difficult to imagine the New Sociology in dialogue with mainstream educators. But the second point I sought to build carried a more substantial problem. With this exegesis I hoped to ground my claim that the critique of Positivism adhered to epistemic privilege. Here I can return to this concern.

In his critique, Giroux never made an explicit claim supporting the notion of epistemic privilege. How then can I suggest that this critique implied an adherence to epistemic privilege? From a linear logical point of view, one proposition (p) implies another proposition (q) if and only if for the former to be true that latter must also be true. Symbolically, this reads straightforwardly, 'p' IFF 'q'. In this instance I am claiming that for the New Sociology's critique of Positivism to be true, the notion of epistemic privilege must also be true. In my unpolished sketch of epistemic privilege I highlighted two propositions: 1) the notion that different views of reality were associated

< 117 >

with the different sides of the socially dominant/dominated dichotomy; and 2) the notion that the dominated view was less distorted than the dominant. Applied here, roughly put, I would suggest that the New Sociologists could critique Positivism as a dominant ideology if and only if 1) they took their view to represent the view of the dominated; and 2) they took their view to be less distorted (or "more objective") than the dominant positivist view.

These last two propositions I take to be fairly evident in Giroux's critique of the culture of Positivism. Anyone at all familiar with the New Sociology would see their proclaimed alliance with the dominated as obvious (I hope). The notion of their view being less distorted than the dominant is only problematic if the New Sociologists are read into the ever present philosophical epistemological debates as naive (or cynical) relativists. While not obvious, I take the worry of relativism to be beside the point in the New Sociology. Lest there be any doubt, I'll address each of the propositions of epistemic privilege in turn.

Before considering on which side of the dominant/dominated dichotomy Giroux's view stood, let me make it clear that Giroux accepted this dichotomy as a description of social positions. Recall the claim that, "In a simple sense, a paradigm might be viewed as in opposition or in support of the dominant ideology" (p. 49). Simply by describing "the dominant ideology," Giroux suggested not only was the dominant/dominated dichotomy viable, but that what was dominant could be seen in the singular (i.e., "the" dominant). The use of a singular article may seem a small point, but Giroux did consistently use the singular when referring a "dominant ideology," and it might signify an ironically unidimensional view of the social hierarchy. At the minimum, ascribing a view of "the dominant" in a description of a whole society suggests that not all people are dominant—meaning someone must be among the dominated.

As for which side of the fence Giroux was on, reconsider some of the dangers he saw emanating from "the positivist mode of rationality": "it denies the world of politics and lacks a vision of the future; [and] it denies the possibility that human beings can constitute their own reality and alter and change that reality in the face of domination" (p. 45). Having repeatedly criticized the culture of Positivism for not addressing ethical issues, and having made clear that the dominant educational ideology was supporting the culture of Positivism (and vice-versa), it seems obvious that Giroux's vision of the future was intended to combat domination itself. Later arguing for "emancipatory praxis," it is evident that the change in reality Giroux sought to advance was a change in the interest of the dominated. Given that Giroux accepted world views as constructed from specific social positions, there are two possible "places" from which his view could originate. His view could either be that of a supra-societal benevolent being, or that of the dominated. And given that his rejection of Positivism partially lay in its ostensible tendency to make itself

< 118 >

universal, it seems the first of these two options could be considered an unlikely reading. It is a safe assumption that Giroux was consistent and, therefore, we should take his view to have been constructed at least partially from the position of the dominated.[3] Thus, Giroux at least seems to have been committed to the first proposition of the epistemic privilege position.

Giroux's employment of a Marxist conception of ideology, noted above, should make it clear that he was also committed to a second proposition of the epistemic privilege position. Having referred to the positivist "mode of rationality" as "the fundamental false consciousness of our time" (p. 45), Giroux had explicitly suggested that the perspective his critique offered was certainly less distorted than that of the culture of Positivism. The view of his critique being less distorted was also apparent in the visualist metaphors Giroux used to explain the distortions of educational Positivism. For example, note Giroux's suggestion that,

> this (positivist) form of rationality prevents us from using historical consciousness as a vehicle to unmask existing forms of domination as they reproduce themselves through the "facts" and common-sense assumptions that structure our view and experience of the world. (p. 45)

In suggesting forms of domination could be "unmasked," Giroux explicitly asserted that a more clear (i.e., less distorted) view of reality was offered by his own critique.

Giroux's deployment of both propositions of epistemic privilege I take to be an evidentiary example of my claim that the legitimacy arguments advanced in the radical critique of Positivism imply a notion of epistemic privilege. In this case, the notion of epistemic privilege wasn't always left implicit, as in Giroux's claim that states of consciousness are embodied and his subsequent focus on unmasking the views of the educational elite. But from a commonsense view, however tainted that may be by analytical logic, it is difficult to see how one could generally advance charges of false or unjust legitimacy without implying that an alternative view offers a less distorted understanding of the basis of the legitimacy in question. Since my concern here is limited to how the New Sociology employed claims based on a presumed epistemic privilege, this more general analytical question need not be pushed further. For now, having raised the general question, I take it to be sufficient to have shown how at least one of the central figures of the New Sociology based his arguments on epistemic privilege.

Incommensurate paradigms

The third notion I take to have been corollary to the New Sociology's critique of Positivism, the notion of incommensurate paradigms, initially can be addressed quite readily. As is probably clear by now, the New Sociologists

< 119 >

often relied on Kuhn's conception of differing scientific paradigms, as in Giroux's critique of the culture of Positivism. In a sense, in opposing dominant ideology as if it was a paradigm, the New Sociology's critique was itself taken and self-presented as a paradigm. Subsequent texts in the sociology of education and curriculum explicitly introduce radical sociologies of school knowledge as a paradigm, with inclusions of both the general notion that various paradigms exist within each field, and with the more specific inclusion of the New Sociology's works as fitting in a so-called "critical," "radical," or "conflict" paradigm. Because of its centrality in the educational academic commonsense, I don't think it is necessary to examine the New Sociology's deployment of the general notion of a paradigm in any more detail.

However my interest is not simply in the general notion of paradigms. My concern here is centered specifically on the idea that scientific paradigms are incommensurate. Although it is difficult to grasp the fullness of the notion of incommensurability between paradigms, Thomas Kuhn employed a rough characterization of the problematic with linguistic metaphors, likening the problem to that of translating between two languages (see Kuhn, 1970, Feyerabend, 1970). While we can say that knowledge of two languages is necessary for translation, argued Kuhn, we cannot say that such knowledge is sufficient (after all, simply being bilingual, even fluently so, does not a translator make) nor that there is always such a thing as a full translation. In effect, incommensurability could be seen as the recognition that some things said in one language could not be said in another, and that attempts to do so would result literally in "nonsense." When applied to scientific paradigms, according to Kuhn, what could be seen, tested, measured and hypothesized in one paradigm would simply not be recognized as a problem (or question) in another.

This claim, advocated by both Kuhn and Paul Feyerabend since the early 1960s, is almost always (unfortunately) ignored in educational textbook presentations of "paradigms." More specifically, as with the notion of epistemic privilege, the New Sociology rarely, if ever, explicitly suggested that its research was incommensurate with its nemesis—Positivism. For both Apple and Giroux, the critique of Positivism was the basis of a claim that a new paradigm was needed. According to these critics, the New Sociology offered visions that brought to light issues they took to have been missed in traditional studies of school knowledge. Despite the strength of their criticisms, however, it is not at all clear that Apple and Giroux believed that people in the dominant paradigm could not see the issues being raised by the radical critique. Simply raising previously ignored issues does not constitute a commitment to incommensurability. To argue that two paradigms are incommensurate is to suggest that what one "sees" from the perspective of one paradigm *cannot* be "seen" from the perspective of another. Because of this, it is

< 120 >

necessary to support more fully my claim that the notion of incommensurate paradigms was corollary to the New Sociology's critique of Positivism.

It is possible to sketch the issue at hand by considering how these writers explicitly discussed what their perspective offered educational research. In his review of two British volumes in the sociology of education, for example, Apple (1978) formulated the difference between the New Sociology and traditional studies of the relationship between schooling and the economy as follows:

> What happens inside the school at a cultural level must be understood before we can understand what happens outside school on an economic level.... Others, especially the political economists of education, have studied the schools in a way that stresses the economic role of educational institutions. Mobility, selection, the reproduction of the social division of labor, and other similar outcomes are the prime subjects of their analyses. Conscious economic manipulation by those in power is often seen as a determining element. While this is certainly important, it gives only one side of the picture. The economistic position is less adequate in appraising how the schools achieve these ends. *It cannot fully illuminate what the mechanisms of domination are and how they work in day-to-day school life.* (p. 496, emphasis added)

Clearly Apple saw the cultural perspective he advocated as offering images which could not be addressed in studies of mobility and the like. Speculatively, it is safe to assume that Apple had traditional quantitative studies in mind here (perhaps even those of the Neo-Marxists Bowles and Gintis). Moreover, we do find Apple explicitly making the claim that such studies "cannot fully illuminate" what he was concerned with studying.

Such a position was also taken by Giroux. For example, in his review of the New Sociology and its relation to curriculum, Giroux (1981b) questioned whether an actual "paradigm" had been established in curriculum because the critiques of "the Dominant model" were varied and emanated from vastly differing perspectives but, nevertheless, that the dominant paradigm was incapable of addressing the questions he sought to ask. He suggested, for example, that "[t]he learning-psychology perspective fails to examine the way schools legitimize certain forms of knowledge and cultural interests" (p. 98). As we have seen, Giroux's perspective was explicitly intended to examine "the way schools legitimize" many forms of knowledge and cultural interests.

Another marker of the position which presumed that a "new" language was necessary to illuminate issues traditional educational research ignored, was the New Sociology's use of a philosophical and theoretical language foreign (both literally and metaphorically) to their U.S. peers. This was an issue which Giroux addressed directly. In characterizing the difficulties faced by the New Sociology in curriculum, he said,

< 121 >

> The new language may be difficult, but it is necessary because it enables its users to develop new kinds of relationships in the curriculum field and to raise different kinds of questions. (p. 103)

Asking questions that cannot be asked in one language, and attempting to answer them in another is the very maneuver described by Feyerabend and Kuhn in their explanations of what incommensurability was all about.

Further clarity on this can be seen in what Giroux had to say about the possibilities of his "New Sociology of Curriculum":

> curriculum models must develop forms of understanding that relate experience of social meanings to wider societal parameters in order to be able to judge their claims to the truth ... (And) ... The dominant technocratic curriculum paradigm may be aging, but it is far from an historical relic. The struggle to replace it with principles and assumptions consistent with the vision of the new sociology of curriculum movement will be difficult indeed. But one thing is certain. The struggle for a new mode of curriculum rationality cannot be approached as a technical task only. It must be seen as a social struggle deeply committed to what Herbert Marcuse has aptly termed "... the emancipation of sensibility, reason, and imagination in all spheres of subjectivity and objectivity." (p. 106)

Here, Giroux's reference to a new mode of analysis which could not only be a question of technical tasks was an oppositional reference to what he saw as the dominant paradigm in curriculum (the "positivistic" technocratic model). While this paradigm had not yet been displaced (nor is it yet), it was clear that Giroux sought to replace it with an alternative paradigm. This was also clear simply by considering the title of Giroux's paper, "Toward a New Sociology of Curriculum," and by the label "New Sociology of Education." Further, in this passage, the New Sociology was seen as necessary to judge educational Positivism's claims to truth.

The question here becomes, "Even if the New Sociology was necessary to raise political, ethical, and cultural issues, as these authors suggested, does that mean that the New Sociology was based on a notion of incommensurability?"

As with the notion of epistemic privilege, I want to argue that this critique of Positivism logically implies incommensurability. Directly put, for this central claim (that the New Sociology was necessary to raise these previously ignored issues) to be true, it also had to be true that the New Sociology was incommensurate with traditional educational Positivism. After all, if these ignored issues could have been addressed within the traditional educational research paradigm, a "new" one would not have been necessary. The possibility of raising political and ethical issues within Positivism was directly rejected with Giroux's notions that basic tenets of Positivism, such as sharply

< 122 >

distinguishing between fact and value, were impossible, and that Positivism had resulted in an ethical failing. It is on these thoughts that I base my claim that the notion of incommensurate paradigms was corollary to the New Sociology's critique of Positivism.[4]

Summary of the philosophical corollaries

I have argued so far that the New Sociology's critique of Positivism carried with it three corollary philosophical notions, the notions of science as inherently oppressive, of epistemic privilege, and of incommensurate paradigms. But my use of the term "corollary" has referred to two separate types of interconnection. In the case of the notion of positivistic science as oppressive, I used the term corollary to cover an instance in which the critique of Positivism provided the basic premises and proposition from which the New Sociology logically derived its argument that the use of a strict science in educational research was oppressive. In the other two cases I used the term corollary to refer to instances in which the New Sociology's critique of Positivism logically implied adherence to the notions of epistemic privilege and incommensurate paradigms. With each of these different meanings of the term "corollary," however, there was a similarity. Whether speaking of logical derivations or implications, the relationships I have just demonstrated between the New Sociology's critique of Positivism and other philosophical tenets were elucidated from the arguments constructed within the critiques themselves. In this sense these corollary relationships were textual or linguistic.

The purpose of analyzing the New Sociology's critique of Positivism through such linguistics lenses was twofold. First, I needed to show that these three philosophical notions were, in one sense or another, corollary to this critique. Second I chose to use an analytical language in this section which mirrors, or mimics, a mode of analysis I take to be currently commonplace in the philosophy of education in the United States. For evidence of its dominance, if I were to defend my choice, I would point to the conscious importation of British analytical philosophy into United States philosophy of education by such thinkers as R. S. Peters, Israel Scheffler, and Jonas Soltis— from the late 1950s into the 1960s. The influence of this mode of thinking in the United States is much broader than simply in educational philosophy (evidenced by the role of symbolic logic in mainstream U.S. epistemology). But the institutional position of Scheffler and Soltis at Harvard and Columbia (two of the then quite prestigious graduate institutes of education), has meant that a significant number of current professors of educational philosophy were students of this mode of analysis. I could also point to the great number of articles written from this perspective in journals such as *Educational Researcher* and *Educational Theory*. After all, even among radical scholars, the rise of

< 123 >

Analytical Marxism in the 1980's, which carries its own ties to British analytical logic, has found a significant audience among educational theorists as well (myself included; see Ladwig, 1991).

With this choice of analytical lenses made apparent, I would like now to consider how we might expect (and have seen) mainstream educational theorists to respond to the corollary notions of the New Sociology's critique of Positivism.

Typically, among radical educational theorists, the arguments I have constructed as corollary to the New Sociology's critique of Positivism have been taken to be on "secure" philosophical grounds. From more conventional philosophical perspectives, though, these radical positions continue to be problematic. Roughly put, analytical philosophers see in these notions problems of incoherence. To be brief, the notion of incommensurability seems questionable the instant it is clear that in demonstrating that two paradigms are untranslatable, we are in fact making translatable claims. In this regard, when Feyerabend (1970) speaks of the incommensurability between classic celestial mechanics and the special theory of relativity, and proceeds to do so by describing in which instances these paradigms would not be able to make translatable claims about similar phenomenons, it appears that Feyerabend himself has made just such a translation (see Seigel 1980a, 1980b). The notion of epistemic privilege encounters a similar logic when it is connected with the idea of relative knowledge claims. Here relativist ideas are seen as self-refuting because some sort of a nonrelative claim seems to have been made the instant relativity was proclaimed (see Mannheim, 1936 and Mills, 1963 for a counter argument). The notion that positivistic science simply supports the status quo and is oppressive when applied in conditions of social oppression (such as in contemporary schooling) becomes questionable from the view that considers social science to be value neutral once it reaches the stage of verifying propositions or hypotheses (or from the historical memory which reminds us of the liberatory role science played for those living under the Church's medieval reign) (Dale, 1991).

From a textually bound analytical perspective, I also take these propositions to be quite problematic. Bluntly stated, neither the notion of incommensurability, nor the position of "epistemic privilege," nor the idea of interest laden forms of oppressive knowledge hold up to philosophical scrutiny—unless, of course, you radically alter your notion of what philosophy is in the first place. It is by considering how the radical critiques altered philosophical perspectives that an understanding of these claims can be substantiated. Philosophy, in these radical critiques, is not the philosophy of Descartes as he individually pondered melting wax, the mind/body distinction, and the existence of God. Philosophy, for the radical critique, is a social matter.

Each of these corollary notions I take to be describing social phenomena.

< 124 >

As sociological matters, these arguments are much less dubious and have been readily supported. Within the context of Kuhn's historical analysis, for example, the notion of incommensurability arguably holds up (Lakatos and Musgrave, 1970). Within the context of Lukács's cultural critique of capitalism, or within Harding's feminist critique of social science, the notion that "epistemically" privileged knowledge is "less distorted" than conventional knowledge certainly seems quite plausible (that is, knowledge about specific modes of oppression and exploitation produced from the perspectives of those who are being oppressed and exploited seems reasonable in Harding's (1986, 1991) construction of it). Within trenchant capitalistic societies where science has been used by powerful corporate interests, I have no doubt that empirical/analytical knowledge has oppressed people. But neither Kuhn, nor Lukács, nor Harding, nor Habermas defend these ideas simply on the philosophical grounds of the Anglo-Analytic philosophy of educational philosophy.

While I am tempted to simply leave this recognition of divergent interpretations of these philosophical arguments in the reader's lap, I would like to make one further observation about these philosophical debates in anticipation of the last section of this paper. That is, I'd like to highlight a difference between what I term the "conventional" or "mainstream" philosophical perspective and the "radical." Notice that the archetypical image of the conventional (Anglo-Analytic) philosopher was of one man (Man) employing self-reflective logical deductive reasoning to persuades his readers (e.g., Rene Descartes and his Meditations). But the archetypical radical arguments came with socio-historical, that is context-specific, arguments about the relation between knowledge claims and social contexts (Kuhn, Harding, Habermas). In the first, the conventional image, philosophy is largely a matter of textually limited deductive introspection; but in the second, the radical, philosophy has become a matter of employing social observations within a logical argument. In these context-specific radical arguments, there is a heavy reliance on "empirical" claims—that is, with a rather loose interpretation of what I mean by "empirical," arguments which make claims about large (societal level) groups of people "outside" of any philosophical text. Hence, I roughly draw out a distinction between an introspective philosophical rhetoric of demonstration (conventional philosophy) and a social scientific rhetoric of evidence (radical philosophical critique).

The point in constructing this distinction is not to make some grand claim about the nature of philosophical arguments as opposed to scientific arguments. I only intend this as a heuristic device to name what is a key difference between what (some) radical and (some) mainstream philosophers of education think philosophy is all about. The importance of this difference, for me, is limited to how I see it restricting the commensurability between

< 125 >

these groups of academics. It is interesting to note that each of the arguments I outlined above, the New Sociology's arguments supporting the corollary notions of their critique of Positivism, was supported by empirical claims about society. Apple's suggestion that educational Positivism was oppressive relied on its application in a society marked by oppressive relations; Giroux's argument that the New Sociology offered an epistemically privileged position from which one could critique the dominant positivistic curricular paradigm relied on the claim that "objectivity" and "value-neutrality" were socially more legitimate (and hence held higher status) within the educational academy (and the society at large); and the notion that the New Sociology was incommensurate with educational Positivism relied on the claim that schools (in fact) operate on a cultural level which traditional research could not examine. To the extent that these arguments could be supported, then, support could not be found in a philosophical text, nor in a textually bound philosophical critique. In this regard, it is not surprising that when read through the lens of Anglo-Analytic philosophy these arguments met with some communicative difficulties.

Having framed this essay with an initial concern about how well the critique of Positivism has served radical sociologists of education in altering mainstream educational research, I would like to turn in the following section to a somewhat more practical question about the deployment of the New Sociology's critiques of Positivism. That is, I would like to examine the openly political-strategic interest of these critiques. As with the previous section of this analysis, I shall employ an analytical language specific to political aspects of the critique of Positivism; but my assumed position will shift. Where my concern in the previous section was one of understanding how mainstream educational researchers might make philosophical sense of the New Sociology my position could be seen as having been that of an outsider (with some empathy and partial alliance with the mainstream). But in the following section, I seek to question the political strategy employed by the New Sociology as a member of the "alternative paradigm." In the following section I position myself as one who agrees with the goal of radically transforming the terrain of educational research.

If there is such as thing as the "we/they" or "us/them" distinction in these debates (with the New Sociology identified as the "we" or "us"), I would characterize the difference between the analytical positions in these two sections as follows. When trying to understand how the mainstream might interpret the radical critique, I attempted to view these matters as one of "them." (I am not proclaiming nor even suggesting that I have actually done this well). But below, I question the strategy of the founding members of New Sociology in terms of understanding how "we" might have better articulated our agenda in the field of educational research. As I suggested in the introduction to this

< 126 >

analysis, I do not think the New Sociology has been all that intelligent in its strategy. In the following section, I try to make more clear why.

POLITICAL QUESTIONS

Here my focus on the U.S. context is perhaps most striking. Where early English sociologists of school knowledge sought to connect the sociology of education and curriculum studies within English sociology of education (successful or not), in the United States, the sociology of school knowledge merged with an ongoing critique of extant educational research. As many have noted, struggles in the U.S. educational academy of the time were being waged along two fronts (Apple, 1978).

On the one hand, an overtly "political" agenda was being advanced by Neo-Marxist educational critics against an educational research establishment perceived to be in "liberal" support of an unjust status quo. This battle was to be found in a number of educational subdisciplines. In the history of education, authors such as Clarence Karier and Michael Katz had advanced distinctly Marxist analyses of the class-based expansion of American schooling. In the sociology of education, Martin Carnoy, Samuel Bowles, and Herbert Gintis (among others) had advanced a Marxist agenda. (It might also be possible to argue that the interest in understanding alienation in the late 1970s was in part sparked by a philosophical interest in the young Marx's writings.)

On the other hand, ethnographic and ethnomethodological studies of schooling were being advanced against the predominantly quantitative educational research tradition in the United States. Though ethnographic work in education has long been part of the U.S. educational research landscape (at least since the works of Jules Henry), the late 1960s and early 1970s saw a rapid influx of anthropological methodologies into research on schooling. The works of Cicourel and his colleagues and a host of other "lesser known" qualitative researchers, such as Louis Smith and Ray Rist, were becoming commonplace in educational research by the mid-1970s.

While separate, both of these struggles held out "Positivism" as an opponent. It is into both of these struggles that the sociology of school knowledge was imported from England. It is with the merger of Neo-Marxist, ethnographic educational research and English sociology of school knowledge that a peculiarly American radical sociology of school knowledge was set against mainstream "positivist" educational research. Holding out Paul Willis's (1978) *Learning to Labour* as an exemplar, for example, Apple called for the development of the New Sociology in the States by building on both the Neo-Marxist and the qualitative traditions. Writing in 1978, he suggested that "(t)he current growth of these two traditions—one 'structural' (political-economic) and the other 'interpretive' (ethnographic and ethnomethodological)—could lead to the kind of cultural and economic program I am articulating here" (p. 498).

< 127 >

Here we can see the explicit conjunction of what many have seen as competing analytical traditions in a (relatively) unified attack on educational Positivism. Here we can question the strategic wisdom of seeking unification through mutual opposition.

An important question comes to mind when considering the strategic and tactical issues of this maneuver: how is it that radical sociologists of school knowledge found sufficient mutual interests within the "structural" and "interpretive" traditions to explicitly seek their conjunction? After all, simply having a common enemy does not necessarily provide any sense of unity—as both the U.S. politics of the 1980s and the growth of post-structural/postmodern analysis in the academy have reminded the Left. As I argued earlier, this move carries with it a host of analytical and conceptual dilemmas (see Chapter One). Stated differently, I would rephrase this issue by asking, "Other than the Marxist (Hegelian) penchant for dialectical unification of opposites, what preconceptions of the New Sociology made this agenda seem plausible in the first place?"

Self-isolation

For expressly political struggles in the United States (and perhaps elsewhere), there is a legacy of compromise which consistently haunts revolutionary visionaries. The essential(ized) value of compromise is, of course, hailed as a cornerstone of American republican democracy. Liberal educational discourses teach us to value the ability to always find room for give and take. But from the perspective of those who see an "establishment" (in lay terms) or a hegemonic ideological rationality (in popularized Gramscian intellectual terms), from the point of view of those fighting on the side of the oppressed, there is a fine line between compromise and cooptation. For those with a faith in revolutionary possibilities, attempts to bring together opposites forfeit the Great Leap forward. Fear of being coopted often empirically corresponds, so it would seem, with a tendency toward dogmatic adherence to radical orthodoxy.

In Marxist debates of the New Sociology, the question of how much the radical educational research program had been coopted was cast in the terms of debates which questioned the "primacy" of the economic dimensions of social reproduction. For Apple, to propose a program entailing a theoretical synthesis of both economic and cultural propositions was to push the frontiers of cooptation. From the perspective of those in radical quarters (or at least those who wished to be seen as radical), the validation of both the "structural" and the "interpretive" risked violation of the radical orthodoxy.

But a defender of the New Sociology would see a different story. It is clear from Apple's inscription of the development of these two traditions in educational research that the radical academic struggle against Positivism paralleled

< 128 >

the analytical framework brought into the radical sociologies of school knowledge. Broadly speaking there is some analytical consistency between the conceptual dichotomies of the radical sociologies of school knowledge and this academic maneuver. Most obviously, in the search for possibilities of political transformation, in the search for a nondeterministic alternative to the 1970s theories of social, cultural, and economic reproduction, the New Sociology's acceptance of the structure-agency dichotomy was central. From this one conceptual perspective alone, these two research traditions, ostensibly corresponding to each side of this conceptual anathema, offered the possibility of a dialectical, transcendent resolution. Hence, it seems, the seeds of plausibility of Apple's program were planted well within the conceptual developments of his field.

Underneath the story told by a defender of the New Sociology's cultural turn, there also seems to be a latent political strategy. By arguing that both of these opposing educational research traditions offered valuable insights into the processes of schooling, the U.S. New Sociology simultaneously employed an old political strategy of inclusion. The validation of multiple perspectives has, of course, been a long-standing political strategy unapologetically used to enlarge a following.

Openly declared or not, it is clear the New Sociology reaped benefits from such a strategy. In the radical program of Apple, there was something for both the orthodox Marxist and the "nonpolitical" ethnographer. Embedded in the New Sociology's cross-disciplinary rhetoric, which nominally drew from philosophy, social theory, curriculum, sociology, and many other disciplines, the conjunction of theoretical opposites carried the potential of a popularist (albeit academic) appeal. Given the New Sociology's success in reaching a wide array of educational audiences (and to a lesser degree sociological audiences), and the significant inclusion of radicals within mainstream venues (such as AERA), the strategy of inclusion seems to have met with some success.

Accepting the truth seen in both these perspectives, those of the radical orthodox and the New Sociology defender, it is exactly the earlier success of RSSK which have created the position from which I can now argue that the radical sociology of school knowledge faces the threat of stagnation. It is by juxtaposing the philosophical arguments advanced in the New Sociology's critique of Positivism to the stifling research trends in radical sociologies of school knowledge I analyzed earlier that I find reason to question the New Sociology's political strategy. Stated differently, if we assume correspondences between philosophy and politics, it is possible to understand the trends of, or developments internal to, the radical sociologies of school knowledge as homologously linked to the U.S. New Sociology's critique of Positivism.

Returning to the New Sociology's philosophical critique of Positivism, the idea of incommensurability and the negative assessment of quantitative, generalizable "science" has paralleled two trends I noted earlier: the lessening dialogue with mainstream educational research, and the continued reliance on qualitative methods. Connecting these trends with the critique of Positivism is rather straightforward. On the one hand, belief in incommensurability corresponds with little effort being made to enter into dialogue with the "mainstream." As I noted earlier, this observation is more true of "second generation" critical scholars than of the "founding fathers." But when the radical agenda is buttressed with an implicit acceptance of the notion of incommensurability, this lack of dialogue makes sense. After all, if translation is impossible, why bother trying communication?

On the other hand, the rejection of "objective facts" and the disposition to view quantitative analysis as emulating that form of science which (ostensibly) necessarily oppresses "Others" corresponds with the almost exclusive reliance on qualitative analyses.[5] Apple (1986b) himself has noted this connection in his warning that radical educational research may have taken its criticism of Positivism a bit too far. As he frames it,

> The Habermasian criticism that science is a form of domination, while partly justifiable, has led many people to neglect the empirical economic, political, cultural, and educational data that are available and that could provide important support for our arguments about the growing inequalities in the larger society and in schools themselves. (p. 15)

But even as Apple has relied on data available from other sources, that reliance continues to remain limited to data which has been produced by others.

The appropriation of facts created by research which has been guided by differing theoretical agendas has proven a long-standing dilemma for the social sciences; and it is interesting to find one so keenly aware of the social genesis of facts, such as Apple, advocating (however cautiously) this methodological procedure. As Bourdieu, Chamboredon, and Passeron (1991) pointed out in 1968,

> Anyone who has ever tried to carry out secondary analysis of material collected in relation to another problematic, however neutral-seeming, knows that even the richest of data can never fully and adequately answer questions for which, and by which, they were not constructed. It is not a question of challenging on principle the validity of using second-hand material, but rather of recalling the epistemological conditions of this work of *retranslation*, which always deals with (well or badly) constructed facts and not with data. (p. 36)

Problems of retranslating data are not, of course, limited to those encountered in doing the analysis. When members of one's audience are people who have

< 130 >

personal knowledge of the epistemological gap between data and interpretation—i.e., when one is speaking in part to a research community—it is reasonable to expect a skeptical reception of reinterpreted data.

Moreover, the affinity between qualitative research and academic endeavors currently appealing to many radical educational researchers remains quite strong. Be it feminist politics (the personal is the political), cultural interpretations, so-called post-structural literary studies, or narrative studies, there seems to be a persistent intellectual disposition among radical educational researchers which pushes away quantitative empirical work. The once explicit, but now presumed, criticisms of science as an oppressive force simply provide justification to avoid work on which mainstream educational research communities heavily rely.

This constellation of philosophical dispositions and research practices portrays social practices whose effects are of dubious political merit. In effect, I would suggest that, to some degree, radical sociologists of school knowledge have silenced themselves. Given the initial political intents of the field, and especially its interest in altering the terrain of educational research, it seems to me that the critique of Positivism has corresponded to and buttressed questionable tactics.

Aiding the enemy

Self-assigned isolation is not the only political question I would like to raise about the radical educational critique of Positivism, however; nor is it one toward which I am unsympathetic. Candidly stated, I can see some benefit from self-marginalization—there may be strength and free space to be gained from symbolically creating a unity in opposition to the "dominant." But the New Sociologists' critique of Positivism inscribed another unity besides its own. And I find little reason to think this move was at all politically wise.

Broadly speaking, the label "Positivism" has been mistakenly applied to most mainstream curricular research. By ubiquitously attributing the label "Positivism" to virtually all mainstream work, the radical critique strengthens its nemesis with an erroneous unity.

To be more specific, I concur with mainstream philosophers who point out that the label "Positivism" is something of a misnomer. While there are many similarities between Positivism (as it is formally understood in social theory) and traditional educational science, there are also some significant differences between them (cf. Phillips, 1987). For example, it may be true that traditional educational researchers take themselves to be measuring objective, value-free facts. But the objectivity sustained in Positivism is not necessarily the simplistic reflect-the-world-out-there notion of objectivity educational researchers employ. Many sociological "Positivists" (e.g., Durkheim) do not take facts to be value free. So, when Giroux suggests that researchers who take themselves to be simply describing value-free facts are positivistic, both Giroux and those researchers are mistaken. Much of this research is not positivistic; but it is, forgive my bluntness, simplistic.

Hence, when the critique of "Positivism" (as it has been understood by many "critical" educational scholars) is applied to those traditional educational researchers who recognize that measures do not reflect "reality" and "facts" are not "value-free," a "category mistake" is made. Traditional educational researchers who understand knowledge to be socially constructed and value-laden take the critical argument to be simply wrong—the New Sociology's critique of Positivism is descriptively inaccurate when applied to the more sophisticated of the mainstream empiricists. What is simply bad research is not named such and left defended by default. When grouped together, traditional research remains strong in the unity radical critiques give it (an inverted educational Aesop's fable, perhaps).

There is also a second category mistake generated by the New Sociology's critique of Positivism which has significant strategic consequences. I am referring to the different senses of what the radical and mainstream educational theorists mean by philosophy and its familial terms. Where I earlier pointed out that the image of philosophy in the radical philosophizing was largely a matter of social observation and critique, I was concerned generally with problems of communication. Here, though, I am concerned specifically with the possibility that radical critiques have simply given opponents the linguistic capacity to create symbolic confusion. In employing a different understanding of what one assumes in claiming works to be "philosophical," it seems to me that radical critics may have simply given mainstream defenders pathways for sidetracking major issues.

Let me be more specific by way of an example taken from a slightly different academic debate (which seems to me to be outlined by a similar dynamic). As feminist theorists have increasingly taken seriously the notion that knowledge claims can be distorted by one's social position and have pushed this further to advocate "epistemic privilege," they (like the New Sociologists) have rewritten what they take to be epistemological. Where feminist critiques apply a partial, social view of "epistemology," mainstream (masculine) social theorists see a psycho-social phenomenon presented dogmatically as universal "epistemological" truth. By simply using the word "epistemology," such critiques affect a categorical confusion which has mainstream respondents charging the marginalized critics with self-refutation. Often, these debates continue further with the marginalized spokesperson focusing his/her attention on a topic which could have been avoided in the first place—as if the issue of whether "epistemic privilege" should be seen as self-refuting is going to be raised when one empirically contrasts differing accounts of oppressive and violent social phenomenon!

< 132 >

When Audre Lorde says that "the master's tools cannot dismantle the master's house," we could say she is using the master's tools to make that claim; but why would we, when it is clear she is describing the struggle of powerless people to be able to raise their own voices, and speak on their own terms, about the exploitation and oppression they are fighting? But when Giroux charged that the dominant analytical language in education could not adequately address the moral and political questions he sought to raise, and proceeded to do so in what was then an obscure philosophical discourse understood by fewer people (probably) than any other discourse he could have used, he invited those "philosophically"-minded academics to read his words through their own restricted understanding of reality. Without a healthy dose of explanation as to how radical notions of "philosophy" and "epistemology" differ from more mainstream understandings, mainstream respondents are given a means by which to buffer themselves from the main lines of the radical critique.

In making explicit these political questions I cannot help but be cognizant that in many ways these charges depend on what has come before them. From my personal experiences, and from all that I have read about political strategy, I feel keenly sensitive to the need for expressly political struggles to be mindful of time and space. At a time when educational research has only begun to recover from powerful conservative attacks (with Diane Ravitch and Checker Finn having played watchdog over federal research dollars), and at a time when radical voices seem scarcely heard outside of the protected and privileged environment once afforded the Academy, I do not intend to open radical educational researchers to unproductively damaging critique. Nor do I intend to ignore the obvious fact that I would not be able to raise these issues were it not for these past struggles and the space their successes have given me. But, at the same time, I do intend to enter into a critique of radical educational research in the attempt to understand the limits and possibilities of future radical research endeavors. I do want to make clear, though, that I present these criticisms at a specific historical juncture and take their validity to be based only on that specificity and my own strategic estimation of what would be politically useful in the near future.

With these concerns in mind, with the recognition that academic struggles take place within social environments bounded by historically specific dimensions of space-time, I would like to turn to the third analytical section of my reexamination of the critique of Positivism.

SOCIOLOGICAL QUESTIONS

To speak of the conceptual and political arguments of this small body of academics as strategies in a social field, and to place them within dimensions of time and social space, is to approach the debates of the radical sociologies of

< 133 >

school knowledge from a perspective I have woven together from dual partial appropriations of the works of Pierre Bourdieu and, to a lesser extent, Michel Foucault. Though vastly different in many respects, my appropriations of these two thinkers are meant to complement one another. By using the logic of social practice to analyze the sociology of school knowledge as a social field and simultaneously using the logic of discursive regularities to question homologous epistemological arguments, my "sociological" reading of the critique of Positivism simultaneously addresses what more traditional disciplinary boundaries would label the sociological and the philosophical. Such would be true in an analysis built from German Critical Theory as well. But unlike Critical Theory which privileges philosophical rhetoric, my appropriation of French "post-structuralism" privileges the scientific rhetoric of sociology and history. In this analysis, the limits of epistemology are accepted and philosophical or political proclamations are transformed into empirical questions. Admittedly, this use of so-called post-structural analysis is perhaps unique.

The arguments of the critique of Positivism are by now, for many, quite familiar. After all, they have reappeared since the mid-1970s with an astounding regularity in radical sociologies of school knowledge. Where Neo-Marxists, interpretations of curricular texts reject the "empiricism" of traditional educational research, they have aped the notion that science is oppressive and supplanted it with their own qualitative readings of educational ideology. Where post-structural feminist critiques of school knowledge have drawn on feminist theories which pronounce the pedagogic control of phallocentric rationality, they have turned the Critical attack on itself and highlighted the ambiguities and limits of knowledge and social identities. And with every announcement of a need for a new analytical framework, the silhouette of incommensurability and epistemic privilege appears on the frontiers of the theoretical shadow cast. Recent debates among radical curricular scholars seem amazingly similar to those that once formed the lines of communication between the radical and the mainstream in educational research.

My interpretation of these arguments, through my sociological lens, begins with an initial dual rejection of my past interpretations. This dual rejection has been well articulated by Bourdieu (1991b) in his sociological analysis of the philosophy of Martin Heidegger. In Bourdieu's words,

> Any adequate analysis must accommodate a dual refusal, rejecting not only any claims of the philosophical text to absolute autonomy with its concomitant rejection of all external reference, but also any direct reduction of the text to the most general conditions of its production. (p. 2)

My earlier appropriations of analytical philosophical procedures and leftish political strategizing, when isolated, risked ignoring the correspondences and

< 134 >

regularities formed in the reality of their simultaneous existence in a social field.

Hence, where U.S. sociologists of school knowledge argue against the psychologically based quantitative curricular research associated with the dominant traditions of American educational research, my sociological interpretation sees both a series of substantive claims and social strategies to distinguish radical curricular work from its Other. Where positions informed by Critical Theory argued against dichotomous splits (the micro versus macro, the objective versus subjective), and instead relied on their own so-called dialectical understanding, I see both social stances and re-establishment of the hierarchical principles on which status in academic fields are based. Simplistically, if we assume that radical educational scholars perceive themselves to be in a subordinate position within the field of educational research, their stance of attacking the foundations of that field is not surprising. (This does not imply that "mainstream" research is without its rhetorical strategies.)

So where the multiplicities of various radical educational works can be understood and highlighted in a post-structural frame, regularities are also evident. Multiple and fragmented intellectual stances (manifestations of mental structures) can be empirically examined for possible correspondences with partially equivalent social positions (held within a social structure). Through this analysis, by asking how the critique of Positivism constructed a social identity of radical sociologies of school knowledge, I seek to further question whether anything has actually changed in the structural social relations of educational research.

There is an analytical turn taken here that needs to be underscored. While radical sociologists of school knowledge have long attempted to reflectively understand their work in relation to its social function, the focus of this reflection has most often been on social formations in "the society at large." The sacred tripartite "race, gender, and class" has been used by radical scholars to question their work in relation to these larger social differentiations. In educational research this has become most blatantly apparent in the formulation of a so-called "Critical Ethnography," whose relation to ethnography is perhaps more tenuous than its fragile connection to Habermasian Critical Theory, where interpretations of micro-level social interactions are blindly linked to macro-level unequal relations of power. But these analytical gymnastics leap over many other social fields in their attempt to connect the macro and the micro.

There are a few exceptions to this in the sociology of school knowledge. Most notable here are Wexler (1987) and Lather (1991), both of whom have taken the "post-structural turn." Wexler's "social analysis" importantly questions the role of the New Sociology in the intersection of class mobility and the academic field. Lather's reflective analysis of feminist research and pedagogy

< 135 >

centrally questions "emancipatory research" and its legitimacy in academia. Both of these authors inscribe the mid-level social arena of the academy as objects of their analyses. But each of these analyses maintains undue or blind analytical loyalty to their intellectual heritage. Where Wexler's suggested analyses of social identities continues to remain, by and large, framed by the conceptual lens of class, Lather's focus in reflectivity forfeits any hopes of constructing research whose legitimacy would be recognized by anyone other than those who are already converted. Nevertheless these two theorists foreshadow the opening of multiple social fields as objects of sociological analysis.

In this section of my analysis I add another level of correlation between the critique of Positivism and its deployment; what I would call an extra-textual level. This level carries yet another meaning of the term "corollary"— a level of meaning which refers to empirical, social correspondence. In discussing the political strategies of the New Sociology I briefly hinted at some of these corollary connections. There I linked self-isolating trends in the New Sociology's research with the notion of incommensurate paradigms. But there are many more.

Consider, as an example, the New Sociology's appropriations of European social philosophy and critique. For Apple there was the self-declared adherence to a Gramscian cultural Marxism, with multiple references to other English and German Leftists such as Raymond Williams and Jürgen Habermas. For Giroux there was his early, and quite comprehensive, rearticulation of the Frankfurt School Critical Theory. More recent analyses in the field have, as is the case here, turned to the currently faddish French social theory. Reading this literature seems quite like an excursion into the intellectual history of the radical Europeans. Lacan, Barthes, Foucault, Lukács, Arendt, Habermas, Gramsci, Williams, Anderson, Derrida, Perry, Marcuse, Adorno, Horkheimer, Giddens, Merleau-Ponty, Bourdieu, Touraine, Thompson, Poulantzas, Offe, and so on: the list of high culture European intellectuals referenced in radical sociologies of school knowledge has been both remarkably long and conspicuous. At a time when many of these European theorists themselves have turned to the insights of the American Pragmatists, it seems at least odd to find U.S. curricular theorists so heavily reliant on work only a few educational scholars would know. What is it that makes this stance plausible?

Logical Positivism, as found in the Vienna Circle, posited the notion that all knowledge claims could be founded on the philosophical investigation of logic. Today, U.S. undergraduate students of logic are taught that philosophy is a "grounding" discipline, the study of which would aid even the most remote or eccentric academic endeavor. The New Sociology's reliance on "philosophical" critique, however irreverent about disciplinary boundaries, corresponds (or is corollary) to the intellectual disposition which places philosophy at ground

< 136 >

zero. Such a correspondence would not make much sense if we focused only on the self-declarations of alliance with the working class, women, or people of color; few of these groups of people would have any use for, or interest in, such ethereal enterprises. But if we emphasize the degree to which such intellectual alignments carry the potential for turning over a profit in the academy—capitalizing on acquired culture is, in many ways, the name of the academic game—the radical appropriation of philosophic discourse appears somewhat predictable. If one wants to remain in an academic field, after all, there are only limited options open for socially distinguishing oneself as oppositional within an academic field dominated by pedestrian science.

Consider also the New Sociology's emphasis on theorizing. For the New Sociology, theory was a nascent aspect of curricular intellectuals' enterprise which allowed them to question what they saw as a preoccupied push for technocratic answers to moral and political educational problems. In place of traditional educational research's blind application of empty quantitative methodologies, we are often told by radical educational theorists, that there is a "need" for theory, or, as the generations of radical sociologists of school knowledge make their way into the field, a "new" theory. The terms of this conceptual "advancement" are part of the radical educational regime of truth: neo-Marxism, reproduction, resistance, relative autonomy, parallelism, non-synchrony, hegemony, ideology-critique, discourse, production, identity politics, post-Marxism, post-structuralism, postmodernism, post-Positivism, and cultural politics are all common educational banners marking the frontiers of the radical theoretical territory.

There are, in almost every scientific discipline, always a few theorists around. In the natural or physical sciences, theorists of physics, chemistry, and biology often work in tandem with those who manage the laboratories. In the human sciences, it is never too difficult to find the social, or psychological, theorist. In the "applied" disciplines of law, medicine, or education, theorists have always played some role. In many ways, theory is what makes an academic academic. The meaning of theoretical practice, however, is not necessarily consistent across all scientific fields.

In the context of the United States, the relations among the disciplines would most likely differ from those Bourdieu (1988) found in his study of the May 1968 crisis in the French Academy. For example, the strength of atheoretical scientism, so characteristic of American sociology, would imply a relative weakness of the power of theory in the U.S. Academy, compared to France. And the power relations between the humanities and the sciences, or between the "pure" and the applied sciences (such as engineering) remain ambiguous to me. Without empirical research I would hesitate to estimate, for example, the influence of Defense Department funding in buttressing the legitimacy of the "applied" fields—including psychology. Nevertheless, the

< 137 >

tendency for radical scholars toward theory has been readily apparent in many disciplines, including law, literature criticism, sociology, and education.

Further, in the "applied" disciplines there is a perceived added emphasis on reproducing a cadre of future practitioners (one need only look at the sheer numbers of degrees given in the "applied" fields, as compared to the "pure," for empirical substantiation of this perception). Placed between the "pure" sciences (both human and physical) and the practical affairs of humans, caught between the Academy and the State, the applied disciplines have each turned to forms of "objectivity" in the pursuit of an allusive dual legitimation.

It is in the context of these multiple relations among the disciplines that the New Sociology's theoretical inclinations were at least partially formed. Doubly placed in the contexts of the American Academy and in a low prestige "applied" field,[6] radical educational academics and their students have taken a stance, instilled in themselves a disposition, which associates theory with opposition to the educational academic hierarchy. But there is an added profit to be gained from theory.

In the traditional model of scientific progress, theory lies always on the frontier of a field. Producing hypotheses to be tested later, the theorist in the "positivist" sciences is guaranteed a vision of the future. So too is the case for those social revolutionaries who seek to anticipate, and lead-on toward, the approach of a Utopian ideal. For the radical academic, theorizing corresponds to the Marxist impulse to be an intellectual for the Vanguard. And so, as their use of philosophic discourse relied on the positivistic placement of philosophy as a grounding discipline, the New Sociology's use of theory cashed in on the positivistic placement of theory in the future.

From these two maneuvers, I would point to an emerging pattern. In its use of philosophy and theory, RSSK has employed the very hierarchical relations of power within the academy and science that Positivism has celebrated. On the one hand, as Logical Positivism held philosophy and logic at the pinnacle of legitimated academic disciplines, the New Sociology cast its critique of Positivism within a highly philosophical discourse, and thereby invested itself with the academic capital associated with the "grounding" discipline. On the other hand, as "positivistic" images hold Theory at the cutting edge of scientific disciplines, the New Sociology has consistently employed theoretical discourse as a major mechanism for opening academic space.

There are, of course, added contingencies that make the reliance on philosophy and theory readily sensible. Here I should note that the simple question of who gets funding in the political economy of research adds a dimension of understanding to considering why radical educational scholars have simultaneously employed dispositions of the Positivism they attacked. Large-scale quantitative sociology is simply much more expensive than theorizing or small-scale, individual-researcher qualitative research. In the context of

< 138 >

a discipline in which the teaching demands of university employment are considerable, simply having the time and money to do other forms of research is not a reality. There seems little reason to believe that any revolutionary research would find a benefactor in the American landscape of ameliorative progress.

I would like to consider one more way in which the critique of Positivism maintained the hierarchical relations Positivism would advocate in educational research. Consider here the dialectical unification of theory and practice so revered in the radical deployment of the language of *praxis*. While often chastised for not making clear its "prescription" for educational practice, the New Sociology has repeatedly maintained that the notion of *praxis* implies a consistency between one's "democratic" politics and one's theory (see Giroux, 1981a; McNeil, 1981). In this regard, some of the New Sociologists, such as Giroux, have warned against detailed prescription and offered only the assurance that in a communal critical reflection, radical teachers would be able to develop their own practice (Giroux, 1981a, p. 219).

At the same time, the New Sociologists have spoken of new paradigms of research and new forms of creating legitimate knowledge, and have criticized those who do not follow the rules the radical theory dictates. And radical educational scholarship hasn't exactly been remiss in its attempt to generally define what some positive educational practice might look like (e.g., Apple, 1986b). Of this I would only point out that it seems odd, even ironic, that perhaps the most uniquely positivistic feature of Comtean social theory, the presupposition that social theorizing and research could make positive claims about how society ought to change, is precisely the goal sought in that educational theory which partially owes its identity to its rejection of "Positivism."

When viewed sociologically, these philosophic maneuvers highlight principles of legitimation within a social field. From this perspective we can see that the radical sociologies of school knowledge follow some of the same principles of legitimation as the culture of Positivism they critique. Rather than damning radical scholars for inconsistency, though, their stances can be seen to correspond to their position within the larger fields of the American Academy and its partial subset, educational research. Where, from a philosophical critique, I questioned the radical proclivity for constructing their arguments in "epistemological" language, here I can understand this as a pragmatic recognition of the currency of philosophic capital in the field. And where I politically questioned the self-isolation of radical educational scholars, here I can sociologically understand over-specialization as a mechanism of self-maintenance and identity formation within a Modernist institution that has yet to yield the missionary trappings of its feudal heritage. The cultivation of a relatively private conceptual language, and the acts of consecration which accompany entrance into all

< 139 >

academic fields, are no less a reality for "politically correct" radical educational scholars than they are for any other discipline.

Within these institutional level observations, the individual daily practices of radical sociologists of education also reveal homologous correspondences to the regimes of academic truth. As Jennifer Gore (1992) has disclosed in her Foucauldian critique of radical and feminist pedagogy (which are philosophically, politically and sociologically very close relatives of RSSK), the self-discipline and stylizing of the radical curricular theorist displays his dual positions as a radical-scholar. Here, on the level of individual practice, the most minute acts signify one's home in social structures.

Bringing the analysis to such a minute, almost microscopic frame (sociologically speaking) raises a fair, general question: "so what?" More specifically, this retort can be translated into multiple responses: So what if the critique of Positivism relied on the principles of hierarchization it criticized? So what if the social strategies of radical sociologists of school knowledge partially conform to those of the Academy? So what if the daily practices of these radicals reveal their ambiguous and multiple social positions? Indeed, so what?

CONCLUSION

I raise the skeptical rhetorical questions to my sociological observations not only out of some intellectual game intended to mimic the open-mindedness of dialogue and critique. These observations are my own, true enough; but so are the skeptical retorts. With this in mind, I would like to offer my general response to these questions and to attempt drawing conclusions from my analysis of the critique of Positivism. As part of this conclusion I shall also articulate, as best I can, why the sociological observations just presented outline an analytical view which can frame a response to my overriding intent of strengthening the persuasiveness of RSSK.

Jürgen Habermas (1981) argues that within every communicative act there are certain background presuppositions which form the basis of a mutually shared life-world. To enter into an ideal-speech situation, says Habermas, we must first presume that the other participant(s) speak with intelligibility, truth, sincerity, and non-coercion. Although Habermas's arguments have been soundly criticized for a perceived overemphasis on the "ideal," his focus on the basis of communication, and his proposed linkage between communication and non-dominating social formations (a position shared with Dewey) serve as a reminder that my general concern about the lack of communication between RSSK and mainstream educational research takes place within its own background cultural horizon.

In Bourdieu's (1977c) framework, these considerations can be understood as recognizing the unspoken assumptions of a field, the *doxa* of American educational research. Again, given the space within which the

< 140 >

radical educational critique of Positivism was constructed, that that critique capitalized on the principles of legitimation it questioned seems only sensible. Here, Marx's reminder, that humans make their own history but the history upon which they build is not of their own making, suggests to me that when radical sociologists of school knowledge proclaim the defeat of Positivism, they have lost sight of their history.

In reexamining the radical educational critique of Positivism I have attempted to raise a number of skeptical questions. I have questioned the persuasive utility and philosophic validity of some of the radical philosophic positions (namely epistemic privilege, the view that science is inherently oppressive, and the notion of incommensurability). I have also questioned the wisdom of unifying political strategies (in which the radical critique potentially weakened itself and strengthened its opponent). However, in reframing both of those analyses within a sociological frame, rejecting the dichotomy I had imposed on the "object" of my study, it may seem that I have also radically relativized both the "original" critique of Positivism and my own critique of the critique. In some ways this perception is correct, and I intend to examine the consequences of such a relativism in the final two chapters; but, for now, by way of a conclusion, I would like briefly to make explicit some of the assumptions implicit in my analyses (some of which are quite nonrelative).

In describing the different analytical frameworks educational philosophers bring to their arguments, I simultaneously attempted to deploy a language understandable for both the radical and mainstream educational theorists. If there was success in that endeavor, it would be due to the degree to which my description adequately matched the presuppositions of either side. Commensurability was implied in my attempt. In pointing to the social basis for a defense of epistemic privilege, I shifted the *telos* of philosophic inquiry away from pursuits of transhistorical, universal truths. A pragmatic unity of knowledge and human inquiry was implied in that move. And in suggesting that the question of whether science is oppressive depends on the social conditions of its enactment, I relied on a commitment to the potential for science to work in emancipatory ways.

In questioning the political strategies of the critique of Positivism, there was obviously a very simple assumption being made: i.e., some strategies work better than others (relative to specific historical junctures). But there was a less apparent assumption made in distinguishing between two kinds of mainstream educational research. Roughly put, I suggested that some so-called positivistic research was done well (by the slowly changing standards of science), but other mainstream research was not. This implies a non-relative image of "good" research. I shall return to this image in the next chapter and there attempt to more fully present an outline of it, but it was always already implicit in my impending turn to the sociological.

< 141 >

To suggest that social actions can be examined sociologically is to suggest that there is at least an intersubjective reality, a cultural playing field if you will, on which those actions are played out. By outlining what might be some of the principles of legitimation structuring educational research in the United States (both radical and mainstream), by suggesting that the social strategies of radical sociologists of school knowledge partially conform to the history they have inherited as academics, and by minutely describing the daily acts which correspond to the social positions of radical educational scholars, I have employed an analysis which makes visible the multiple layers of the conditions of my work. In response to the skeptical "so what?" I call on a position articulated nicely by Bourdieu.

Recognizing that political struggles of educational research are not simply a matter of persuading free, disinterested, rational actors in Rawls's (1971) "original position," there still is a shared basis of those struggles. If the critique of Positivism was correct in suggesting that science is dominant in educational research (and the sociological framework I employed would help answer this question), then the New Sociology's response to that culturally contingent fact did not match its proclaimed goal of transforming that field. Bourdieu (1990a) points out,

> Truth is the stake in a series of struggles of every field. The scientific field . . . has this peculiarity: you have a chance of success in it only if you conform to the immanent laws of the field, that is, if you recognize truth practically as a *value* and respect the methodological principles and canons defining *rationality* at the moment under consideration, at the same time as bringing into battle in the competitive struggles all the specific instruments that have been accumulated in the course of prior struggles. The scientific field is a game in which you have to arm yourself with reason in order to win. (p. 32)

To the extent that RSSK has met with some success corresponds, I'd suggest, to the extent they have conformed to the principles of legitimation they critique.

The moral and political question I implicitly raised in this chapter is whether or not radical sociology of school knowledge has an interest in pursuing further success in its scientific space. Without a definitive answer to this question, and with a commitment to not answer it, I shall attempt instead to synthetically analyze what that pursuit would take.

< 142 >

six

Wherein Lies the Scientific Rhetoric?

WHEN SPEAKING ABOUT STRUGGLES OVER TRUTH Bourdieu has repeatedly employed war metaphors (Bourdieu, 1981, 1991a). And, almost certainly, these metaphors would not be readily accepted by many radical educational thinkers who take offense at anything resembling war or violence. But aside from the connotations of Bourdieu's descriptions of the struggles which continually take place between intellectuals (both within and outside those institutions commonly recognized as the Academy), there lies a recognition that not only are claims to knowledge and truth rarely uncontested within scientific fields, but that specifically scientific struggles are sociologically conducted through that historical construction called "reason."

For me, the intellectual consequences of this position for RSSK is as radically profound as they are obvious. To recognize scientific reason as a historical construction, and to recognize knowledge claims as a central capital over which intellectuals compete, is to impose an epistemological break from philosophy. Reenacting the centuries-old confrontation between science and philosophy, in this chapter, as one way to further assess the discourse in RSSK, I attempt to describe on what ground radical sociologies of school knowledge engage in specifically scientific struggles.

Historically, it is probably no surprise that I raise this question here. At a time when intellectual debates question the end of philosophy, virtue, and Foucault, at a time when sociological theory contemplates giving up its scientific foundation, in short, at a time when the very notion of a "foundation" raises hair on the back of many academic necks, my question addresses, on a micro-level, issues that have been reverberating through the Academy for quite some time.

In this context I cannot claim to have constructed an original approach to this task. There are many points of departure from which I have begun to address this question, some of which have not been brought to bear on RSSK. But it is in this sense, as I specifically question the scientific authority of RSSK through my sociological lens, that I take my contribution to RSSK as unique.

Because this analysis specifically examines the discourses in RSSK as science, and because of the historical conflation of Positivism and science in RSSK, I initiate this sociological reading from a point of departure chosen to emphasize its own understanding of science. That is, I begin this analysis by viewing science as a form of rhetoric. To question the modes of rhetoric in the discourses of RSSK, I then present a distinction between two forms of rhetoric: what I heuristically call a philosophic rhetoric of demonstration and a scientific rhetoric of evidence. Chosen to emphasize the ways in which these discourses have tended to rely mostly on philosophic discourse, and to question the structure of authority in their rhetorical mode, this distinction is admittedly and intentionally polemic.

Placing these discourses, once again, within a sociological reading, I then analyze how radical sociologies of school knowledge have disregarded or failed to meet three basic methodological canons of educational science: falsifiability, generalizability, and validity.[1] (This does not imply that mainstream educational research has met these canons either.) Taking these canons not as some set of methodological norms by which truth is revealed, but as socially legitimating principles, I shall be implicitly arguing that accepting these canons does not necessarily imply committing the sins of Positivism. To make this argument more explicit I conclude this chapter by distinguishing my sociological understanding of science from more philosophical arguments and close with one last observation about RSSK.

SCIENCE AS ONE RHETORIC (AMONG MANY)

To begin, I would like to recognize the limits of my scientific agenda. In the previous chapter I metaphorically suggested that we can understand the claims of the New Sociology as rhetoric, or modes of persuasion. Given my concern for understanding how the different discourses in educational research communicate and persuade one another, this metaphor is perhaps of apparent utility. But this perspective on science is not only mine. The notion that scientific discourse is a form of rhetoric has origins in many disciplines, one of which is the study of rhetoric itself, and has been suggested partially as one way of relating competing knowledge claims.

For example, in an analysis of what it means to treat knowledge claims as forms of rhetoric, Michael Calvin McGee and John R. Lyne begin by echoing similar remarks on Positivism's critics to those I employed earlier (McGee and Lyne, 1987). In a section of their essay subtitled "The difficulty of being positive," McGee and Lyne recall the importation and influence of a general "academic positivism" which saw the transformation of politics into political science and moral philosophy into social science. They also note that Positivism was initially intended to unite all forms of knowledge claims and provide certainty—but that these hopes were never accomplished. The continued existence of Positivism, according to McGee and Lyne, has been largely (though not entirely) as an epithet created by its opponents. Commenting on the shift toward a scientific academy, they suggest,

> This state of affairs alarmed those academics whose work could not be scientific—artists, literati, rhetoricians, metaphysicians, and most historians. Nervous pliants from such quarters helped mask the fact that the rhetoric of the positivist movement never quite produced the projected unity. Positivism was kept alive more in the minds of opponents than in the daily practice of scientists, becoming in the end more epithet than signifier, more the ghost of horrified imaginations than a coherent body of thought ... [And] ... This is not to say that positivism was entirely the child of threatened imaginations. Rather, it simply did not exist as a unique and coherent philosophical position after the breakup of the Vienna Circle. (p. 383)

According to McGee and Lyne, the major influence of Positivism has not been as a philosophical position, but as "an attitude toward the ideal relationship of the fields of knowledge," an attitude they term "scientism" (p. 383). What these authors describe as scientism seems virtually the same as Giroux's culture of Positivism. To convey this similarity, their description is worth quoting at length:

> The story of scientism is at once cold, calculating, and romantic. The greatest miseries of humanity have been caused by irrational belief in magic, religion, and other intellectually indefensible rubbish. Reason, understood as virtually equivalent to scientific method, can save humanity. Science is universal in the sense that the logic of its inquiry is the same in any domain where knowledge is possible. The universal objective of inquiry is explanation and prediction. An event is explained by showing that it occurred as the result of laws, rules, conditions, and so makes prediction possible. Inquiry is "value-free" or "value-neutral"; it strives to be as objective as possible, showing how to change circumstances to produce results, but never recommending that one particular policy be selected. *Scientists* may offer value judgments, but *science* is mute on the problem of decision, for no "ought" claim can be derived from knowledge of facts. No claim will be acknowledged as fact until is has been verified by

observation, and no proposition will be treated seriously even in theory unless it is possible to envision the conditions of its verification. (p. 383)

McGee and Lyne argue further that recognition of the failure of scientism, the failure to provide a unified basis for deciding between competing knowledge claims, has lead many academics toward rhetoric and the rhetoric of inquiry.

To find such a description of the current state of academic affairs that is so similar to those found in my own field is somewhat comforting. Even if the New Sociology's critique of Positivism didn't radically undermine main-stream educational science, it seems the New Sociology may have been on to something. But McGee and Lyne offer a much different cure for the ills of the academy than do any of the current discourses in RSSK.

Outlining four possible "routes" toward rhetoric, McGee and Lyne propose, of course, their final option: a path in which rhetoric is taken as a means to adjudicate or negotiate between competing knowledge claims—when competition results from exigencies in academic communities "as part of the natural evolutionary process of science," in response to interfield or interdisciplinary competition for material resources of knowledge production, or simply as the consequence of interfield debates among those who study the same thing, or as a result of having experts comment or give advice in the public interest (p. 385–87). These authors continue at length to defend their choice of route and to argue for understanding rhetoric as a means of negotiating between knowledge claims—not as a means of unifying knowledge claims.

Whatever managerial role McGee and Lyne propose for rhetoric as a discipline is pragmatically not of import to my agenda; but their position on science is of most concern to me. According to them, this mode of rhetoric is not opposed to science, but rather sees scientific inquiry as one type of rhetoric. In their own words,

> We prefer this last route to rhetoric of inquiry because it exposes and features a dialectical tension that is only implicit elsewhere. Other arguments lose the issue because they make it appear that rhetoric is setting itself against the rigor and reliability of a practice that results in the largesse of technology. Rhetoric in fact values scientific discourse, if only because the scientific method is a powerful and persuasive form of argument. But it is neither the only nor the most persuasive in all situations (p. 389).

Of course, for those more familiar with science, the notion that there is a "natural evolution" of science or that there is such a thing as "the scientific method," may seem troubling. However the dialectic tension McGee and Lyne see in their proposal nicely captures, for me, the social chasm that seems to lie between RSSK and mainstream educational research. As they explain,

> The dialectic that undergirds the turn to rhetoric in contemporary letters lies in an opposition between passionate and prejudiced social reason (traditionally associated with the rhetoric of the marketplace and forum) and the antirhetoric of cool, comfortably neutral technical reason (associated in the public mind with computing machines and sterile laboratories). (p. 389)

Where McGee and Lyne are concerned with largely analytical categories in this depiction (even as they speak of socially associated meanings), my concern is more context specific. Given that it is possible to recognize science as one form of rhetoric, and not a means for unifying knowledge, what kind of rhetoric has been employed in RSSK?

RHETORICAL TENDENCIES IN THE FIELD

Earlier, in Chapter Five, I introduced a distinction between the two conceptions of philosophic discourse—that associated with (mainstream) analytical educational philosophy and that associated with radical social critique. On the one hand, analytical philosophy is largely restricted to deductive introspection. In this form of philosophic discourse, beginning from stated premises, arguments are largely constructed within the limits of logical coherence and deductive reasoning, building toward a conclusion. On the other hand, radical social critique builds its premises and arguments from a continual dialogue with empirical (social) observation. In this latter form of philosophic discourse, observations of the social world are explicitly conducted through theoretical interpretation.

Here I would like to reconsider these forms of philosophic discourse through a more stark distinction drawn between what I call the philosophical rhetoric of demonstration and the scientific rhetoric of evidence. The difference between these two modes of persuasion can be understood readily through a visualist analogy.

Imagine the intellectual in the place of the clergy, presenting a view or image of the world from the elevated pulpit. Speaking out over the masses, this philosophical rhetorician proceeds to critique the world outside the halls of the church. His sermon is lengthy and full of references to the evils of external secular life—the life where contact must be made with the non-initiates.

The mode of presentation in these sermons is of course connected with the spatial geography of the church's habitat, but it is the mode of discussion which is of concern here. Presenting "the vision" held of the outside world (through allegory, reason, and appeal to supposedly shared subjective experiences), this intellectual for the masses attempts to persuade his audience that His is the real Truth. As my label suggests, this rhetoric relies heavily on philosophical, a priori, analytical demonstration. External references are made, but the basis of persuasion lies in the eloquence of the presentation—in the artistic, poetic construction of reality. (Justice and equality are often banners of the ultimate appeal.) In a sense, in the extreme form, this rhetoric is hermetically sealed, enclosed. Connection with its message can only be made through a leap of faith, a will to truth.

On the other hand, the promise of science potentially lies in its differing rhetorical mode. In contrast to my Church analogy, I think an alternative image can be found in the court room—the secular home of truths. Here persuasion does not wholly rely on demonstration. Here an appeal must be made to evidence. Here the model is not of a sermon, nor even a dialogue between two parties. A mutually accepted (socially constructed) view of evidence, acting as a third party arbiter, is the result of a process of triangulated communication. Questions left unresolved in the abyss of incommensurate knowledge claims can be mutually opened to possibilities of empirical matters.

To me, the most significant difference between the philosophical rhetoric of demonstration and the scientific rhetoric of evidence lies in the way in which each rhetorical mode constructs authority. In the philosophical rhetoric of demonstration, authority lies in the positions of the author, the speaker; whereas, in the scientific rhetoric of evidence authority is dispersed— if "evidence" is explicitly (and partially) framed and deconstructed. (In a court room, the explicit framing of evidence is manifested by the role of purposely prejudiced contending legal representatives—the lawyers.)

In drawing this more stark distinction between philosophic and scientific rhetorical modes, and reconsidering the rhetoric of RSSK, something of an irony appears. Where before I suggested that the philosophical claims of the New Sociology relied heavily on empirical observation, here I would argue that even though this reliance is obvious, within the discourses of RSSK appeals to socially recognizable "evidence" are rather limited. Given this, it seems to me that where the New Sociology imported an alternative view of philosophy in the endeavor to critique empirical social phenomena, its rhetoric has remained a philosophic rhetoric of demonstration. I am not suggesting that empirical observations are not made in these discourses, but I am questioning the degree to which radical sociologies have presented observations in a form their Others might recognize as "evidence" supporting the claims they make.

This charge may seem to recapitulate Liston's criticism that Marxist educational theorists have not empirically verified their claims. But I raise this criticism in the context of viewing science as a form of rhetoric to emphasize the difference I see between Liston's concern and my own. Unlike Liston, I am not calling on a "realist epistemology." Rather, by focusing on the rhetoric of RSSK I would simply reframe Liston's critique as evidence of my claim that the discourses in RSSK have failed to present empirical observations which are socially recognized as "evidence" by their Others. Even with his explicit political sympathy for Marxist theory, Liston doesn't see evidential support in the Marxist educational discourse.

< 148 >

There is of course a very important issue raised here. Given that radical sociologies of school knowledge do make social observations, the question at hand is what counts as evidence for the theoretical claims being made by these discourses. With this issue in mind, the historical struggle of ethnography and qualitative methodologies to gain acceptance in U.S. educational research stands as one reminder that within the "larger" field there are continually struggles over what counts as evidence. Of course, these methodological battles continue with, for example, Lather's arguments for recognizing "catalytic validity." Such struggles can be seen as successful redefinitions of what counts as evidence. But the question then becomes, for me, if these new methodologies are presenting evidence that counts, for whom does it count?

Since my concern here is with the persuasiveness of radical sociologies of school knowledge, and since I wish to further support my claim that the discourses in RSSK have not employed a socially recognizable scientific rhetoric of evidence, I turn now to an analysis that begins from something of a different point of departure and attempt to show the ways in which mainstream educational research canons can deny the radical discourses of RSSK's scientific authority.

BEING READ THROUGH CANONS NOT OF ONE'S CHOICE

Before beginning this analysis, I should justify its strategy. Here I shall be following Bourdieu's notion that within scientific fields, relatively stable canons of methodology form the doxa and orthodoxy which regulate what gets consecrated as scientific capital. In this view, the scientific field is not at all a level playing field, but it is a field of unequal power relations in which legitimating principles function to the advantage of those in "higher" relative positions of power. If this view is correct, and if the traditional methodological canons of educational research serve the interest of mainstream researchers, then viewing radical research through mainstream canons ought to tell us something about the persuasive capacity of that research within the mainstream. In effect, when I suggest that the rhetoric of RSSK has not been a scientific rhetoric, I am presuming that it is mainstream orthodoxy/doxa which has defined what counts as scientific. Thus, I take what follows not only as evidence for the tendency toward philosophical rhetoric, but also as further evidence for my claim that radical sociologies of school knowledge have not been that persuasive to the mainstream.

Unfortunately for these radical discourses, being identified as holding only limited scientific capital can be done in rather short order with only three conventional criteria for educational science: falsifiability, generalizability, validity. Below, I'll consider each of these criteria in turn, giving a brief outline of what each means (here) and then screening the discursive strands in RSSK to see if each criterion is met.

Roughly put, the Popperian notion of falsifiability is intended to delimit the kinds of claims which can be scientifically tested. The basic idea here is pretty simple. Because science is supposed to build on past empirical inaccuracies, there has to be some way in which theoretical claims can be said to be inaccurate (Popper, 1968, pp. 40–42). In other words, there at least has to be the possibility of showing a theory to be wrong.

In Chapter Two I have already argued that with its cultural turn to recognizing resistance and human agencies which oppose the hegemonic control of Capital, the Structural Neo-Marxist discourses in RSSK, particularly the ever expansive Parallelist Position, have virtually guaranteed that whatever is observed relative to the functioning of hegemony will confirm their theories. Similarly, by basing their theoretical construction on the notion of "contradictions," Carnoy and Levin, Ginsburg, and Aronowitz and Giroux also have proposed theories which defy this scientific tenet. Unfortunately, when structural feminists argue that Patriarchy functions in contradictory ways, they too fall on the non-scientific side of Popper's dichotomy. Likewise, when each of the post-structural variants begin to speak of multiple and contradictory subjectivities, they have moved beyond the realm of falsifiability.

Hence, on the level of broad societal claims (in the case of the structural arguments), or in terms of their "basic" claims about subjectivities (for the post-structural variants), none of the theoretical discourses of RSSK meet the falsifiability criterion. Of course, these kinds of arguments are only some of the claims advanced in the radical discourses. However, on another level, many more detailed or context-specific claims have been proposed within each of the discourses of RSSK.

For example, among the Structural Neo-Marxist arsenal is the claim that teachers have been de-skilled. Structural feminists suggest that the distribution of school knowledge within classrooms is such that young women and girls are not taken seriously, academically speaking. Post-structurally, Wexler argues that the micro-economy of self-production will define everyday educational processes, and Ellsworth has suggested that the rationalism of critical pedagogy marginalized and silenced students in her class. Each of these claims, I suggest, could be drafted in a way which would make them susceptible to the falsifiability criterion. That is, I think it is possible to imagine studies by which these claims potentially could be shown to be wrong. But have reasons or evidence been given to suggest that such phenomena occur across many social contexts? I think not.

Here the conventional notion of generalizability presents some serious problems for the research in RSSK. As conventional research wisdom would have it, the qualitative or interpretive evidence upon which these claims have been largely substantiated does not suffice for believing that these phenomena are generally true. This isn't to say they are not generally true, but that evidence hasn't been forthcoming to show that they are. In fact, unfortunately, the basic tenet of conventional ethnography suggesting that all things are context specific works directly against generalizing.

Where Apple largely bases his claim about de-skilling on an interpretive analysis of one science curricular package and one qualitative study, to my knowledge there have been no studies done in multiple contexts to show that the technologies Apple sees as de-skilling are in fact de-skilling large numbers of teachers. (Of course Apple also has the further historical problem of showing that teachers actually once had the skills he says they have lost.) Kelly and Nihlen have already suggested that there is a need for data to support the qualitative insight that, within classrooms, school knowledge is differentially distributed along gender lines. (Between classroom school knowledge differentiation according to gender, of course, has been substantially documented.) While Wexler has offered some qualitative evidence for his claim, there is no evidence beyond his own. And while Ellsworth's interpretation of her classroom's use of critical pedagogy may be true, the generalizing force of her arguments depends on her theoretical assertions about the historical relationship between rationalism and its creation: Others.

Each of these arguments, I think, is based on strong analytical claims. Furthermore, there is reason to believe each of them may be true across many contexts, in many classrooms; but from the evidence presented by the field to date, I do not think it would be safe to assert any of these things are generally the case (although, based on my own observations, I do think Kelly and Nihlen's claim is a relatively safe bet). Here the field's heavy reliance on qualitative evidence, which has been so fruitful in further developing more detailed and nuanced theoretical claims, becomes seriously restrictive. Without evidence gathered (constructed) from within multiple classrooms, none of these claims stands a chance of meeting the conventional criterion of generalizable substantiation.

This leaves, I think, the more general concern about these theories' validity. While there are many types of validity about which mainstream educational researchers worry (construct validity, internal validity, face validity, etc.), the general issue of validity concerns the very simple question of whether or not radical sociologies of school knowledge have presented interpretations of data that mainstream researchers are likely to see as valid representations of what actually goes on in schools. Lather (1991) has discussed the problems raised when one theoretically maintains that individuals can be seen as holding a false consciousness (pp. 67–68). As Lather suggests, claims about false consciousness need significant justifications for privileging the theorist's interpretations of social actions over those of the people being researched.

But beyond this one theoretical notion, there is yet another more general problem for the field; namely, as radical theories, these discourses are presenting general arguments most people are not exactly going to readily accept as valid. In Chapter Two, I pointed out how Hargreaves (1982) questioned Anyon's interpretations of behaviors she took to be "resistance." Conventional ethnographic wisdom suggests that multiple interpretations of data need to be generated and analyzed, through a process of ruling out those interpretations that only marginally "fit" the data. Since each of the discourses of RSSK has advanced a "new" theoretical perspective, and since only Lather has presented possible interpretations which were ruled out, the data presented in these discourses is almost all only that which fits the interpretation each theory advances. For mainstream researchers who aren't exactly amenable to these interpretations in the first place, there has been no methodological defense given for the claims advanced in these discourses (Erikson, 1990, pp. 136–38, 152–62).

Overall, this brief analysis suggests, I think, that when viewed through the philosophical-scientific dualism I imposed above, the rhetorical mode of radical sociologies of school knowledge is clearly not recognizable by mainstream educational research as scientific. Such conventional methodological charges could be expected from a "positivist," of course; but they also suggest, I think, a crucial political point that many radical sociologists of education have missed.

The missing element in these discourses, I think, is an acceptance of the need to construct defensible evidence. Armed with the view that evidence is not innocent and always created out of particular world-views, these radical intellectual clergy have come to an immensely arrogant conclusion: that it is up to them to mold evidence. The view in these discourses, I think, is that since evidence is not innocent, and since we know research works in particular interests, it is in the (our) masses' interest to have our evidence molded to the reality we see.

But socially recognizable evidence is rarely presented. This style of rhetoric erases the possibility of having the audience view the evidence themselves—"directly?" (knowing that it is not innocent). If presented in/through the scientific rhetoric of evidence, however, it would be possible to appeal to evidence as a third party arbiter. It is this appeal that I take to be restricted within the sociologies of school knowledge.

ON THE LIMITS OF THE FIELD'S
SOCIALLY RECOGNIZABLE EVIDENCE

I do not mean to dismiss the issue of what ought to count as evidence here. This is, of course, a central concern when making arguments about a lack of presenting evidence. However, I think one could argue that while the radical discourses have entered into the debate of what counts as evidence, making the issue problematic or unsettled, they also have filtered what little evidence they presented through a theoretical framework few would be willing to accept prior to empirical persuasion. By arguing that a scientific discourse appeals to "evidence," I am simultaneously arguing that its evidence is socially recognized as evidence.

Nor do I mean to suggest that the radical sociologies of school knowledge have presented no data which can be commonly recognized as evidence. While I think this is generally the case, there are exceptions. But even these exceptions have their rhetorical limits. For example, in his *Teachers and Texts*, Apple (1986b) presents a political economic analysis of textbook publishing which incorporates quite a few standard statistical measures of the textbook industry. There we find Apple citing measures of the textbook industry's profits and income, and proportional measures of how much of the market is made up by individual States (pp. 81–105). In all, Apple employs these data to begin an analysis of the production-consumption circuit of school knowledge. However, even with this analysis, Apple himself recognizes the limits of his research. As he puts it,

> This points to a significant empirical agenda as well. What is required now is a long-term and theoretically and politically grounded ethnographic investigation that follows a curriculum artifact such as a textbook from its writing to its selling (and then to its use.) Only then will we have a more accurate portrayal of the complete circuit of cultural production, circulation, and consumption. (p. 104)

As much as I applaud Apple's recognition of the empirical limits of his analysis, his proposed research agenda still seems to me limited. Assuming that a "theoretically and politically grounded ethnographic" study would generate claims mainstream educational research would take to be valid (a big assumption I think),[2] and assuming that this study does construct "a more accurate portrayal of the complete circuit of cultural production, circulation, and consumption," what would a portrayal of *one* artifact have to say about an entire national industry? Once again, such an agenda would continue radical sociology of school knowledge's tenuous treatment of the generalizability issue.[3]

Another problem arises when it is recognized that radical *historical* analyses of teaching also provide recognizable empirical support for their claims. To take Apple as an example again, consider his historical argument that teaching has been constructed within the patriarchal hegemonic definitions of "women's work." To support this claim Apple has, among many other sources of data, presented the text of a teacher's contract from 1923 (Apple, 1986b, pp. 73–74). This contract explicitly restricts women's private behaviors, and I think lends credence to Apple's overall arguments. But as a *historical* analysis, such research will continually face the question, how do we know this is still relevant in schools today? In the United States, after all, exploring frontiers has often meant leaving history behind us (both literally and metaphorically), and teacher

< 153 >

contracts do not look the same as they used to. This means such arguments are in the position of having to persuade readers that even after relatively visible social movements have asserted themselves and been publicly associated with some social change (such as the women's movement over the past two decades in the United States), these kinds of historical critiques still carry contemporary validity. While historically minded researchers may find such analyses persuasive, I suspect many don't. As historical analyses, the data presented in such research do not necessarily provide evidence of what is happening now.

Given that there continue to be strong debates over what constitutes acceptable evidence in U.S. educational research (Eisner and Peshkin, 1991), and given that many radical educational researchers are centrally located in these debates, it may seem odd that I have attempted to apply standards of evidence which these radical discourses reject. Below I would like to justify this strategy. Roughly speaking I will explain how understanding science as a specific form of rhetoric within a social field can justify the use of traditional canons of science without accepting, nor expecting, any settlement on the philosophical foundations of science.

ON SOCIALLY RECOGNIZABLE EVIDENCE AS A (NON-STANDARDIZED) STANDARD

The argument that socially recognizable evidence can serve as a third party arbiter, and hence both reinforce the persuasive capacity of a discourse and open up the lines of authority established in a rhetoric, may seem to be a very dangerous argument. Since I know of no other authority on which I can build specific justifications for this idea, I suppose I must assume responsibility for this claim. But I have not come to this position out of a vacuum, and I do have some preliminary, general thoughts on its defense. This defense I offer as one point of departure for constructing a methodology for RSSK.

As a preliminary specification, I would like first of all to make explicit that I take this claim as a tactical stance within a field (in a particular socio-temporal context) I see as having drifted too far toward politically vanguardist and sociologically irrelevant theorizing.

If I can at all predict reactions of those in RSSK based on my sociology of it, I would expect two types of responses. From readers of Critical Theory, and subsequent secondary attacks on "empirical/analytical" inquiry, this argument might be seen as a reinstallation of the heartless technical rationality and blind empiricism associated with Positivism. For believers in an identifiable external reality, this probably would be seen as equating "truth" with the conventional whims of a social community. Unfortunately for both of these readings, readings which I take to be misguided by the overly philosophic dispositions of RSSK, I think the sociology of knowledge has provided ample evidence that such concerns are socio-historically incorrect.

< 154 >

Self-named educational critical theorists who link an epistemological cognitive interest of control with science (as one form of "instrumental action") might argue that constructing socially recognizable evidence within contemporary U.S. educational research would mean generating empirical/analytical knowledge that is less open to human understanding than hermeneutic discourse (a strange claim for anyone who recalls coming to hermeneutics for the first time). Aside from the philosophic critiques of the Habermasian distinction on which this claim would be based, there is for me a more compelling reason to reject this view. That is, sociological studies of science have shown that scientific practice is not based on instrumental action. As Karin Knorr-Cetina (1981) has argued, based on her study of scientific laboratories,

> Through the notion of instrumental action, Habermas establishes a link between the fundamental nature of his technical interest and actual scientific practice: surely we would expect a form of action to somehow manifest itself in the scientist's dealings with nature as observed in the laboratory. However, when we actually look at the laboratory, we find none of the monologic, presuppositionless (with respect to the meaning of signs) and formally rational behaviour Habermas postulates for science. (p. 143)

While I hesitate to join Knorr-Cetina in suggesting that Habermas would cause us to expect actual scientific practices to match his analytical distinctions, her work does poignantly remind me of the dangers involved in presuming that analytical arguments generated in epistemological studies have some sort of direct connection with social practice as it is actually lived. Moreover, I think this is a fair warning for those radical educational theorists who continue to transform analytically created distinctions into categories of social practice.

From an opposing philosophical pole, radical educational theorists who believe that "reality" is some sort of "fundamental source of control over the arbitrariness of belief" might suggest that in emphasizing the need to create "socially recognizable" evidence I have opened the door to scientific anarchism or epistemological relativism. My rejections of this view are two: 1) if the epistemological foundations of such a realist view are sound, and if evidence in some way is controlled or constrained by reality, then I see no reason to worry that whatever gets socially recognized as evidence would stray from "reality;" and 2) if the realist epistemology is wrong, then I see no other option than a socially recognizable base for distinguishing what counts as evidence. As with my rejection of the Habermasian fret, I would simply point out that the sociology of knowledge, as well as the history and sociology of science, have offered ample evidence that what counts as evidence has always been a function of what is socially recognized as such. If such criteria

< 155 >

leads to arguments and debate about what constitutes evidence, all the better. *Vive Le Crise!* (Bourdieu, 1988b).

This is not to say that there has been no debate about methodological concerns about how one constructs evidence in which radical sociologists of education have taken part. For example, Roman and Apple's article, "Is Naturalism a Move Away from Positivism" (Roman and Apple, 1990), was presented as part of a debate about objectivity and subjectivity in qualitative inquiry. But the issues raised in such debates (to which Roman and Apple did not respond) have not been about evidence for the claims made. The issues raised, it seems to me, continue to focus only on ontological and epistemological issues without attempting to assess the claims being made, i.e., without questioning "evidence."[4]

On such epistemological and ontological questions, however, I choose to remain agnostic. While I do think it is imperative to raise such issues as part of the practice of knowing, I also think the more important issues raised by the Foucauldian linking of power and knowledge are those connected to power. Here, facing the postmodern possibility that nothing really does lie outside the text, facing the possibility that realist philosophers are wrong, the question of what type of authority is constructed in the texts of RSSK becomes crucial to me. Here I would like to begin a defense of my postulation that evidence can serve to disperse, or open up, authority structures in a text.

To do this I would like to consider two illustrative texts as evidence on which to base a comparative analysis. Both texts in name address the possibility of a radical pedagogy. The first is taken from the discourse (related to RSSK) known as Critical Pedagogy:

> Pedagogy as defined within the traditions of modernism, postmodernism, and postmodern feminism offers educators an opportunity to develop a political project that embraces human interests that move beyond the particularistic politics of class, ethnicity, race, and gender. This is not a call to dismiss the postmodern emphasis on difference as much as it is an attempt to develop a radical democratic politics that stresses difference within unity. This means developing a public language that can transform a politics of assertion into one of democratic struggle. Central to such a politics and pedagogy is a notion of community developed around a shared conception of social justice, fights, and entitlement. This is especially necessary at a time in our history in which the value of such concerns have been subordinated to the priorities of the market and used to legitimate the interests of the rich at the expense of the poor, the unemployed, and the homeless. A radical pedagogy and transformative democratic politics must go hand in hand in constructing a vision in which liberalism's emphasis on individual freedom, postmodernism's concern with the particularistic, and feminism's concern with the politics of the everyday are coupled with democratic socialism's historic concern with solidarity and public life. (Giroux, 1991, p. 56)

< 156 >

Compare the following passage from a post-structural feminist critique of critical pedagogy discourse:

> Our classroom was not in fact a safe space for students to speak out or talk back about their experiences of oppression both inside and outside of the classroom. In our class, these included experiences of being gay, lesbian, fat, women of color working with men of color, White women working with men of color, men of color working with White women and men. Things were not being said for a number of reasons. These included fear of being misunderstood and/or disclosing too much and becoming too vulnerable; memories of bad experiences in other contexts of speaking out; resentment that other oppressions (sexism, heterosexism, fat oppression, classism, anti-Semitism) were being marginalized in the name of addressing racism—guilt for feeling such resentment; confusion about levels of trust and commitment surrounding those who were allies to another group's struggles; resentment by some students of color for feeling that they were expected to disclose "more" and once again take the burden of doing the pedagogic work of educating White students/professor about the consequences of White middle-class privilege; and resentment by White students for feeling that they had to prove they were not the enemy. (Ellsworth, 1989, pp. 315–16)

Similarities within each of these texts, I think, are evident. Each is centrally concerned with understanding experiences and conditions of oppression. Each takes pedagogy as a political endeavor. Each grapples with problems of difference and diversity among and between multiple social groups. And each addresses practical concerns of political agendas. Essentialized, it might even be possible to say that each of these texts addresses a common phenomenon. But what are the phenomena being discussed in these texts?

In the critical pedagogy passage there are references to "Pedagogy as defined within modernism, postmodernism, and postmodern feminism," a "radical transformative politics," and "a public language." But these are references made with a "call" to radical transformative politics, i.e., within imperative statements. Indeed, almost all of the critical pedagogy passage is an imperative about what is needed in a radical transformative political agenda.

There are some descriptive statements in this critical pedagogy passage as well, though. The reader is told, for example, that,

> in our history . . . the value of such concerns (a shared conception of social justice, rights, and entitlement) have been subordinated to the priorities of the market and used to legitimate the interests of the rich at the expense of the poor, the unemployed, and the homeless.

This clearly is a statement about the conditions of "reality." But what is the referent? Personally, I actually agree with this description, if we are talking about the United States since, say, 1776. But aside from the general reference to vague public categories such as "the rich," "the poor," "the unemployed," or "the homeless," I really don't know about what this critical pedagogue is talking. To the degree that I understand this as a struggle for developing "a public language," a project I would strongly defend, I can accept the basic idea here. But still, I see nothing in these discourses which I could point to as evidence. And for anyone who doesn't agree with this political agenda, I can only vaguely imagine trying to offer them something with which to engage in such claims.[5]

In the post-structural feminist discourse, however, it is clear from the beginning that the "object" of the discourse is, at least partially, one classroom. The opening statement is a general characterization of the class experience:

> Our classroom was not in fact a safe space for students to speak out or talk back about their experiences of oppression both inside and outside of the classroom.

The next sentence presents the issues which were not raised in the class (but presumably were raised elsewhere):

> In our class, these included experiences of being gay, lesbian, fat, women of color working with men of color, White women working with men of color, men of color working with White women and men.

The remainder of the passage presents the reasons these issues were not raised in class. Presuming the reasons listed in this post-structural feminist passage were actually spoken by class members outside of class, one could take this passage as presenting evidence. I could easily imagine class members talking about the issues and reasons raised in this passage. And I could easily imagine explaining to someone who doesn't share the political agenda of this discourse what might have been going on in the class and why the theoretical/political issues raised in the post-structural feminist discourse are important (and real).

On what authority does each of these texts speak? I would argue that in the critical pedagogy passage, readers are faced with two choices. One could either agree with the portrayal of reality (that priorities of the market have subordinated issues of justice) or not. But without a clear point of reference on which potential mutual agreement could be reached, I would suggest that readers are faced with a leap of faith (potentially a rather large leap for those who disagree). In the post-structural feminist passage, however, there is at least the possibility of readers accepting as reality that the issues the author raises were in fact not discussed in class, but were in fact raised elsewhere. So even if one does not agree with the overall arguments of the post-structural feminist analysis (and I am personally quite skeptical about it),[6] there is at least the potential of entering into dialogue based on a shared, mutually accepted understanding of the reality about which we are speaking. Hence the notion that evidence can serve as a "third party" arbiter.

< 158 >

I should emphasize that I am not making what I understand to be a philosophical argument. I am not suggesting that "socially recognizable evidence" always would function as a mutual point of departure between competing views, nor am I simply saying that all radical discourse requires evidence. I am suggesting, however, that in the current context, if U.S. RSSK wishes to persuade more people than those who already agree with radical perspectives, and if one group of people these discourses wish to persuade is "mainstream educational researchers," then presenting socially recognizable evidence would be both consistent with the "democratic" emphasis on dialogue and nonauthoritarian discourse and potentially more persuasive.

A BREAK FROM PHILOSOPHY

Throughout my discussion of the ways in which radical sociologies of school knowledge have not met conventional canons of educational science, my concern was with constructing "socially recognizable evidence." This phrase, of course, carries a host of implications. If read through analytical philosophical lenses this perspective might seem dangerously close to the notion of "justified true belief." Or, pushing this slant further, many conventional so-called philosophers might see the simple imposition of a naive epistemological relativism. From the perspective of an educational philosophy which has yet to find a way out of endless relativism versus objectivism debates, this perspective on my work may seem valid. Sociologically, however, such universalistic and reductive claims are evidence that in the endeavor to construct social sciences, philosophy has its limits.

The distinction which separates my reading of RSSK's lack of persuasiveness in the U.S. field of educational research from Liston's (1988a) claims for an epistemologically necessary empirical verification is homologous to the historical break between sociology and philosophy (Bourdieu, 1991a). The grounding of this analysis has been constructed in opposition to both the positivist image of science as a mirror of reality and the conventionalist image of science as purely a social construct. Unlike Liston, who seeks more or less accurate models of some underlying reality in an "epistemological discourse designed to ground and to justify science in and by a normative methodology tied to a logical reconstruction of the progress of science,"[7] I view struggles of scientific authority as taking place within a field of unequal power relations in which methodological canons are the effect. In this view, the epistemological positions advanced under the authority of philosophy are simultaneously accepted at their word, as manifestations of the "native view," and constructed as social facts. Hence when I impose conventional notions of scientific methodology on radical sociologies of school knowledge it is in the sociological attempt to describe some of the legitimating principles by which radical educational theories would be deemed nonscientific.

< 159 >

This analysis, of course, is not without its own subtext. If the New Sociology's critique of Positivism was on to something, I would suggest it is in the recognition that U.S. educational research is indeed a field in which there is a struggle over scientific authority. And if the critique was mistaken, it was in part mistaken in the miscalculation of the marginal return on its investment in philosophic discourse.

In his history of science, Georges Canguilheim (1988), one of Bourdieu and Foucault's teachers suggested that,

> It should be laid down as a general principle in the history of science that discord and rivalry within the scientific community can never totally impede communication, certainly not since the seventeenth century." (p. 71)

This historical observation is for me quite telling. Entering into the educational Academy in the wake of two decades of "Paradigm Wars" (Gage, 1989), there are indeed many theoretical avenues open to current students of RSSK. Each of these rhetorical paths would open lines of communication within some social contexts to be sure. But it seems odd for a field of inquiry so concerned with understanding, and perhaps altering, unequal power relations to have left one of the most persuasive rhetorics in the hands of those against whom it struggles.

While there are many theoretical and analytical implications of viewing science as a form of rhetoric, there is one main implication which needs to be clearly put forward. Just as Rorty (1979) turned away from analytical philosophy in his much discussed turn toward more edifying philosophic endeavors, I would suggest that RSSK would benefit by a turn away from addressing the debates and tensions in radical theorizing in its now traditional form. Even as advocates of radical agendas continue to address the challenges of "newer" theoretical positions, the tendency to do so within a logic of debate that remains internal to RSSK continues to risk the self-isolation and self-defeat I identified with the earlier critique of Positivism (e.g., Morrow and Torres, 1994). While a Critical call for a continuing dialectical interrogation between empirical and political concerns seems undoubtedly wise, it seems even wiser to build on the past successes of radical academic struggles to construct a discourse even more persuasive than past dialectical inquiries have been. As Rorty noted of the aporias of the analytical philosophical agenda, there seems little reason to expect that the theoretical tensions within RSSK are going to be solved with ever more philosophical reasoning. And as Rorty asked of his colleagues in philosophy, I would ask that students of RSSK change the subjects and objects of our debates.

< 160 >

seven

Constructing a Science with an Attitude

"How am I able to obey a rule?"—if it is not a question about causes, then it is about the justification for my following the rule in the way I do.

If I have exhausted the justifications I have reached bedrock, and my spade is turned. Then I am inclined to say: "This is simply what I do."
— Ludwig Wittgenstein, *Philosophical Investigations*, § 217

I N THE OPENING PASSAGES OF THIS BOOK, I hinted at the possibility of constructing a concerted, strategic research program that might better address the initial agenda set for the radical sociology of school knowledge. I also positioned the field in relation to the potential role RSSK could play in the current global context of expanding educational systems, growing modern state apparatuses, and persistent (and growing) social and economic inequalities. Predictably, I am not the first to see this potential in RSSK (e.g., Karabel and Halsey, 1977a), nor would I be the first to suggest that current research in RSSK is not up to this task (e.g., Wexler, 1987). If there is but one justification for taking up these previously recognized themes once again, it would be in the hope of illuminating a path not yet taken in the endeavor to better understand the relationship between school knowledge and power.

In this chapter I will outline what I take to be a basic framework of such a new path, explicating current methodological stances and theoretical premises which seem promising for furthering the agenda of RSSK. However, before turning to that explication, it is necessary to position the proposed strategy in relation to the multidimensional aspects of the social reality in which these words are actions.

WHERE DOES THIS CONSTRUCTION FIT?

To begin on a philosophical plane, I would like to suggest that the dispositions toward questions of "truth," "reality," and the "foundations of science" I am advocating here are consistent with those positions articulated by a host of well-known philosophers, social theorists, and social epistemologists. For example, although many philosophic examples are readily available, it is interesting to note that when asked to explain her philosophical positions in relation to questions of "essentialism," Gayatri Spivak's (1993) response is to reframe the issue as a strategic one, employing philosophy as an explicitly strategic venture. Further, Bourdieu's (1993; Bourdieu et al., 1990) analyses of science and his notion of a "science that causes trouble" are also explicitly constructed in relation to his understanding of practice as a strategic logic. And in the midst of constructing his own approach to reconstructing the philosophy of science, Fuller's (1993a, 1993b) "social-epistemology" strongly pursues the consequences of understanding science as rhetoric and issues related to the broader task of constructing knowledge. In this light, in the shadow of Marx's Eleventh Thesis, I take the implications of my stance toward ethereal philosophical debate to be a matter for a history not yet written.

On a sociological plane, I have already noted the growing recognition of schooling as an institutional site of the world cultural system. I should note also that the interest in the sociology of culture which questions the relationships among social groups, symbolic representations of culture, and social stratification hold immediate implications for analyses of school knowledge (and vice-versa). As sociologists of culture continue to explore the importance of cultural dimensions of institutional differentiation, social exclusions, and the construction of the modern *polis* (Lamont, 1992; Lamont and Fournier, 1992; Lamont and Lareau, 1988), the need for a more complete understanding of the role schooling plays in constructing the initial cultural framing of social groups (for each generation) becomes increasingly evident.

On a political plane, it is very clear that schooling plays a central role in each modern state, in terms of constructing citizens and the basic norms, beliefs, and dispositions that make up each nation's unique identity(ies). In this sense, if there is one contribution post-structural analyses have offered RSSK, it is the reminder that some of the basic terms of our earlier debates are more and more irrelevant. Where the early New Sociology of Education might have been able to construct criticisms of schooling as controlling institutions, it is now evident that currently available political options render some early concepts moot. As we approach the turn of the millennium, it seems to me humans do not face the question of whether or not we have controlling institutions; but rather, we face the question, "What kind of controlling institutions do we want?"

< 162 >

On an academic plane, I have gone to great lengths to demonstrate how academic discourses are continually constructed in accordance with a social and analytical logic that is specific to the Academy. I must make it very clear that I do *not* take this observation as a criticism in itself. I accept working within the terms of the Academy as an effect of an institutionalization I would heartily defend. For individual academic projects or whole academic fields in which there is an explicit interest in attempting to influence social movements beyond the walls of the Academy (such as RSSK), however, I would argue there is a great and very specific need to monitor the degree to which research serves any social interests. To the degree academic interests carry the potential of overriding any others, I believe intentionally political academics must continually ask what other interests are served by academic debates. To the extent this work may have pressed colleagues to ask this question anew, I take this work to have served one of its key intents.

On a professional plane, specific to the field of education (but assuredly with its analogous counterparts in other fields), I would like to point out that while RSSK has constructed a multitude of hermeneutic and critical knowledge claims about the relationship between power and curriculum, as a profession educators actually have very, very little technical knowledge on which systemic alternatives could be built. Here the U.S.-centric nature of this work shows one of its weakest points. It might be plausible, from a U.S. view, to justifiably rebuff any calls for technical knowledge. But in nations where socialist governments have explicitly and purposefully *asked* for alternative curricular knowledge that would fulfill the requirements of bureaucratic and state sanctioned probabilistic rationality, to my knowledge no one has widely proffered any viable alternative options that have met even the basic tenets of technical demands. To the extent that radical educational criticisms hold out hope for newer, more just societies, I would argue, the advocates of such criticisms have invested themselves with a responsibility yet to be fulfilled.

On a scientific plane, I would point out that my acceptance of science as one means of constructing critically informed technical knowledge simply takes up the challenge social and cultural studies of science have enabled (Harding, 1993). From the works of many socially interested scholars, it is clear there are many alternative images and purposes of science yet to be made widely actionable. While I would hardly suggest that the need for a strong feminist movement is over, I do think feminists' theoretical and political approaches to science are an indication of what can be accomplished (e.g., Haraway, 1986; Harding, 1986, 1991). The interconnections between the technical knowledge created in feminist sciences and the socio-legal battles won in the world's women's movements serve as a continuing reminder of what can be done.

< 163 >

And on a personal plane, I would like to make it very clear that the agenda I am about to present has been constructed on the assumption that all of the various stances and positions I have described so far (and more) are going to continue to be taken and defended, rightfully. In fact, the agenda of reconstructing a science with an attitude, constructed in service of the wider agenda of radical educational research, is wholly interdependent on the existence of a wide-ranging and self-sustaining field of radical educational research and practice. It is with a collective interest in the forefront of this agenda that I repeat that I take constructing science with an attitude to be a stance that is both historically specific and strategic.

STRATEGIC METHODOLOGICAL STANCES

Following Sandra Harding (1987), I would identify "methods" as "techniques for gathering evidence" (and, I should add, thereby constructing whatever data is gathered as evidence), as opposed to "methodology," which "is a theory and analysis of how research does or should proceed" (p. 3). This distinction is part of Harding's argument that what have developed as unique feminist methodologies have, at the same time, continued to employ traditional, historically androcentric methods. I take my project to be a theory of methodology to the extent that I have "applied" one sociological framework to the research in RSSK in an analysis of how its research has been done.

To the extent feminist methodologies have demonstrated that the master's tools can be used to bring down the master's house, it seems that a wider, heterodoxic stance toward methodology could only aid RSSK. I should note that calling for a methodological heterodoxy differs substantially from philosophical calls for methodological pluralism (such as Roth, 1987), in that the very notion of heterodoxy is built from a recognition of the power relations both internal and external to any one specific scientific field (Bourdieu, 1988b). With this explicit recognition of extant power relations, the utility of re-thinking radical methodological dispositions becomes clear. That is, despite recent attempts to reconstruct the relation between power and research method (Gitlin, 1994), RSSK and wider realms of radical educational research have maintained a rather limited set of research practices.

What I offer below are what I take to be methodological points of consideration for choices that are made in the process of constructing a science with an attitude. I would imagine any one of the propositions I outline below could stimulate long debates. If *any* substantive debate results from these being brought forward, they would have served their purpose. I have categorized these points of consideration into three types of choices: choices about research methods, about sources of methods, and about procedures.

< 164 >

On choosing methods
I. Choosing methods in accordance with the nature of the claim at issue

As any educational researcher is well aware, there is a host of debates about the relative strengths and weaknesses of various methods for meeting the tenets of research. There is no need to delineate already widely discussed issues here, except to remind radical educational researchers that even while they may hold a strong disdain for such technical criteria, it is often technical criteria that become the Achilles' heel of radical research claims. I raise this issue of technical criteria first, as a way of acknowledging the prominence of technical rationality outside of radical social fields. Acknowledging this technical reality simply means being very clear about calculating one's losses from the beginning.

II. Choosing methods in accordance with the intended audience and range of desired influence

I have been told, "Research is pedagogical," and I agree. But the issue at hand is for whom is our research intended to be pedagogical? If the radical agenda is to impact on systems of education, then it seems to me systemic knowledge is going to be needed. Politicians, policy makers, and managers do not always rely on generalized knowledge simply because of some misguided beliefs in objectivity or "neutrality" but because they deal with generalized systems. Generalized, systemic solutions to the well-documented social ills of our school systems, solutions that can be publicly defended, are recognized as sorely needed in many countries. The quicker socially recognizable evidence might be constructed, the quicker possible systemic solutions might be defended.

On choosing methodological sources
III. Poaching mainstream issues

Obviously one of the most crucial questions to face when constructing a research project is topic choice. If that choice is made solely in relation to past radical educational research, the likelihood of choosing a topic of narrow interest increases dramatically. Of course, making a narrow choice does serve many purposes; but there is ample space for a more publicly recognized range of radical research to develop. Possibly a good example lies in one of the more influential moves in U.S. sociology of education over the past decade: i.e., the turn toward critically examining tracking (streaming). The debates signalled by Oakes's (1985) widely read research continue to this day *and* have influenced many school-based restructuring reforms across the industrialized world.

IV. Poaching mainstream tools

For whatever reason the methodological tendencies of RSSK have developed,

< 165 >

it is unfortunate that other possibilities have not been explored. The possibilities of "measuring" educational inequality have been demonstrated repeatedly in the sociology of education, and it is from the mainstream that the first attempts to apply such approaches to an examination of classroom curriculum practices has come (e.g., Gamoran, 1989; Gamoran and Nystrand; 1991). The methods and methodological tools of mainstream sociology of education are clearly well placed to provide a widely recognized scientific basis for studying the hypotheses and claims of RSSK (Ladwig and Berends, 1994). The point in doing so is at least twofold: on the one hand, the technical refinement process of disconfirming or confirming past theoretical claims can only aid in the process of specifying and clarifying one's research agenda; on the other hand, to do so in a language that has broad appeal can only aid the process of expanding the persuasive capacity of RSSK.

I should note that I expect this particular proposition will be the most unpalatable for radical educational researchers. In anticipation of the criticisms which will try to suggest that proposing an amalgamation of radical theory and mainstream methods somehow violates the basic tenets of radical inquiry, I would remind readers of the early Frankfurt School use of primitive survey devices *and* suggest that the perception of methodological violence is only plausible if one presupposes radical social science is somehow pure.

On choosing procedures
V. Attending to some conventional formalism

The traditional procedures of accumulative sciences have long been rejected by many social scientists—but not all, of course. Here I would simply like to propose that some fairly conventional steps in knowledge construction would be of great assistance in the current context. Many of the rapid changes in educational policy and practice over the past decade or so assuredly have had some impact on the production of socio-educational inequality. At the same time, there have been a plethora of studies (both mainstream and radical) which have monitored the impact of some of these shifts in policy and practice.

Given these circumstances, at least three types of conventional literature reviews and meta-analyses would be very helpful at the current juncture: first, a general accounting of what is currently known about extant educational practices (curricular and extracurricular) and their impact on equity would prove invaluable as a way of situating the work of RSSK within broader studies of socio-educational inequality; second, a more specific meta-analysis of the equity implications of current so-called "restructuring" curricular reforms in relation to the knowledge produced by RSSK would also prove invaluable for providing some insight for future topic choices; and third, given the relative success in multicultural curriculum (in terms of having instigated some measurable shifts in curriculum practice), a meta-analysis of the relationships

< 166 >

between multicultural curricular reforms and Bernsteinian-influenced analyses of classification and framing would also provide an overview of one potential site of important curricular insight.

At the time of this writing, each of these "reviews" has yet to be done; and each would provide RSSK with valuable bases for further study—in terms addressed by much wider audiences than are currently favored. While such reviews do submit to the conventional formalism of accumulative science, they also serve as important strategies of stocktaking and regrouping.

VI. Building collective productions

Aside from ideological and political inclinations that value collective action, there are some very pragmatic issues in trying to maintain support for radical research agendas. Assuming for the moment questions of fiscal resource are fairly evident to those in the field, I would like to point out that precisely since much of RSSK has been built from research that has respected the context-specific nature of education, the field has also produced highly divergent research products which make them very difficult to compare and contrast, except in very general and abstract terms. One strategy for building both the generalizability of one's research findings *and* for constructing more widely comparable studies (beyond the specific issue of generalizing any one claim), lies in the possibility of purposefully constructing what I counterintuitively would call "comparative case-studies" or multi-context studies based on the collective work of multiple researchers. Such study designs are fairly common in other areas of study, but have yet to be employed in RSSK.

VII. Building collective strategies/explicit division of labor

The sociology of science has repeatedly documented the ways in which science informally builds collective strategies and divisions of labor. All I am pointing to here is that a more explicit collective strategy might be built among radical educational researchers.

On understanding the limits of our ability to choose

While I have labeled the above criteria "choices," I want to explicitly acknowledge that no one makes such choices in a vacuum—that was the point of demonstrating the analytical constraints on past choices. That is also the point here of trying to open up available, sanctionable options beyond what current conventions allow.

STRATEGIC THEORETICAL POSITIONS

In Chapter Two I argued that the theoretical framework within Structural Neo-Marxist discourses in RSSK has developed into a logically inconsistent and politically dubious matrix of conceptual filters. While I have not

< 167 >

subjected each of the other discursive strands related to RSSK to the same level of detailed theoretical critique, I have noted some "scientific" limits of each strand's theoretical framework. That is, when read through mainstream educational science tenets, each discursive strand's theoretical framework seems to limit the degree to which socially recognizable evidence could be constructed. Structural radical discourses which, from their relatively macro-level frame, speak in general terms about "contradictory" relations are susceptible to the charge that they will never be wrong (confounding falsifiability). Post-structural radical discourses, from a micro-level frame, defy generalizability almost by definition. And attempts to join the "macro" and the "micro" at a theoretical level have left what many perceive to be a priori interpretive filters which simply screen out those parts of "reality" which don't fit radical political agendas.

In response to this situation, I would like to outline briefly one viable theoretical framework already available to the field. Beginning with Young's (1971b) early call to analyze the principles of selection and organization that underlie the curriculum in relation to the institutional setting of the school and the wider society, there is a statement of a sociological problem of significant interest. Placed within a radical agenda, rather than by prespecifying any particular set of social dimensions (such as class, race, or gender), one could open the theoretical lens to an analysis of social group formations and correspondences with unequal power relations. Such an approach carries many benefits, the first being that such questions have long been a central focus in sociological inquiry. Politically, this eliminates worries about the a priori primacy of any one social dimension. Empirically, this would allow a "test" of the radical claims that the distribution of school knowledge corresponds with societal relations of unequal power. And, theoretically this also would be parsimonious. In such a theoretical view, there is but one central conceptual concern: unequal power relations.

Of all the theoretical frameworks available to the field, there seems to me only a few which would allow for building on such a parsimonious view empirically. Each of the structural accounts (and the post-structural feminist account) currently employed in U.S. radical sociologies of school knowledge posits a priori social dimensions, and would thus prematurely impose its analytical view. The current post-structural accounts do place analytical primacy on actual cultural practices and in this view seem advantageous. However, in the attempt to persuade a mainstream educational community that (I suspect) will continue to ignore non-generalizable research, current post-structural work would fail to make it through the mainstream "scientific" screen. This may seem to eliminate all of the available options—except (of course), the one I have been attempting to employ throughout this project.

< 168 >

Recognizing the need for a theoretical frame that is simultaneously opera-tive at multiple "levels" of social reality and which explicitly examines the basic analytical framework of the sociology of knowledge (connecting social structures and "mental" structures), many scholars have already noted the util-ity of Bourdieu's basic conceptual framework of capitals, *habitus*, and fields—along with his early analyses of pedagogy as symbolic violence—for the overall analysis of educational inequality (Jenks, 1993; Mehan, 1992). Here I would simply note that when taken broadly as a "cultural difference" theory in which unequal power relations are centrally recognized, the Bourdieuian interrela-tion of knowledge, institutions, and reflexive sociological practice (e.g., Bourdieu, 1993; Bourdieu et al., 1993) are readily interwoven with Bernstein's (1977a) analyses of classification and framing (Ladwig, 1994b). Such a frame-work also clearly shares theoretical points of departure with current main-stream sociological explanatory frameworks (e.g., Coleman, 1988, 1990).

Clearly, detailing the specific dimensions of such a theoretical framework requires much more extrapolation than space allows here—but the basic dimensions of the framework should be evident. Whether or not one chooses to rely on Bourdieu, four basic points of departure seem crucial for RSSK. As a general theoretical outline for radical sociologies of school knowledge, I would delineate the following four basic requirements:

1. a broad frame of cultural difference in which schools are seen as institu-tional cultural "filtering" and "transmission" devices, with

2. a central focus on power as a basic medium through which social identi-ties are formed and contested, and

3. a conceptual apparatus that examines "multi-level" relations, connecting the micro-, mezzo-, and macro- "levels," with

4. a central focus on the relation between social and "mental" structures.

This is obviously just a rough outline of the theoretical needs of RSSK, and none of these points is original with this work, but they are sufficient to propose some further points related to the theoretical needs of constructing a science with an attitude.

Because much of what has been documented above entails decades-old arguments and debates that center on issues which to this date remain unre-solved (and in many cases have simply been rearticulated under "newer" names), I would like to point out many of the current faddish debates in social theory are simply not on this agenda. Worrying about whose theory better explains the role of agency, or whose theoretical ancestry has been unrespect-fully overlooked in the attempts to continually push the frontiers of justice, are addressed only to the degree that a politically realistic marginal gain might be expected from the effort that goes into constructing such arguments.

< 169 >

In my outline of the theoretical needs of RSSK, the central focus on the culture/institution relation is premised on a recognized interrelation of economic, social, and overtly political spheres of social reality. That is to say, because virtually every dimension of social life is seen to have a cultural "background" (including economics and the property relations that govern economic relations); I would simply note that by accepting culture as a central focus no more specific social sphere is ruled out.

WHY THE ATTITUDE?

In 1991, when I began thinking about trying to find a way to productively push the boundaries of the fields to which I had initially turned in my own studies of U.S. society, the proposition of making one's position explicit was being taken very seriously by my colleagues. Current thinking might emphasize the many problems that come with engaging in explicit declarations of authorial position; but in the endeavor to list out the characteristics used to understand and "fix positions," there is also a possibility of acknowledging one's own historical space. My first attempt produced the following passage:

> However framed by Grand proclamations about the conditions of "our times," my task by necessity and by choice must remain partial, limited, small. Though much more limited than the host of issues raised within the Grand Frame, I wish to respond to several issues in this thesis. As these issues emanate from separate and disparate intellectual and social fields, each will be considered as a distinct point of departure signalling distinct paths that have partially converged and led me toward this study. Linearly presented below, these points of departure are rooted intellectually in social philosophy, the history of science, social theory, the sociology of school knowledge, and curriculum theory.
>
> But these heady enterprises are not engaged in a social vacuum. About this I wish to be quite clear: my purpose in pursuing this work is personal *and* political. The source of my personal interest can be objectively found in the autobiography of a white, non-religious, heterosexual, able-bodied, North American man whose birth virtually coincided with the construction of the Berlin Wall; whose first memories are of Alabama red clay, white hoods, burnings crosses, and terror in the eyes of my very, very young Black friends; whose earliest recalled television images were of the Vietnamese jungles and murdered Viet-Cong; whose first understanding of government came in the witnessing of the 1968 Democratic convention/riot in Chicago and Watergate; whose adolescence was spent fighting a school and culture in a self-destructively chosen hallucinatory milieu; who was commanded by law to open my Self to potential selective service in the American War machine.
>
> A political outlook from such a history is probably not surprising. And such a self-selected presentation of one's past is, of course, not innocent. But, I must be honest in openly declaring the moral outrage and cold anger harbored from being brought into a society whose ideological mythos is nothing less than a blatant lie. It is this anger that has motivated my studies

< 170 >

in education, curriculum, and social theory. It is this motivation that, at least in part, guides my work.

While I might be able to excuse the posturing and individualistic, self-important nature of this passage to youth and a rather silly masculinity, dispositions against which my own struggles continue, the anger of which I spoke then is not something I care ever to temper as a matter of personal styling (combining that anger with a little more humility and compassion is another matter, of course).

Is this an attitude? Yes, of course it is. As anyone who studies social inequality in the industrialized world would be well aware, although many changes have occurred over the past three decades, if any progress has been charted in the struggle to alter past injustices at all, that progress has been minimal at best. With the fall of the Wall, and the globalization of market capitalism and so-called representative democracies, the institutional mechanisms which industrialized countries use to produce that inequality are also going global. Academic dispositions and past political struggles remind me that any future lasting changes are probably going to be as difficult to achieve and as slow in coming as have all others that have occurred in my lifetime. Nevertheless, if the generation of scholars (and other servants of our states) who share a historical memory similar to my own are going to hold the goal of an equitable social justice firmly in hand, it is clear to me that we will need an attitude.

< 171 >

notes

CHAPTER ONE: INTRODUCTION

1. To the extent evidence might be available to test negative assessments of RSSK's persuasiveness, in addition to the claims of the field's forefathers, one could examine simple citation patterns in identifiably mainstream educational research journals. For example, taking a sample of books and journal articles often taken as part of RSSK's heritage (Apple, 1978, 1979b; Bernstein, 1977a; Bourdieu and Passeron, 1977; Bowles and Gintis, 1976; Giroux, 1979; Liston, 1988b; McCarthy, 1990; Sharp and Green, 1975; Wexler, 1987; and Young, 1971c), and using the odd years from 1975 to 1993 inclusive, as points of reference, one can note a total of 1535 citations recorded in the *Social Science Citation Index*. Of these 1535 citations, only *nine* are in journals sponsored by the American Educational Research Association. Despite all the methodological problems of making such sample choices, such blunt numbers I assume help make a point.

CHAPTER TWO: CONSTRUCTING THE FIELD

1. In naming this logic "additive," I mean only to suggest that the analytical categories of the Parallelist Position were added together—not that such logic implies notions of added dimensions of oppression. For an explanation of the latter use of the term "additive" see McCarthy (1990, pp. 82–84).

2. For those seeking a more complete review, I would recommend a combination of texts: Karabel and Halsey's (1977a) introduction to their edited volume *Power and Ideology in Education* (pp. 1–85); Wexler (1987); and Whitty (1985).

3. It is interesting to note that Young (1971b) was highly critical of Perry Anderson's (1969) Marxist analysis of the English academic curricula because of Anderson's structuralism.

4. More complete analyses of these texts abound, but for those interested, I would point out a few. For a general discussion of the field, and the role of Bowles and Gintis's work in it, see Karabel and Halsey (1977a). There Karabel and Halsey also offer an early interpretation of the significance of Bernstein's work.

   For an early and thoughtful review of Bernstein's *Class, Codes, and Control, Vol III*, see Apple and Philip Wexler (1978). Later revisitations of Bernstein's works are also worthy of note, including Atkinson (1985). Even more recently, with the publication of Bernstein's (1990) *The Structuring of Pedagogic Discourse: Class, Codes, and Control, Vol. IV*, there is something of a third wave of reanalyses. See Sadovnick (1991) and Apple (1992).

   For early interpretations of Bourdieu and Passeron's *Reproduction*, see Apple (1979b, esp. pp. 29–34); Dimaggio (1979); Giroux (1983a); and Schwartz (1977). Later, recent interpretations of Bourdieu have argued that these early interpretations were mis-readings, (see, for example, Wacquant (1989)). For Bourdieu's own comments on this, consider his response to some early criticisms, recently published in his new preface to the second English edition of *Reproduction* (1990), in which he notes recent research done in the United States which seems to validate his theory and says,

> This empirical validation of the model outlined in *Reproduction* in the very society that was for so long held up as its living refutation would appear to be worth all the proofs and procedures of conventional empiricist methodology. And we shall not despair that America loses yet another parcel of its "exceptionalism" when this loss contributes to the greater unity of social science. (p. xi)

For an interpretation of Willis's *Learning to Labor*, see Apple (1979a) and Giroux (1981c; 1983b). I would like to point out, as well, that if one wants a good reading of these texts it is perhaps best to go directly to them. Reading these secondary sources is mostly a way of finding out about the conceptual framework of the interpreter.

5. By suggesting that *Reproduction* received more attention, I mean that direct secondary analyses of this work were abundant in U.S. radical sociology of school knowledge literature. At the same time, *Reproduction's* overall framework was usually rejected. See, for example, Apple (1982c, esp. p. 45) and Giroux (1983a).

6. I should note that my attempt to briefly outline Bourdieu and Passeron's (1990) arguments about legitimacy radically simplifies them, and in a sense does them symbolic violence. To give a slightly broader sense (and I should emphasize the *slightly* qualifier here) of the context from which these arguments come, consider the paragraph from which I extracted the just cited quote:

> Thus, to understand that the social effects of the common or learned illusions which are sociologically implied in the systems of relations between the educational system and the structure of class relations are not illusory, it is necessary to go back to the principle which governs this system of relations. Legitimation of the established order by the School presupposes social recognition of the legitimacy of the School, a recognition resting in turn on misrecognition of the delegation of authority which establishes that legitimacy or, more precisely, on misrecognition of the social conditions of a harmony between structures and habitus sufficiently perfect to engender misrecognition of the habitus as a product reproducing what produces it and correlative recognition of the structure of the order thus reproduced. Thus, the educational system objectively tends, by concealing the objective truth of its functioning, to produce the ideological justification of the order it reproduces by its functioning. (p. 206)

If one questions my reluctance to enter into "secondary" debates about how the "primary" texts of the radical sociology of school knowledge ought to be read and understood, and my chosen disposition to treat secondary readings as empirical fact, be sure that choice is based on a rationally calculated recognition that the marginal analytical return of such debates geometrically declines as one moves further down the axis from the primary point of origin.

7. This is not meant to imply these structural accounts all held the same conception of "class." In fact, I have argued elsewhere that they held vastly differing conceptions of class, a fact U.S. sociologists of curriculum seem to have conveniently ignored. See Ladwig (1994b).

8. The reception of Bourdieu's work into the U.S. educational research community was perhaps more strongly impeded than it would have been in England. While some of Bourdieu's own articles had been translated and were available in U.S. sociological literature, until the translation of *La Reproduction*, the availability of Bourdieu and his colleagues' analyses of education were limited to those made available by the London New Sociologists, and the publication of Karabel and Halsey's *Power and Ideology*.

9. In *Ideology and Curriculum* (1979b), Apple's treatment of the State is largely limited to questioning the role of governmental funding (esp. in chapter 6, pp. 105–122). But as

< 174 >

Apple himself pointed out in *Education and Power* (1982c), his later analyses considered the State much more fully and directly (pp. 28-30). Apple's prior focus on the economy and culture and subsequent turn to focusing on the State was also evident in the title of his 1982 edited volume, *Cultural and Economic Reproduction in Education* (London: Routledge and Kegan Paul). There is something of a symbolic congruence here in that this volume's subtitle was "Essays on Class, Ideology, and the State." Included in this volume were two essays, by Martin Carnoy and Roger Dale, which centered on Marxist analyses of the State.

10. Unlike Hargreaves, I am willing to assume that Anyon ruled out other possible interpretations before presenting hers—with the possible exception of the Foucauldian one. But since Foucault's *Discipline and Punish*, the work most noted for its articulation of the "self-disciplining" argument, would have just been translated into English at the time Anyon would have analyzed her data, one couldn't really expect Anyon to have considered this interpretation (unless we would expect her to have relied on a few comments Bernstein made along the similar lines in his works). *Discipline and Punish* first appeared in English in 1977.

11. This is not to reject the possibility of broadening the notion of "materialist" to include biological determinist arguments about gender as Materialist/Marxist feminists have done. Here I am referring only to the "materialism" on which the Marxist focus on the means and modes of economic production is based (i.e., the materialism advocated in the U.S. New Sociology).

12. It is interesting to note that as early as 1983, Philip Wexler was arguing for a direct examination of extant political movements in the United States, and that one of the major movements he saw as significant was the fundamentalist Christians'. Given the timing, and the subsequent rise of the New Right in part because of its alliance with religious conservatives in the United States, this seems a remarkably alert observation. See Wexler (1983).

13. Of course, we could also point out that a significant number of gay and lesbian activists in the United States are politically quite conservative. I should also note the possibility of a latent homophobia.

CHAPTER THREE: DECONSTRUCTING THE FIELD

1. I should note that the vision of a fractured field I present in this chapter is not intended to imply that prior to 1983 the field wasn't fractured, merely that when viewed through "post-structural" lenses these later radical U.S. educational discourses clearly do not form a linearly developing, singular agenda. Had I employed a post-structural frame in analyzing RSSK produced prior to 1983, I suspect the picture presented in Chapter Two would have been substantially different from the depiction it now conveys; but, to my knowledge, such an analytical frame was not common at the time. The point in constructing these two chapters in this manner is not to make some claim about "the field," but rather to underscore the methodological consequences of one's theoretical choices.

2. I should note that people who cannot (biologically) have children, or the possibility of genetically manufactured "test-tube" children, may be seen as problematic for Grumet's universalization. But the phrase "relative to this possibility," of course, leaves a good deal of room for interpretive inclusion—and a basis for defending biological reproduction as an "essentially" human(e) capacity/experience.

3. The reference to identifying men as "the only persons with the capacity to know" is built on arguments which suggest that the uncertainty men experience in relation to childbearing (men can never give birth and therefore do not "know" it, and men are never "really" certain who their children are) results in the specifically masculine need to create "certain" knowledge. For better articulations of this argument see Grumet (1988); Chodorow (1978); O'Brien (1981). Grumet's argument in part builds on O'Brien's.

4. As a personal note, I would want to point out that to me this inversion of "evidence," when understood as an ironic denial of masculine epistemology (with the words of a male author), is simply brilliant.

5. McCarthy (1990) speaks with two voices on this topic, depending on which portion of his book one reads. In the chapter which presents his nonsynchronous proposal, McCarthy suggests that the Parallelist Position is open to an additive interpretation: "this model unfortunately had often been construed in a static and simplistically additive way" (p. 82). But in his introductory chapter, his criticism is more direct as he suggests that the Parallelist Position *is* additive:

   > But the parallelist approach to the analysis of social difference . . . offers an "additive" model of the intersection of race, class and gender which does not address issues of contradiction and tension in schooling in any systematic way. (p. 9)

   Potential reasons for this double-mindedness, I think, are understandable when one considers the contexts in which McCarthy, the author, constructed his text(s)—as a student and (subsequently) a young professor.

6. I should note that at one point, when discussing his use of the word "contradictory" (in a footnote), McCarthy (1990) explicitly draws on both deconstruction and a Hegelian structuralism. (n. 3).

7. Wexler's criticisms of the New Sociology are sometimes taken to be relatively obtuse. For interesting, and telling, comments on the reception of his criticisms and for a quite clear and cutting rearticulation of them, see Wexler (1983). For one example of how Wexler's work has been received, and for what I think is an insightful critique, see Hunter (1991).

8. Permit one juxtaposed intervention here: Aside from seeming appropriate given the context, my sociological observational mode can't resist pointing out that at the time Wexler was speaking of disjuncture and ruptures, Ronald Reagan was enforcing deregulation and increased competition in the U.S. state apparatus (the airlines). This strategy for opening seems, to many Leftists, risky business; but when translated into the educational realm as policies of "choice," such endeavors as Debbie Meyers's attempt to open Central Park East were possible. So while Wexler's language and the theoretical apparatus being constructed under the rubric of avant-garde faddish post-structuralism may seem inherently deconstructive *ad absurdum*, in the social realm some "space" for "radical" intervention was being created.

9. For something of a cumulative representative of Lather's work in this effort, see her *Getting Smart: Feminist Research and Pedagogy with/in the Postmodern*, 1991.

   I should also note here that Lather inscribes her work as postmodern, not (usually) post-structural. For the purposes of this project I shall not attempt to distinguish between these two labels—although if I had to I would point to the separate disciplinary/ national contexts within which each of these labels arose. My choice of labels is consciously based on attempts to 1) link my project with particular concerns in social theory; 2) privilege a particularly sociological way of thinking about social matters and social research; and 3) simultaneously side-step issues endogenous in debates about postmodernism that I take to be less relevant to my concerns (such as questions of whether or not we are in a postmodern age—a question I prefer to leave to history). To justify my temporary conflation of Lather's postmodernism with post-structuralism, I would point out that Lather herself uses the terms interchangeably (see p. 4).

10. Citing Giroux (1988, p. 178). It might be interesting to note that when Giroux reprinted the article in which these charges were made, the "careerism" charge was dropped. See Aronowitz and Giroux (1991, p. 132).

11. This list of Special Interests Groups (SIGs) in the American Educational Research Association was culled from that organization's newsletter/mouthpiece, *Educational Researcher*, Vol. 20, No. 4 (May 1991), 42. In all, as of the publication of this list, there were 76 SIGs from which to choose.

< 176 >

CHAPTER FIVE: WAS THE CRITIQUE OF POSITIVISM A MISTAKE?

1. I use war metaphors here intentionally to simultaneously mimic the stances taken by the radical critics and to signify theoretical argumentation in relation to academic struggles over the symbolic representation or classification of everyday life. Of these struggles Bourdieu (1988a) writes,

> In fact, like the social field taken as a whole, the university field is the locus of a classification struggle which, by working to preserve or transform the state of the power relations between different criteria and between the different powers which they designate, helps create the classification, such as it may be objectively grasped at a given moment in time; but the representation which the agents have of the classification, and the force and the orientation of the strategies which they may deploy to maintain or subvert it, depend on their position in the objective classification (p. 18).

> (And) This struggle may not be apparent as such, and a particular agent or group of agents may threaten the credit of other members of the field by their very existence (for example, by imposing new modes of thought and expression, and criteria of evaluation favorable to their own productions), without setting themselves up consciously as rivals, even less as enemies, and without resorting to strategies deliberately directed against them (p. 282).

Recognizing struggles in the academy, in part, as struggles over symbolic capital, it would be possible of course to ascribe even less flattering metaphors to such actions. After all,

> Symbolic capital is the product of a struggle in which each agent is both a ruthless competitor and supreme judge (and therefore, in terms of an old opposition, both *lupus* and *deus*) (Bourdieu, 1990b, p. 136).

> See Bourdieu (1989a).

2. I should note here that Giroux's employment of a Marxist conception of ideology was consistent with that version of "ideology" found within Critical Theory, which carried with it a partial critique of a more Orthodox Marxist conception of ideology.

3. I think I should note two things about this reading. First, Giroux was clearly cognizant (and has long been) that power relations in society are multidimensional and that the dominant/dominated dichotomy carries problematic reductionist dilemmas. Second, I say his position was constructed *at least partially* from the position of the dominated because Giroux was also explicitly concerned with understanding the role of the intellectual as distinct from other societal roles. As is almost always the case, in trying to interpret critical analyses through linear logical lenses, this analysis faces the same problems that Giroux saw as a tendency in positivistic rationality.

4. It might be of interest to some readers that this claim could not be maintained, I think, if based on the positions of other educational critics of positivism, such as Thomas Popkewitz. Popkewitz (1984) was no less a critic of positivism, but his position was one which explicitly suggested that multiple paradigms were useful for educational research. In this regard, he named himself "willing to adopt a liberal-democratic perspective to the problem of social science" (p. 54).

5. In addition to what I have presented in the foregoing chapters, this can be verified simply by looking at the published studies done by Apple's numerous doctoral students. When these studies explicitly focus on presenting empirical evidence, it is almost exclusively qualitative evidence.

6. Suggesting that education is a low status field would hardly be news to anyone in education. But having spoken to some physicists who also proclaim their field to be low status, I

< 177 >

make this claim by relying on the economics of value—which infer, on one dimension of the Supply and Demand equation, an inverse relationship between the quantity of a commodity and its value. With education producing massively disproportionate numbers of bachelor, masters, and doctoral degrees, it does not take a genius to realize that educational scholars are, as the saying goes, "a dime a dozen."

CHAPTER SIX: WHEREIN LIES THE SCIENTIFIC RHETORIC?

1. These three labels, of course, signify what are in fact very complicated matters for educational researchers. My use of them in this chapter, however, shall be limited to their more commonsense understandings in order to simply open the debate about the scientific rhetoric of RSSK. As evidence that these analytical concerns are current within educational research see Liston (1988a, 1988b) on the issue of falsifiability, and Linn (1986) and Erikson (1986) on the issues of generalizability and validity.

2. I suggest that it is a big assumption to expect mainstream educational researchers to accept the interpretations of "radical" researchers as valid based on both my own personal observations of educational researchers and on published admonishments of researchers such as those by Hargreaves who seem to presume that research about ideological mechanisms is somehow more suspicious than "non-ideological" research (whatever that is).

3. This isn't meant to imply that radical educational research doesn't deal with generalizability. But it does suggest that a reliance on ethnography within mainstream educational research would continue to be susceptible to typical generalizability criticisms. For example, one of the ways in which radical educational research could currently address generalizability is by arguing that since its general depiction of societal structures is accurate (for example, naming the entire United States "capitalist" seems safe enough), any specific interpretive claims which are based on this general depiction would be generalizable across other contexts in which the same conditions were obtained. In essence, though, this strategy requires relying on a critique seen as highly theoretical (such as Marxism) and which most non-radicals would reject out of hand. While I might have little trouble accepting such a strategy, anyone who tends to reject all things Marxist would probably not accept it. Even more starkly, it is clear such strategies would not be persuasive to anyone who believes the only way to "test" reality is with quantitative methods.

4. One notable exception to this would be Olneck and Bill (1980).

5. Under the assumption that this discourse is talking about something more than academic politics, I have purposely ignored the only slightly veiled and explicit references to the ideas of other radical theorists—which are made with varying degrees of moral support.

6. My skepticism of Ellsworth's argument lies in her claim that the "rationalist" assumptions of critical pedagogy are based on "reason," and that "As long as educators define pedagogy against oppressive formations in these ways the role of the critical pedagogue will be to guarantee that the foundation for classroom interaction is reason" (p. 304).

   On the one hand, I don't think it is safe to join two opposing thinkers such as Liston and Giroux under the same label with respect to their position on "reason." And on the other hand, I'm not persuaded that how critical pedagogy textually defines itself has anything to do with social practices conducted under textual (logical, written) assumptions. Similarly, when Ellsworth suggests that the position she advocates "leaves no one off the hook" (p. 322), I wonder if such a position might be socially impossible.

7. These words represent one pole against which Bourdieu struggles in his sociology of science. See Bourdieu (1991a).

< 178 >

bibliography

Acker, S. (1987a). "Sociology, Gender and Education." In S. Acker, et. al., eds. *Women and Education: World Yearbook of Education 1984* (pp. 64–78). London and New York: Kogan Page and Nichols.

Acker, S. (1987b). "Feminist Theory and the Study of Gender in Education." *International Review of Education*, 33(3): 419–35.

Acker, S., Megarry, J., Nisbet, S., and Hoyle, E., eds. (1987). *Women and Education: World Yearbook of Education 1984*. London and New York: Kogan Page and Nichols.

Agar, M. (1980). *The Professional Stranger*. New York: Academic Press.

Alexander, J., ed. (1990). *Durkheimian Sociology: Cultural Studies*. Cambridge: Cambridge University Press.

American Educational Research Association. (1991). Special Interest Groups *Educational Researcher*, 20 (4): 42.

Anderson, P. (1969). "Components of National Culture." In A. Cockburn and P. Anderson, eds. *Student Power* (pp. 214–84). Harmondsworth: Penguin.

Anyon, J. (1979). "Ideology and United States History Textbooks." *Harvard Educational Review*, 49(3): 361–86.

———. (1980). "Social Class and the Hidden Curriculum of Work." *Journal of Education*, 162(1): 67–92.

———. (1981a). "Social Class and School Knowledge." *Curriculum Inquiry*, 11(1): 3–42.

———. (1981b). "Schools as Agencies of Social Legitimation." *Journal of Curriculum Theorizing*, 3(2): 86–103.

———. (1981c). "Elementary Schooling and Distinctions of Social Class." *Interchange*, 12(2–3): 118–32.

———. (1983). "Workers, Labor and Economic History, and Textbook Content." In M. W. Apple and L. Weis, eds. *Ideology and Practice in Schooling* (pp. 37–60). Philadelphia: Temple University Press.

———. (1984). "Intersections of Gender and Class: Accommodation and Resistance by Working-Class and Affluent Females to Contradictory Sex Role Ideologies." *Journal of Education*, 166(1): 25–48.

Apple, M. W. (1973). "School Reform and Educational Scholarship: An Essay Review of *How Effective Is Schooling*." *Journal of Educational Research*, 66(8): 368–81.

———. (1974). "The Process and Ideology of Valuing in Educational Settings." In M. W. Apple, M. J. Subkoviak, and H. S. Lufer Jr., eds. *Educational Evaluation: Analysis and Responsibility* (pp. 3–34). Berkeley, California: McCutchan Publishing Corp.

———. (1976). "Curriculum as Ideological Selection." *Comparative Educational Review, 20* (2): 209–15.

———. (1978). "The New Sociology of Education: Analyzing Cultural and Economic Reproduction." *Harvard Educational Review, 48*(4): 495–503.

———. (1979a). "What Correspondence Theories of the Hidden Curriculum Miss." *The Review of Education, 5*(2): 101–12.

———. (1979b). *Ideology and Curriculum.* London: Routledge and Kegan Paul.

———. (1980). "The Other Side of the Hidden Curriculum: Correspondence Theories and the Labor Process." *Journal of Education, 162*(1): 47–66.

———. (1981). "Reproduction, Contestation, and Curriculum: An Essay in Self-Criticism." *Interchange, 12* (2–3): 27–47.

———. (1982a). "Reproduction and Contradiction in Education: An Introduction." In M. W. Apple, ed. *Cultural and Economic Reproduction in Education* (pp. 1–31). Boston: Routledge and Kegan Paul.

———. (1982b). "Curriculum Form and the Logic of Technical Control: Building the Possessive Individual." In M. W. Apple, ed. *Cultural and Economic Reproduction in Education,* (pp. 247–74). Boston: Routledge and Kegan Paul.

———. (1982c). *Education and Power.* London: Routledge and Kegan Paul.

———. (1986a). "Curriculum, Capitalism, and Democracy: A Response to Whitty's critics." *British Journal of Sociology of Education, 7*(3): 319–27.

———. (1986b). *Teachers and Texts.* New York: Routledge.

———. (1988a). "Social Crisis and Curriculum Accords." *Educational Theory, 38*(2): 191–201.

———. (1988b). "Facing the Complexities of Power: For a Parallelist Position in Critical Educational Studies." In M. Cole, ed. *Bowles and Gintis Revisited: Correspondence and Contradiction in Educational Theory* (pp. 112–30). London, New York, and Philadelphia: Falmer Press.

———. (1989). "Regulating the Text: The Socio-Historical Roots of State Control." *Educational Policy, 3*(2): 107–23.

———. (1991). "Educational Policy and the Gendered State." *The Review of Education, 14*(2): 17–19.

———. (1992). "Education, Culture, and Class Power: Basil Bernstein and the Neo Marxist Sociology of Education." Educational Theory, 42(2): 127–45.

———. (1993). *Official Knowledge: Democratic Education in a Conservative Age.* New York: Routledge.

Apple, M. W., ed. (1982). *Cultural and Economic Reproduction in Education: "Essays on Class, Ideology, and the State."* London: Routledge and Kegan Paul.

Apple, M. W. and Beyer, L. E. (1988). "Social Evaluation of Curriculum." In M. W. Apple and L. E. Beyer, eds. *The Curriculum* (pp. 334–50). Albany: State University of New York Press.

Apple, M. W. and Weis, L. (1983a). "Ideology and Practice in Schooling: A Political and Conceptual Introduction." In M. W. Apple and L. Weis, eds. *Ideology and Practice in Schooling* (pp. 3–33). Philadelphia: Temple University Press.

< 180 >

————. (1983b). *Ideology and Practice in Schooling*. Philadelphia: Temple University Press.

Apple, M. W. and Wexler, P. (1978). "Cultural Capital and Educational Transmissions." *Educational Theory*, 28(1): 34–43.

Arnot, M. (1984). "A Feminist Perspective on the Relationship Between Family Life and School Life." *Journal of Education*, 166(1): 5–24.

Arnot, M. and Whitty, G. (1982). "From Reproduction to Transformation: Recent Radical Perspectives on the Curriculum from the USA." *British Journal of Sociology of Education*, 3(1): 93–103.

Aronowitz, S. and Giroux, H. A. (1985). *Education under Siege*. South Hadley, Massachusetts: Bergin and Garvey Publishers.

————. (1991). *Postmodern Education*. Minneapolis: University of Minnesota Press.

Atkinson, P. (1985). *Language, Structure, and Reproduction: An Introduction to the Sociology of Basil Bernstein*. London: Methuen.

Ball, S. (1981). *Beachside Comprehensive*. Cambridge: Cambridge University Press.

Barton, L. and Walker, S., eds. (1982). *Race, Class, and Education*. London and Canberra: Croom Helm.

Benavot, A., Cha, Y–K., Kamiens, D., Meyer, J. W., and Wong, S–Y. (1991). "Knowledge for the Masses: World Models and National Curricula, 1920–1986," *American Sociological Review* 56: 85–100.

Berger, P. and Luckmann, T. (1966). *The Social Construction of Reality*. New York: Doubleday & Company.

Bernstein, B. (1971a). "On the Classification and Framing of Educational Knowledge." In M. F. D. Young, ed. *Knowledge and Control* (pp. 47–69). London: Collier-Macmillan.

————. (1971b). *Class, Codes, and Control Vol. I, Theoretical Studies towards a Sociology of Language*. London: Routledge and Kegan Paul.

————. (1975). *Class, Codes, and Control Vol. III, Towards a Theory of Educational Transmissions*. London: Routledge and Kegan Paul.

————. (1977a). *Class, Codes, and Control Vol. III*, Second Edition., *Towards a Theory of Educational Transmissions*. London: Routledge and Kegan Paul.

————. (1977b). "Class and Pedagogies: Visible and Invisible." In J. Karabel and A. H. Halsey, eds. *Power and Ideology in Education* (pp. 511–34). New York: Oxford University Press.

————. (1977c). "Social Class, Language, and Socialisation." In J. Karabel and A. H. Halsey, eds. *Power and Ideology in Education* (pp. 473–86). New York: Oxford University Press.

————. (1982). "Codes, Modalities, and the Process of Cultural Reproduction: A Model." In M. W. Apple, ed. *Cultural and Economic Reproduction in Education* (pp. 304–55). Boston: Routledge and Kegan Paul.

————. (1990). *The Structuring of Pedagogic Discourse: Class, Codes, and Control Vol. IV*. London and New York: Routledge.

Bernstein, B., ed. (1973). *Class, Codes, and Control Vol. II, Applied Studies towards a Sociology of Language*. London: Routledge and Kegan Paul.

Best, R. (1983). *We've All Got Scares*. Bloomington: Indiana University Press.

Beyer, L. E. (1983). "Aesthetic Curriculum and Cultural Reproduction." In M. W.

< 181 >

Apple and L. Weis, eds. *Ideology and Practice in Schooling* (pp. 89–113). Philadelphia: Temple University Press.

———. (1986). "The Reconstruction of Knowledge and Educational Studies." *Journal of Education*, 168(2): 113–35.

———. (1988). *Knowing and Acting.* London: Falmer Press.

Beyer, L. E. and Apple, M. W., eds. (1988). *The Curriculum.* Albany: State University of New York Press.

Boli, J. and Ramirez, F. (1986). "World Culture and the Institutional Development of Mass Education." In John G. Richardson, ed. *Handbook of Theory and Research for the Sociology of Education* (pp. 65–90). New York: Greenwood Press.

Boli, J., Ramirez, F., and Meyer, J. W. (1985) "Explaining the Origins and Expansion of Mass Education," *Comparative Education Review* 29: 145–70.

Bourdieu, P. (1971a). "Intellectual Field and Creative Project." In M. F. D. Young, ed. *Knowledge and Control* (pp. 161–88). London: Collier-Macmillan.

———. (1971b). "Systems of Education and Systems of Thought." In M. F. D. Young, ed. *Knowledge and Control* (pp. 189–207). London: Collier-Macmillan.

———. (1977a). "Symbolic Power." In D. Gleeson, ed. *Identity and Structure: Issues in the Sociology of Education* (pp. 113–19). Nafferton, England: Nafferton Books.

———. (1977b). "Cultural Reproduction and Social Reproduction." In J. Karabel and A. H. Halsey, eds. *Power and Ideology in Education* (pp. 487–510). New York: Oxford University Press.

———. (1977c). *Outline of a Theory of Practice*, trans. Richard Nice. Cambridge: Oxford University Press.

———. (1981). "The Specificity of the Scientific Field." In C. C. Lemert, ed. *French Sociology: Rupture and Renewal Since 1968* (pp. 257–92). New York: Columbia University Press.

———. (1982). "Schooling as a Conservative Force: Scholastic and Cultural Inequalities." In E. Bredo and W. Feinberg, eds. *Knowledge and Values in Social and Educational Research* (pp. 391–407). Philadelphia: Temple University Press.

———. (1983). "The Forms of Capital." In J. G. Richardson, ed. *Handbook of Theory and Research for the Sociology of Education* (pp. 241–57). New York: Greenwood Press.

———. (1984). *Distinction*, trans. Richard Nice. Cambridge, Massachusetts: Harvard University Press.

———. (1988a). *Homo Academicus*, trans. Peter Collier. Stanford, California: Stanford University Press.

———. (1988b). "Vive la Crise!: For Heterodoxy in Social Science." *Theory and Society*, 17: 773–787.

———. (1989a). "Social Space and Symbolic Power," trans. Louie Wacquant. *Sociological Theory*, 7(1): 14–25.

———. (1989b). *La Noblesse d' État: grandes écoles et esprit de corps.* Paris: Ed. de Minuit.

———. (1990a). *In Other Words: Essays Toward a Reflexive Sociology*, trans. and ed. Matthew Adamson. Stanford, California: Stanford University Press.

< 182 >

————. (1990b). *The Logic of Practice*, trans. Richard Nice. Stanford, California: Stanford University Press.

————. (1991a). "The Peculiar History of Scientific Reason." *Sociological Forum*, 6(1): 3–26.

————. (1991b). *The Political Ontology of Martin Heidegger*. Stanford, California: Stanford University Press.

————. (1991c). *Language and Symbolic Power*, edited and introduced by John B. Thompson, trans. Gino Raymond and Matthew Adamson. Cambridge, Massachusetts: Harvard University Press.

————. (1993). *Sociology in Question*, trans. Richard Nice. London: Sage Publications. Bourdieu, P., Chamboredon, J. C., and Passeron, J. C. (1968). *Le Métier de Sociologue*. Paris: Mouton-Bordas.

————. (1991). *The Craft of Sociology*, ed. Beate Krais, trans. Richard Nice. Berlin and New York: Walter de Gruyer.

Bourdieu, P. and de Saint-Martin, M. (1974). "Scholastic Excellence and the Values of the Educational System." In J. Eggleston, ed. *Contemporary Research in the Sociology of Education* (pp. 338–71). London: Methuen.

Bourdieu, P. and Passeron, J. C. (1977). *Reproduction in Education, Society, and Culture*, trans. Richard Nice. Beverly Hills: Sage.

————. (1979). *The Inheritors: French Students and Their Relation to Culture*, trans. Richard Nice. Chicago and London: University of Chicago Press.

————. (1990). *Reproduction in Society, Education, and Culture*, Second Edition. London: Sage.

Bourdieu, P., Passeron, J. C., and de Saint Martin, M. (1993). *Academic Discourse: Linguistic Misunderstanding and Professional Power*. trans. Richard Tesse. Cambridge: Polity Press.

Bowers, C.A. (1986). "The Dialectic of Nihilism and the State: Implications for an Emancipatory Theory of Education." *Educational Theory*, 36(3): 225–32.

Bowles, S. and Gintis, H. (1976). *Schooling in Capitalist America*. New York: Basic Books.

Bredo, E. and Feinberg, W., eds. (1982). *Knowledge and Values in Social and Educational Research*. Philadelphia: Temple University Press.

Brubacker, R. (1985). "Rethinking Classical Theory: The Sociological Vision of Pierre Bourdieu." *Theory and Society*, 14(6): 745–74.

Canguilheim, G. (1988). *Ideology and Rationality in the History of the Life Sciences*, trans. Arthur Golhammer. Cambridge, Massachusetts, and London: The MIT Press.

Carnoy, M. (1982). "Education, Economy, and the State." In M. W. Apple, ed. *Cultural and Economic Reproduction in Education: Essays on Class, Ideology, and the State* (pp. 79–126). London: Routledge and Kegan Paul.

Carnoy, M. and Levin, H. (1985). *Schooling and Work in the Democratic State*. Stanford: Stanford University Press.

Cherryholmes, C. H. (1988). *Power and Criticism*. New York: Teachers College Press.

Chodorow, N. (1978). *The Reproduction of Mothering: Psychoanalysis and the Sociology of Gender*. Berkeley: University of California Press.

Christian-Smith, L. K. (1987). "Gender, Popular Culture, and Curriculum." *Curriculum Inquiry*, 17(4): 365–406.

————. (1990). *Becoming a Woman through Romance*. New York and London: Routledge.

Cicourel, A. and Kitsuse, J. I. (1977). "The School as a Mechanism of Social Differentiation." In J. Karabel and A. H. Halsey, eds. *Power and Ideology in Education* (pp. 282–91). New York: Oxford University Press.

Clifford, J. and Marcus, J. E., eds. (1986). *Writing Culture: The Poetics and Politics of Ethnography*. Berkeley: University of California Press.

Cole, M., ed. (1988). *Bowles and Gintis Revisited: Correspondence and Contradiction in Educational Theory*. London, New York, and Philadelphia: Falmer Press.

Coleman, J. S. (1988). "Social Capital in the Creation of Human Capital." *American Journal of Sociology*, 94: 95–120.

————. (1990). *Equality and Achievement in Education*. Boulder: Westview Press.

Collins, R. (1979a). "Functional and Conflict Theories of Educational Stratification." In J. Karabel and A. H. Halsey, eds. *Power and Ideology in Education* (pp. 118–36). New York: Oxford University Press.

————. (1979b). *The Credential Society*. New York: Academic Press.

————. (1990). "The Durkheimian Tradition in Conflict Sociology," In J. Alexander, ed. *Durkheimian Sociology: Cultural Studies* (pp. 107–28). Cambridge: Cambridge University Press.

Connell, R. W., Ashenden, D. J., Kessler, S., and Dowsett, G. W. (1982). *Making the Difference*. Sydney: Allen and Unwin.

Culley, M. and Portuges, C., eds. (1985). *Gendered Subjects: The Dynamics of Feminist Teaching*. Boston: Routledge and Kegan Paul.

Dale, M. (1991). "Social Scientific Knowledge and Explanation in Educational Studies." *Educational Theory*, 41(2): 135–52.

Dale, R. (1974). "Phenomenological Perspectives and the Sociology of the School." In M. Flude and J. Ahiers, eds. *Educability, Schools, and Ideology*, (pp. 175–89). New York: Wiley and Sons.

————. (1982). "Education and the Capitalist State: Contributions and Contradictions." In M. W. Apple, ed. *Cultural and Economic Reproduction in Education* (pp. 127–61). Boston: Routledge and Kegan Paul.

Dale, R., Essland, G., and MacDonald, M., eds. (1976). *Schooling and Capitalism: A Sociological Reader*. London: Routledge and Kegan Paul.

Davies, I. (1971). "The Management of Knowledge: A Critique of the Use of Typologies in the Sociology of Education." In M. F. D. Young, ed. *Knowledge and Control* (pp. 267–88). London: Collier-Macmillan.

Dawe, A. (1970). "The Two Sociologies." *British Journal of Sociology*, 21(2):207–18.

de Lauretis, T. (1986a). "Feminist Studies/Critical Studies: Issues, Terms, and Contexts." In T. de Lauretis. *Feminist Studies/Critical Studies* (pp. 1–19). Bloomington: Indiana University Press.

————. (1990). "Upping the Anti (*sic*) in Feminist Theory." In M. Hirsch and E. Fox Keller. *Conflicts in Feminism* (pp. 255–70). New York: Routledge.

de Lauretis, T., ed. (1986b). *Feminist Studies/Critical Studies*. Bloomington: Indiana University Press.

Delamont, S. (1989). *Knowledgeable Women: Structuralism and the Reproduction of Elites*. London and New York: Routledge.

< 184 >

de Tocqueville, A. (1956). In R. D. Heffner, ed. *Democracy in America*. New York: Mentor Books.

Dimaggio, P. (1979). "Review Essay: On Pierre Bourdieu." *American Journal of Sociology*, 84(6): 1460–73.

Dimaggio, P. and Useem, M. (1982). "The Arts in Class Reproduction." In M. W. Apple, ed. *Cultural and Economic Reproduction in Education*, (pp. 181–201). Boston: Routledge and Kegan Paul.

Dinnerstein, D. (1976). *The Mermaid and the Minotaur: Sexual Arrangements and Human Malaise*. New York: Harper and Row.

Dreeben, R. (1977). "The Contribution of Schooling to the Learning of Norms." In J. Karabel and A. H. Halsey, eds. *Power and Ideology in Education* (pp. 544–50). New York: Oxford University Press.

Eisner, E. and Peshkin, A, eds. (1991). *Qualitative Inquiry in Education*. New York: Teachers College Press.

Ellsworth, E. (1989). "Why Doesn't This Feel Empowering? Working Through the Repressive Myths of Critical Pedagogy." *Harvard Educational Review*, 59(3): 29–324.

———. (1990). "Correspondence." *Harvard Educational Review*, 60(3): 388–405.

Epstein, C. F. (1988). *Deceptive Distinctions*. New Haven and London: Yale University Press.

Erikson, F. (1990). "Qualitative Methods." In American Educational Research Association. *Research in Teaching and Learning, Vol. 2*, (pp. 75–194). New York: Macmillan.

Esland, G. M. (1971). "Teaching and Leaning as the Organization of Knowledge." In M. F. D. Young, ed. *Knowledge and Control* (pp. 70–117). London: Collier-Macmillan.

Everhart, R. B. (1983). *Reading, Writing, and Resistance*. Boston: Routledge and Kegan Paul.

Feyerabend, P. (1970). "Consolations for the Specialists," In I. Lakatos and A. Musgrave, eds. *Criticism and the Growth of Knowledge*, (pp. 197–230). London: Cambridge University Press.

Flude, M. and Ahiers, J., eds. (1974). *Educability, Schools, and Ideology*. New York: Wiley and Sons.

Foucault, M. (1973). *The Order of Things*. New York: Vintage.

———. (1977). *Discipline and Punish*, trans. Alan Sheridan. New York: Pantheon.

Fraser, N. (1989). *Unruly Practices*. Minneapolis: University of Minnesota Press.

Frazier, N, and Sadker, M. (1973). *Sexism in School and Society*. New York: Harper and Row.

Fuller, S. (1991). *Social Epistemology*. Bloomington: Indiana University Press.

———. (1993a). *Philosophy of Science and its Discontents*. Second Edition. New York: Guildford Press.

———. (1993b). *Philosophy, Rhetoric, and the End of Knowledge: The Coming of Science and Technology Studies*. Madison: University of Wisconsin Press.

Gage, N. L. (1989). "The Paradigm Wars and Their Aftermath—A 'Historical' Sketch of Research on Teaching Science 1989." *Educational Research*, 18(7): 4–10.

< 185 >

Gamoran, A. (1987). "The Stratification of High School Learning Opportunities." *Sociology of Education*, 60(3): 135–55.

———. (1989). "Measuring Curriculum Differentiation." *American Journal of Education*, 97: 129–43.

Gamoran, A. and Mare, R. (1989). "Secondary School Tracking and Educational Inequality." *American Journal of Sociology*, 94(5): 1146–83.

Gamoran, A. and Nystrand, M. (1991). "Background and Instructional Effects on Achievement in Eighth-Grade English and Social Studies." *Journal of Research on Adolescence*, 1: 277–300.

Gaze, N. L. (1989). "The Paradigm Wars and their Aftermath—A Historical Sketch of Research on Teaching Since 1989." *Educational Researcher*, 18(7) 4–10.

Giddens, A. (1979). *Central Problems in Social Theory.* Berkeley, California: University of California Press.

Ginsburg, M. B. (1988). *Contradictions of Teacher Education and Society.* London and New York: Falmer Press.

Giroux, H. A. (1978). "Writing and Critical Thinking in the Social Studies." *Curriculum Inquiry*, 8(4): 291–310.

———. (1979). "Toward a New Sociology of Curriculum." *Educational Leadership*, 37(3): 248–53.

———. (1981a). "Pedagogy, Pessimism, and the Politics of Conformity: A Reply to Linda McNeil." *Curriculum Inquiry*, 11(3): 211–22.

———. (1981b). "Forward a New Sociology of Curriculum." In H. A. Giroux, A. Penna, and W. Pinar, eds. *Curriculum and Instruction* (pp. 98–108). San Francisco: McCutchan.

———. (1981c). "Schooling and the Culture of Positivism: Notes on the Death of History." In H. A. Giroux *Ideology, Culture, and the Process of Schooling* (pp. 37–62). Philadelphia: Temple University Press.

———. (1981d). *Ideology, Culture, and the Process of Schooling.* Philadelphia: Temple University Press.

———. (1983a). "Theories of Reproduction and Resistance in the New Sociology of Education." *Harvard Educational Review*, 53(3): 257–93.

———. (1983b). *Theory and Resistance in Education.* South Hadley, Massachusetts: Bergin and Garvey.

———. (1984). "Marxism and Schooling: The Limits of Radical Discourse." *Educational Theory*, 34(2): 113–35.

———. (1985). "Toward a Critical Theory of Education: Beyond a Marxism with Guarantees—A Response to Daniel Liston." *Educational Theory*, 35(3): 313–19

———. (1988). "Border Pedagogy in the Age of Postmodernism." *Journal of Education*, 170(3): 162–81.

Giroux, H. A., ed. (1991). *Postmodernism, Feminism, and Cultural Politics.* Albany: State University of New York Press.

Gitlin, A., ed. (1994). *Power and Method: Political Activism and Educational Research.* New York: Routledge.

Gore, J. M. (1989). "The Struggle for Pedagogies: Critical and Feminist Pedagogy Discourses as 'Regimes of Truth.'" Paper presented at The Eleventh Annual Conference on Curriculum Theory and Practice, Bergamo Conference Center, Dayton, Ohio, 18–22 October 1989.

< 186 >

————. (1992). *The Struggle for Pedagogies*. London and New York: Routledge.

Gramsci, A. (1971). *Prison Notebooks*, eds. and trans. Quitin Hoare and Geoffrey Nowell Smith. New York: International Publishers.

Greenacre, M. J. (1984). *Theory and Applications of Correspondence Analysis*. New York: Academic Press.

Grumet, M, R. (1988). *Bitter Milk*. Amherst, Massachusetts: University of Massachusetts Press.

Habermas, J. (1971). *Knowledge and Human Interest*, trans. Jeremy Shapiro. Boston: Beacon Press.

————. (1981). *Theory of Communicative Action*, Vol. 1, trans. Thomas McCarthy. Boston: Beacon Press.

Hall, S., Hobson, D., Lowe, A., and Willis, P., eds. (1980). *Culture, Media, Language*. London: Hutchinson.

Haraway, D. (1986). *Primate Visions*. London and New York: Routledge.

Harding, S. (1986). *The Science Question in Feminism*. Ithaca and London: Cornell University Press.

————. (1991). *Whose Science? Whose Knowledge?* Ithaca: Cornell University Press.

Harding, S., ed. (1987). *Feminism and Methodology*. Bloomington, Indianapolis, and Milton Keynes: Indiana University Press and Open University Press.

————. ed. (1993). *The "Racial" Economy of Science: Towards a Democratic Future*. Bloomington: Indiana University Press.

Hargreaves, A. (1982). "Resistance and Relative Autonomy Theories: Problems of Distortion and Incoherence in Recent Marxist Analyses of Education." *British Journal of Sociology of Education*, 3(2): 107–25.

Henriques, J., Hollway, W., Urwin, C., Venn, C. and Walkerdine, V. eds. (1984). *Changing the Subject*. London and New York: Methuen.

Henry, J. (1954). "Docility, or Giving Teacher What She Wants," *Journal of Social Issues*, (1954): 33–41.

————. (1963). *Culture Against Man*. New York: Random House.

————. (1972). *On Education*. New York: Vintage Books.

————. (1973). *On Sham, Vulnerability, and Other Forms of Self-Destruction*. New York: Vintage Books.

Hicks, E. (1981). "Cultural Marxism: Nonsynchrony and Feminist Practice." In L. Sargent, ed. *Women and Revolution*, (pp. 219–38). Boston: South End Press.

Hirsch, M and Fox Keller, E., eds. (1990). *Conflicts in Feminisms*. London and New York: Routledge.

Hofstader, R. (1962). *Anti-Intellectualism in American Life*. New York: Random House.

Huebner, D. (1970). "Curriculum as the Accessibility of Knowledge." Paper presented at the Curriculum Theory Study Group, Minneapolis, Minn., 2 March 1970.

————. (1975). "The Task of the Curricular Theorist." In W. Pinar, ed. *Curriculum Theorizing*, (pp. 250–70). Berkeley, California: McCutchan.

Hunter, A. (1991). "Review Essay: *Social Analysis of Education: After the New Sociology*." *Educational Theory*, 41(4): 411–20.

Jackson, P. W. (1977). "Beyond Good and Evil: Observations on the Recent Criticisms of Schooling." *Curriculum Inquiry*, 6(4): 311–40.

Jaynes, G. D. and Williams, R. M., Jr., eds. (1989). *A Common Destiny*. Washington, D.C.: National Academy Press.

Jenks, C. (1993). "Introduction: The Analytic Bases of Cultural Reproduction Theory." In C. Jenks, ed., *Cultural Reproduction*. New York: Routledge.

Karabel, J. and Halsey, A. H. (1977a). "Introduction." In J. Karabel and A. H Halsey, eds. *Power and Ideology in Education* (pp. 1–85). New York, Oxford University Press.

Karabel, J., and Halsey, H. A., eds. (1977). *Power and Ideology in Education*. New York, Oxford University Press.

Keddie, N. (1971). "Classroom Knowledge." In M. F. D. Young, ed. *Knowledge and Control* (pp. 133–60). London: Collier-Macmillan.

Kelly, G. P. and Nihlen, A. S. (1982). "Schooling and the Reproduction of Patriarchy: Unequal Workloads, Unequal Rewards." In M. W. Apple, ed. *Cultural and Economic Reproduction in Education* (pp. 162–80). Boston: Routledge and Kegan Paul.

Kenway, J. (1990). *Gender and Education Policy*. Geelong, Australia: Deakin University Press.

Knorr-Cetina, K. (1981). *The Manufacture of Knowledge: An Essay on the Constructivist and Contextual Nature of Science*. Oxford: Pergamon Press.

Kuhn, T. S. (1962). *The Structure of Scientific Revolutions*. Chicago: University of Chicago Press.

———. (1970). "Reflections on my Critics." In I. Lakatos and A. Musgrave, eds. *Criticism and the Growth of Knowledge* (pp. 231–78). London: Cambridge University Press.

Ladwig, J. G. (1990). "An Alternative Outline for Educational Critical Social Science." Unpublished manuscript, University of Wisconsin–Madison.

———. (1991). "Is Collaborative Research Exploitative?" *Educational Theory, 41*(2): 111–20.

———. (1994a). "For Whom this Reform?: Outlining Educational Policy as a Social Field." *British Journal of Sociology of Education, 15*(3): 341–63

———. (1994b). "The Genesis of Groups in the Sociology of School Knowledge." In B. Pink and G. Noblit, eds. *Continuity and Contradiction*. (pp. 209–29). Cresskill, New Jersey: Hampton Press.

Ladwig, J. G. and Berends, M. (1994). "Testing the Sociology of School Knowledge." A paper presented at the Annum Meeting of the American Educational Research Association, New Orleans, April 1994.

Laird, S. (1988a). "Women and Gender in John Dewey's Philosophy of Education." *Educational Theory, 38*(1): 111–29.

———. (1988b). "Reforming 'Woman's True Profession': A Case for 'Feminist Pedagogy' in Teacher Education?" *Harvard Educational Review, 58*(4): 449–63.

Lakatos, I. and Musgrave, A., eds. (1970). *Criticism and the Growth of Knowledge*. London: Cambridge University Press.

Lakomski, G. (1984). "On Agency and Structure: Pierre Bourdieu and Jean-Claude Passeron's Theory of Symbolic Violence." *Curriculum Inquiry, 14*(2): 151–63.

Lamont, M. (1992). *Money, Morals, and Manners: The Culture of the French and American Upper-Middle Class*. Chicago: University of Chicago Press.

< 188 >

Lamont, M. and Fournier, M., ed. (1992). *Cultivating Differences: Symbolic Boundaries and the Making of Inequality*. Chicago: University of Chicago Press.

Lamont, M. and Lareau, A. (1988). "Cultural Capital: Allusions, Gaps, and Glissandos in Recent Theoretical Developments." *Sociological Theory*, 6: 153–68.

Lather, P. (1984). "Critical Theory, Curricular Transformation, and Feminist Mainstreaming." *Journal of Education*, 166(1): 49–62.

———. (1986). "Issues of Validity in Openly Ideological Research: Between a Rock and a Soft Place." *Interchange*, 17(4): 63–84.

———. (1987). "Feminist Perspectives on Empowering Research Methodologies." Paper prepared for the American Educational Research Association, Washington, D.C., 1987.

———. (1988). "Educational Research and Practice in a Postmodern Era." Paper prepared for the American Educational Research Association, New Orleans.

———. (1991). *Getting Smart: Feminist Research and Pedagogy with/in the Postmodern*. New York and London: Routledge.

Lemert, C., ed. (1981). *French Sociology: Rupture and Renewal Since 1968*. New York: Columbia University Press.

———. (1991) "The End of Ideology, Really." *Sociological Theory*, 9(2): 164–72.

Linn, R. (1990). "Quantitative Methods." American Educational Research Association. *Research in Teaching and Learning*, Vol. 2. (pp. 1–74). New York: Macmillan.

Liston, D. (1984). "Have We Explained the Relationship between Curriculum and Capitalism? An Analysis of the Selective Tradition." *Educational Theory*, 34(3): 241–53.

———. (1985). "Marxism and Schooling: A Failed or Limited Tradition?" *Educational Theory*, 35(3): 307–12.

———. (1986). "On Fact and Values: An Analysis of Radical Curriculum Studies." *Educational Theory*, 36(2): 137–52.

———. (1988a). "Faith and Evidence: Examining Marxist Explanations of Schools." *American Journal of Education*, 9(3): 323–50.

———. (1988b). *Capitalist Schools: Explanations and Ethics in Radical Studies of Schooling*. New York and London: Routledge.

Lukács, G. (1971). *History and Class Consciousness*, trans. Rodney Livingstone. Cambridge, Massachusetts: MIT Press.

Luke, A. (1990). "The Body Literate: Discursive Inscription in Early Literacy Training." Paper of the XII World Congress of Sociology, presented at Madrid, Spain.

Luttrell, W. (1989). "Working-Class Women's Ways of Knowing: Effects of Gender, Race, and Class." *Sociology of Education*, 62(1): 33–46.

Macdonald, J. B. (1981a). "Curriculum, Consciousness, and Social Change." *Journal of Curriculum Theorizing*, 3(1): 143–53.

———. (1988b). "Theory, Practice, and the Hermeneutic Circle." *Journal of Curriculum Theorizing*, 3(2): 130–38.

MacIntyre, A. (1982). "The Idea of a Social Science." In E. Bredo and W. Feinberg, eds. *Knowledge and Values in Social and Educational Research* (pp. 292–310). Philadelphia: Temple University Press.

Maher, F. (1985). "Classroom Pedagogy and the New Scholarship on Women." In M. Culley and C. Portuges, eds. *Gendered Subjects: The Dynamics of Feminist Teaching* (pp. 29–48). Boston: Routledge and Kegan Paul.

Mannheim, K. (1936). *Ideology and Utopia,* trans. Louis Wirth and Edward Shils. New York: Harcourt, Brace & World.

Marcus, G. E. and Fischer, M. M. J. (1986). *Anthropology as Cultural Critique.* Chicago and London: University of Chicago Press.

Marcuse, H. (1978). "On Science and Phenomenology." In A. Arato and E. Gebhart, eds., *The Essential Frankfurt Reader* (pp. 466–76). New York: Urizen Books.

Mazza, K. A. (1981). "Reconceptual Inquiry as an Alternative Mode of Curriculum Theory and Practice: A Critical Study." *Journal of Curriculum Theorizing,* 3(1): 5–89.

McCall, L. (1981). "Does Gender Fit? Feminism, Bourdieu, and Conceptions of Social Order." *Theory and Society,* 21(6): 837–67.

McCarthy, C. (1988). "Reconsidering Liberal and Radical Perspectives on Racial Inequality in Schooling; Making the Case for Nonsynchrony." *Harvard Educational Review,* 58(2): 265–79.

———. (1990). *Race and Curriculum: Social Inequality and the Theories and Politics of Difference in Contemporary Research on Schooling.* London, New York, and Philadelphia: The Falmer Press.

McCarthy, C. and Apple, M. W. (1988). "Race, Class, and Gender in American Educational Research: Toward a Nonsynchronous Parallelist Position." In L. Weis, ed. *Class, Race, and Gender in American Education* (pp. 9–39). Albany: State University of New York Press.

McCarthy, C. and Crichlow, W., eds. (1993). *Race, Identity, Representation in Education.* New York: Routledge.

McGee, M. C. and Lyne, J. R. (1987). "What Are Nice Folks Like You Doing in a Place Like This?: Some Entailments of Treating Knowledge Claims Rhetorically." In J. S. Nelson, A. Megill, and D. N. McCloskey, eds. *The Rhetoric of the Human Sciences* (pp. 381–406). Madison: The University of Wisconsin Press.

McLaren, P. (1988). "Schooling the Postmodern Body: Critical Pedagogy and the Politics of Enfleshment." *Journal of Education,* 170(3): 53–83.

McLellan, D. (1987). *Karl Marx: Selected Writings.* Oxford: Oxford University Press.

McNeil, L. (1981). "On the Possibility of Teachers as the Source of an Emancipatory Pedagogy: A Response to Henry Giroux." *Curriculum Inquiry,* 11(3): 205–10.

McNeil, L. M. (1983). "Defensive Teaching and Classroom Control." In M. W. Apple and L. Weis, eds. *Ideology and Practice in Schooling* (pp. 114–42). Philadelphia: Temple University Press.

———. (1986). *Contradictions of Control.* New York: Routledge and Kegan Paul.

McRobbie, A. (1978). "Working Class Girls and the Culture of Femininity." In Women's Studies Group, eds. *Women Take Issue* (pp. 96–108). London: Hutchinson.

———. (1980). "Settling Accounts with Subcultures: A Feminist Critique." *Screen Education,* 34: 37–9.

Mehan, H. (1992). "Understanding Inequalities in Schools: The Contribution of Interpretive Studies." *Sociology of Education,* 65: 1–20.

Meyer, J. W. (1980). "The World Polity and the Authority of the Nation-State" In A.

Bergesen, ed. *Studies in the Modern World System* (pp. 109–37). New York: Academic Press.

———. (1986). "Types of Explanation in the Sociology of Education." In J. G. Richardson, ed. *Handbook of Theory and Research for the Sociology of Education* (pp. 341–59). New York: Greenwood Press.

Meyer, J. W., Ramirez, F., and Soysal, Y. N. (1992). "World Expansion of Mass Education," *Sociology of Education*, Vol. 65, 128–49.

Mills, C. W. (1963). "Methodological Consequence of the Sociology of Knowledge." In C. W. Mills. *Power, Politics, and People* (pp. 453–68). New York: Ballantine Books.

Mitrano, B. "Feminism and Curriculum Theory: Implications for Teacher Education." *Journal of Curriculum Theorizing*, 3(2): 5–85.

Morrow, R. A. and Torres, C. A. (1994). "Education and the Reproduction of Class, Gender, and Race: Responding to the Postmodern Challenge." *Educational Theory* 44(1): 43–61.

Mulkay, M. (1991). *Sociology of Science: A Sociological Pilgrimage*. Milton Keynes: Open University Press.

Musgraves, P. W. (1972). *The Sociology of Education*, Second Edition. London: Methuen.

Nash, R. (1984). "On Two Critiques of the Marxist Sociology of Education." *British Journal of Sociology of Education*, 5(1): 19–31.

Nelson, J. S., Megill, A., and McCloskey. D. N., eds. (1987). *The Rhetoric of the Human Sciences*. Madison, Wisconsin: University of Wisconsin Press.

Nicholson, L., ed. (1991). *Feminism/Postmodernism*. New York and London: Routledge.

O'Brien, M. (1981). *The Politics of Reproduction*. London: Routledge and Kegan Paul.

———. (1984). "The Commatization of Women: Patriarchal Fetishism in the Sociology of Education." *Interchange*, 15(2): 43–60.

Oakes, J. (1985). *Keeping Track: How Schools Structure Inequality*. New Haven and London: Yale University Press.

Olneck, M. and Bills, D. (1980). "What Makes Sammy Run? An Empirical Assessment of the Bowles-Gintis Correspondence Theory." *American Journal of Education*, 89(1): 27–61.

Phillips, D. C. (1987). *Philosophy, Science, and Social Inquiry*. Oxford: Pergamon Press.

Pinar, W. (1978). "The Reconceptualization of Curriculum Studies." *Journal of Curriculum Studies*, 10(38): 205–14.

Pinar, W., ed. (1975). *Curriculum Theorizing*. Berkeley, California: McCutchan.

Popkewitz, T. S. (1984). *Paradigm and Ideology in Educational Research*. London: The Falmer Press.

———. (1991). *A Political Sociology of Educational Reform*. New York and London: Teachers College Press.

———. (forthcoming). "A Monument to a Field: A Review of *The Handbook of Research on Teacher Education*." *Journal of Teacher Education*.

Popper, K. (1968). *The Logic of Scientific Discovery*. New York: Harper and Row.

Rabinow, P. (1986). "Representations are Social Facts: Modernity and Post-Modernity in Anthropology." In J. Clifford and G. E. Marcus, eds. *Writing*

< 191 >

Culture: The Poetics and Politics of Ethnography (pp. 231–64). Berkeley: University of California Press.

Rawls, J. (1971). *A Theory of Justice*. Cambridge, Massachusetts: Harvard University Press.

Richardson, J. G., ed. (1986). *Handbook of Theory and Research for the Sociology of Education*. New York: Greenwood Press.

Rist, R. C. (1977). "On Understanding the Processes of Schooling: The Contribution of Labeling Theory." In J. Karabel and A. H. Halsey, eds. *Power and Ideology in Education* (pp. 292–306). New York, Oxford University Press.

Roman, L. G. and Apple, M. W. (1990). "Is Naturalism a Move Away from Positivism?" In E. Eisner and A. Peshkin, eds. *Qualitative Inquiry in Education* (pp. 38–73). New York: Teachers College Press.

Rorty, R. (1980). *Philosophy and the Mirror of Nature*. Princeton: Princeton University Press.

Roth, P. A. (1987). *Meaning and Method in the Social Sciences: A Case for Methodological Pluralism*. Ithaca: Cornell University Press.

Sadovnick, A. (1991). "Basil Bernstein's Theory of Pedagogic Practice." *Sociology of Education, 64*(1): 48–63.

Saha, L. J. (1987). "Social Mobility Versus Social Reproduction: Paradigms and Politics in the Sociology of Education." *New Education, 9*(1&2): 14–28.

Schutz, A. (1962). *Collected Papers 1: The Problem of Social Reality*. The Haugue: Martinus Nijhoff.

Schwartz, D. (1977). "Pierre Bourdieu: The Cultural Transmission of Social Inequality." *Harvard Educational Review, 47*(4): 545–54.

Seidman, S. (1991). "The End of Sociological Theory: The Postmodern Hope." *Sociological Theory, 9*(2): 131–46.

Seigel, H. (1980a). "Epistemological Relativism in its Latest Form." *Inquiry, 23*(1): 107–23.

———. (1980b). "Objectivity, Rationality, Incommensurability, and More." *British Journal for the Philosophy of Science*, 31: 359–84.

———. (1987). "Rationality and Ideology." *Educational Theory, 37*(2): 153–67.

Sharp, R. (1980). *Knowledge, Ideology, and the Process of Schooling*. London: Routledge and Kegan Paul.

Sharp, R. (1988). Old and New Orthodoxies: The Seductions of Liberalism. In Michael Cole, ed. *Bowles and Gintis Revisited: Correspondence and Contradiction in Educational Theory* (pp. 189–208). London, New York, and Philadelphia: Falmer Press.

Sharp, R. and Green, A. (1975). *Education and Social Control*. London: Routledge and Kegan Paul.

Shirley, D. (1986). "A Critical Review and Appropriation of Pierre Bourdieu's Analysis of Social and Cultural Reproduction." *Journal of Education*, 168(2): 96–112.

Spivak, G. C. (1988). *In Other Worlds*. London and New York: Routledge.

———. (1993). *Outside in the Teaching Machine*. New York: Routledge.

Stacey, J., Bereaud, S., and Daniels, J. (1974). *And Jill Came Tumbling After: Sexism in American Education*. New York: Dell Publishing.

< 192 >

Steedman, C., Urwin, C., and Walkerdine, V., eds. (1985). *Language, Gender, and Childhood*. London: Routledge and Kegan Paul.

Taxel, J. (1981). "The Outsiders of the American Revolution: The Selective Tradition in Children's Fiction." *Interchange*, 12(2–3): 206–228.

———. (1983). "The American Revolution: An Analysis of Literary Content, Form, and Ideology." In M. W. Apple and L. Weis, eds. *Ideology and Practice in Schooling*, (pp. 61–68). Philadelphia: Temple University Press.

Taylor, C. (1982). "Interpretation and the Sciences of Man." In E. Bredo and W. Feinberg, eds. *Knowledge and Values in Social and Educational Research* (pp. 153–86). Philadelphia: Temple University Press.

Taylor, S. (1989). "Empowering Girls and Young Women: The Challenge of the Gender- Inclusive Curriculum." *Journal of Curriculum Studies*, 21(5) 441–56.

Tyler, S. A. (1987). *The Unspeakable*. Madison: University of Wisconsin Press.

Vallance, E. (1982). "The Practical Uses of Curriculum Theory." *Theory Into Practice*, 21(1): 4–10.

Valli, L. (1986). *Becoming Clerical Workers*. New York: Routledge.

Vulliamy, G. (1976). "What Counts a School Music?" In G. Whitty and M. F. D. Young, eds. *Explorations in the Politics of School Knowledge* (pp. 19–34). Driffield: Nafferton Books, 1976.

Wacquant, L. (1989). "Towards a Reflexive Sociology: A Workshop with Pierre Bourdieu." *Sociological Theory*, 7(1): 26–63.

Walkerdine, V. (1985). "On the Regulation of Speaking and Silence: Subjectivity, Class, and Gender in Contemporary Schooling." In C. Steedman, C. Urwin, and V. Walkerdine, eds. *Language, Gender and Childhood*, (pp. 203–41). London: Routledge and Kegan Paul.

———. (1990). *Schoolgirl Fictions*. London: Verso.

Wallerstein, I. (1990). "Culture as the Ideological Battleground of the Modern World System." *Theory and Culture* 7:31–55.

———. (1991). *Unthinking Social Science: The Limits Nineteenth-Century Paradigms*. Cambridge: Polity Press.

Weedon, C. (1987). *Feminist Practice and Poststructuralist Theory*. Oxford: Basil Blackwell.

Weis, L. (1985). *Between Two Worlds: Black Students in an Urban Community College*. Boston: Routledge and Kegan Paul.

———. (1990). *Working Class Without Work*. London and New York: Routledge.

Weis, L., ed. (1988). *Class, Race, and Gender in American Education*. Albany: State University of New York Press.

Wexler, P. (1981a). "Change: Social, Cultural, and Educational." *Journal of Curriculum Theorizing*, 3(2): 157–64.

———. (1981b). "Body and Soul: Sources of Social Change and Strategies for Education." *British Journal of Sociology of Education* 2(3): 247–63.

———. (1982). "Structure, Text, and Subject: A Critical Sociology of School Knowledge." In M. W. Apple, ed. *Cultural and Economic Reproduction in Education* (pp. 276–303). London: Routledge and Kegan Paul.

———. (1983). "Movement, Class and Education." In L. Barton and S. Walker, eds. *Race, Class, and Education* (pp. 17–39). London and Canberra: Croom Helm.

———. (1987). *Social Analysis of Education*. New York and London: Routledge.

< 193 >

———. (1988). "Symbolic Economy of Identity and Denial of Labor: Studies in High School Number 1." In L. Weis, ed. *Class, Race, and Gender in American Education* (pp. 302–15). Albany: State University of New York Press.

———. (1992). *Becoming Somebody: Towards a Social Psychology of School.* London: The Falmer Press.

Whitty, G. (1985). *Sociology and School Knowledge.* London: Methuen.

———. (1987). "Curriculum Research and Curricular Politics." *British Journal of Sociology of Education,* 8(2): 109–17.

Whitty, G. and Arnot, M. (1984). "Evaluating Curriculum Research." (Xerox copy) In *Issues in Education: The Reproduction of Class and Gender Inequalities* (pp. 80–107). Buffalo: State University of New York Press.

Whitty, G. and Young, M. F. D., eds. *Explorations in the Politics of School Knowledge.* Driffield: Nafferton Books.

Williams, R. (1976). "Base and Superstructure in Marxist Cultural Theory." In R. Dale, G. Essland, and M. MacDonald, eds. *Schooling and Capitalism: A Sociological Reader* (pp. 202–9). London: Routledge and Kegan Paul.

Willis, P. (1977). *Learning to Labour.* Westmead: Saxon House.

———. (1981a). *Learning to Labour,* Second Edition. New York: Columbia University Press.

———. (1981b). "Cultural Production is Different from Cultural Reproduction is Different from Social Reproduction is Different from Reproduction." *Interchange,* 12(2–3): 48–67.

———. (1982). "The Class Significance of School Counter-Culture." In E. Bredo and W. Feinberg, eds. *Knowledge and Values in Social and Educational Research* (pp. 408–22). Philadelphia: Temple University Press.

Winch, P. (1982). "The Idea of a Social Science." In E. Bredo and W. Feinberg, eds. *Knowledge and Values in Social and Educational Research* (pp. 137–52). Philadelphia: Temple University Press.

Wittgenstein, L. (1958). *Philosophical Investigations* Third Edition. trans. G.E.M. Anscombe. New York: Macmillan.

Wittrock, M, ed. (1986). *Handbook of Research on Teaching.* New York: Macmillan.

Yanagisako, S. J. and Collier, J. F. (1987). "Toward a Unified Analysis of Gender and Kinship." In S. J. Yanagisako and J. F. Collier, eds. *Gender and Kinship* (pp. 14–50). Stanford, California: Stanford University Press.

Young, M. F. D. (1971a). "Introduction." In M. F. D. Young, ed. *Knowledge and Control* (pp. 1–18). London: Collier-Macmillan.

Young M. F. D. (1971b). "An Approach to the Study of Curricula as Socially Organized Knowledge." In M. F. D. Young, ed. *Knowledge and Control* (pp. 19–46). London: Collier-Macmillan.

Young, M. F. D., ed. (1971c). *Knowledge and Control: New Directions for the Sociology of Education.* London: Collier-Macmillan.

< 194 >